PICKERS & POETS

John and Robin Dickson Series in Texas Music
Sponsored by the Center for Texas Music History
Texas State University–San Marcos

GARY HARTMAN, GENERAL EDITOR

PICKERS & POETS

THE RUTHLESSLY POETIC SINGER-SONGWRITERS OF TEXAS

Edited by Craig Clifford and Craig D. Hillis

Texas A&M University Press   College Station

Library of Congress Cataloging-in-Publication Data

Names: Clifford, Craig Edward, 1951– editor. | Hillis, Craig D., 1949– editor.
Title: Pickers and poets : the ruthlessly poetic singer-songwriters of Texas
    / edited by Craig Clifford and Craig D. Hillis.
Other titles: John and Robin Dickson series in Texas music.
Description: First edition. | College Station : Texas A&M University Press,
    [2016] | Series: John and Robin Dickson series in Texas music | Includes
    bibliographical references and index.
Identifiers: LCCN 2016014576| ISBN 9781623494469 (cloth : alk. paper) |
    ISBN 9781623494476 (ebook : alk. paper)
Subjects: LCSH: Lyricists—Texas—Biography. | Folksingers—Texas—Biography.
Classification: LCC ML403 .P53 2016 | DDC 782.42092/2764 [B]—dc23 LC
    record available at https://lccn.loc.gov/2016014576

*Special thanks to our friends at Collings Guitars in Austin, Texas,
for the guitar images used in this book.*

CONTENTS

Introduction, by Craig Clifford and Craig D. Hillis | 1

Part One. The First Generation: Folksingers, Texas Style

Too Weird for Kerrville: The Darker Side of Texas Music | 17
   Craig Clifford
Townes Van Zandt: The Anxiety, Artifice, and Audacity
of Influence | 27
   Robert Earl Hardy
Vignette—The Ballad of Willis Alan Ramsey | 36
   Bob Livingston
Guy Clark: Old School Poet of the World | 39
   Tamara Saviano
Kris Kristofferson: The Silver-Tongued Rhodes Scholar | 49
   Peter Cooper
Vignette—Don Henley: Literature, Land, and Legacy | 59
   Kathryn Jones
Steven Fromholz, Michael Martin Murphey, and Jerry Jeff Walker:
Poetic in Lyric, Message, and Musical Method | 61
   Craig D. Hillis
Vignette—Kinky Friedman: The Mel Brooks of Texas Music | 83
   Craig Clifford
Billy Joe Shaver: Sin and Salvation Poet | 85
   Joe Holley
One Man's Music: Vince Bell | 92
   Joe Nick Patoski
Vignette—Ray Wylie Hubbard: Grifter, Ruffian, Messenger | 101
   Jenni Finlay

The Great Progressive Country Scare of the 1970s | 103
  Craig D. Hillis (interview with Gary P. Nunn)
Plenty Else to Do: Lyrical Lubbock | 109
  Andy Wilkinson
Roots of Steel: The Poetic Grace of Women Texas
Singer-Songwriters | 115
  Kathryn Jones
From Debauched Yin to Mellow Yang: A Circular Trip through the Texas
Music Festival Scene | 136
  Jeff Prince
Vignette—Bobby Bridger: "Heal in the Wisdom," Creating
a Classic | 145
  Craig D. Hillis (interview with Bobby Bridger)
Interlude: What Do We Do with Willie? | 148
—I. Willie (An Early Encounter) | 148
  Craig D. Hillis
—II. Willie (On Everything) | 151
  Craig Clifford and Craig D. Hillis

**Part Two. The Second Generation: Garage Bands, Large Bands, and
Other Permutations**

"Gettin' Tough": Steve Earle's America | 161
  Jason Mellard
Lyle Lovett and Robert Earl Keen: Cosmic Aggies | 166
  Jan Reid
Vignette—Walt Wilkins: Spirituality and Generosity | 174
  Craig Clifford (interview with Tim Jones)
Lucinda Williams: Poet of Places in the Heart | 176
  Kathryn Jones
Rodney Crowell: Looking Inward, Looking Outward | 185
  John T. Davis
Vignette—Sam Baker: Short Stories in Song | 192
  Robert Earl Hardy
James McMurtry: Too Long in the Wasteland | 193
  Diana Finlay Hendricks

Part Three. Epilogue: Passing of the Torch?

Drunken Poet's Dream: Hayes Carll | 203
—I. Good Enough for Old Guys | 203
   Craig Clifford
—II. Good Enough for Young Guys | 207
   Brian T. Atkinson
Roll On: Terri Hendrix | 209
   Brian T. Atkinson
From Riding Bulls to Dead Horses: Ryan Bingham | 212
   Craig Clifford (interview with Shaina Post)
Bad Girl Poet: Miranda Lambert | 218
   Craig Clifford
Challenge to Bro Country: Kacey Musgraves | 221
   Grady Smith
Beyond the Rivers | 224
   Craig Clifford

Notes | 231
Selected Sources | 233
Contributors | 243
Index | 251

PICKERS & POETS

INTRODUCTION

Craig Clifford and Craig D. Hillis

Many books and essays have addressed the broad sweep of Texas music—its multicultural aspects, its wide array and blending of musical genres, its historical transformations, and its love-hate relation with Nashville and other established music business centers. This collection of essays focuses on an essential thread in this tapestry, the Texas singer-songwriters that one of the essays in this book, Craig Clifford's "Too Weird for Kerrville," refers to as *ruthlessly poetic*. All songs require good lyrics, but for these songwriters the poetic quality and substance of the lyrics are front and center. We confess that the words "ruthlessly" and "poetic" don't normally go together, but it is, in writing as in songwriting, the unexpected but mysteriously telling phrase that lets us see something from a perspective that we wouldn't ordinarily have access to.

Discerning which songwriters fit into this category is one of the questions that these essays address. Obvious candidates include Townes Van Zandt, Guy Clark, Michael Martin Murphey, Steven Fromholz, Terry Allen, Kris Kristofferson, Vince Bell, and David Rodriguez. Other than the term "Texas singer-songwriters," there isn't a commonly acceptable phrase or genre that properly identifies this singular group of artists. Nevertheless, among people who know and love Texas music, there's a clear sense that there certainly is an identifiable tradition, even if it comes unadorned with a popular-culture moniker.

The notion of the ruthlessly poetic singer-songwriter as it applies to this study had its origins in the coffeehouses and clubs of the late sixties and seventies in Houston, Austin, Dallas, and other Texas cities. In a sense, what these songwriters were doing in small, intimate live-music venues like the Jester Lounge and Anderson Fair in Houston, the Chequered Flag and the Saxon Pub in Austin, and the Rubaiyat and Poor David's Pub in Dallas was similar to what Bob Dylan was doing in Greenwich Village. In the language of the times, these were "folksingers." Unlike Dylan, however, these were folksingers writing songs about their own people and their own origins and singing in their own vernacular to their own people rather than trying to imitate Woody Guthrie's Oklahoma accent and Depression-era sensibilities for the art crowd of New York. This music, like most great poetry, is profoundly rooted.

The rootedness of the Texas singer-songwriters is a recurring theme in this book. Texas writer John Graves quotes Yeats on the subject of roots: "Have not all races had their first unity from a mythology, that marries them to rock and hill?" In *Country Music, U.S.A.*, Bill C. Malone contrasts the urban folksingers like Pete Seeger and Bob Dylan to the genuine folk music of the country music tradition. Whether or not the Texas singer-songwriter tradition highlighted in this book qualifies as part of the country music tradition, it is very much a music of the folk, and its practitioners are very much rooted in their home soil. The urban folksingers of Dylan's variety sang songs about rooted people and they embraced the traditional folk music format, but they often severed their own roots. The folksingers of the Texas coffeehouse scene were writing songs about their own people; they were chronicling their own roots.

In his tribute to Townes Van Zandt, "Fort Worth Blues," Steve Earle says, "You used to say the highway was your home, but we both know it ain't true." Perhaps a curse of sorts, but it's hard to escape your Texas roots when a county was named after your family. Clifford's essay refers to Terry Allen's *Lubbock (on everything)* as a "Yoknapatawpha of the Texas Panhandle." Guy Clark's songs are as rooted in Texas as Eudora Welty's stories are in Mississippi. Fromholz's *Texas Trilogy*, often touted as one of the best works ever written about life in a small Texas town, is unquestionably married to the "rock and hill" of tiny Kopperl, Texas, in Bosque County and to the hearts and hopes of its residents. Popular wisdom has it that the reason there's so much good music coming out of the Texas Panhandle is that there's nothing else to do there, but Andy Wilkinson explains how it's something about the spirit of the place that is the wellspring of the music. Even David Rodriguez's songs, often devoted to attacking Texas, at least Anglo Texas, are so rich in Texas imagery and narrative that it's impossible to think of them without thinking of Texas.

A related topic is the role of venues in the development of this music. The cultural and creative coffeehouse-listening-room environment of the sixties and seventies played an essential role in the nascent styles of these songwriters. And that cultural milieu was shaped not only by the scheduled performances in these venues, but by the picking and singing sessions that often followed those performances.

There are several important questions to address in this context: How did the Texas coffeehouse scene in the late sixties and seventies differ from the Greenwich Village scene that produced Bob Dylan? What constitutes a music scene? What was the intersection of talent, place, and the main currents of American culture (specifically music on a national *and* a regional scale) that created the primordial soup that became the singer-songwriter scene so strongly associated with Texas music in the later twentieth and early twenty-first centuries? Also, in addition to the coffeehouse circuit, Texas has a long-standing affection for music festivals and regional dance halls. Both of these cultural institutions have provided "aesthetic development space" for songwriters over the last forty years. Jeff Prince's essay on the Kerrville Folk Festival and Larry Joe Taylor's Texas Music Festival provides a window on the evolution of Texas music, from the puritanical purity of the early folk era to the rollicking party mentality of contemporary mainstream Texas country. And, last but not least, *Austin City Limits*, founded in 1974 by PBS affiliate KLRN-TV, has played a significant part in this tradition.

How important is this performance-venue, music-media milieu in the emergence and development of this Texas songwriting tradition? If you placed a young Townes Van Zandt down in the Texas music scene in 2016 would he develop into the same kind of songwriter that he became in the 1970s? If young Guy Clark came of age in the world of contemporary I-love-my-truck country music and venues that cater to that music, would he have written "Desperados Waiting for a Train"?

And, of course, as easy as it is to single out the ruthlessly poetic purity of Townes Van Zandt—who, arguably, lived for the sole purpose of writing profound songs—another difficult question arises, a question that all attempts at great artistic expression have to face. Is it really a matter of the purity of artistic intent of these ruthlessly poetic songwriters, or is it the ruthlessly poetic nature of the songs that we care about? A tempting assumption to make is that ruthlessly poetic songwriting implies songwriting that will not be widely accessible, and, as a result, songwriting that will not be hugely successful from a commercial standpoint. As several of the essays in this book mention, Van Zandt once said that he wanted to write songs that were so good no one would understand them. And he probably succeeded, with the end result that many of his songs, however much admired by the aficionados, are not going to appeal to a broader popular audience. We shouldn't reject those songs, just as we shouldn't reject Faulkner's *Absalom, Absalom!* because it's not accessible to a general audience. However, one topic that is central to this book is the relation of the ruthlessly poetic songwriters who lived, and in some cases died, for their songs to those Texas songwriters who have given us ruthlessly poetic songs that are commercially successful. A number of songwriters of various complex motives who seemingly depart from the purity of artistic devotion have written songs of incomparable poetic beauty. Willie Nelson has been a professional songwriter in Nashville; the leader of a Texan revolt against Nashville, which required music that expressed that revolt; an enormously successful performer of cult status; a popular culture icon; and a hero of all aging musicians. But it's hard to deny that he has penned some of the finest songs in the history of Texas music. Likewise, Kris Kristofferson has been one of the most commercially successful songwriters of the late twentieth century and a hugely successful Hollywood actor to boot, but choosing Townes Van Zandt's songs over Kris Kristofferson's because Townes didn't care about money would be tantamount to dismissing Michelangelo's Sistine Chapel because it was commissioned by Pope Julius II. As Robert Earl Hardy's essay on Van Zandt and Peter Cooper's essay on Kristofferson make clear, both of them belong in the pantheon of poetic genius. Ultimately this book is about the music, or, to borrow a phrase, it's "for the sake of the song." In the end, it isn't really a matter of ruthlessly poetic songwriters—it is the ruthlessly poetic nature of the songs that defines the essence of this book.

Of course, the essays in this book are primarily organized around the songwriters—an essay about Townes Van Zandt, an essay about Guy Clark, and so on—but it is not a collection of mini-biographies. It is really about the ruthlessly poetic songs that these songwriters produced, and it's about the songwriters because they produced these songs, whether their motives were ruthlessly poetic or ruthlessly commercial. The lives of these songwriters—their flaws and virtues, inspirations and aspirations, motives and methods—certainly are part of the story of this book, but all of that only matters because those biographical aspects were relevant to the creation of exceptional works.

Another theme that informs these essays is the relationship between poetic songs and poetry in the strict sense. Are these songwriters really poets? Are they writing poetry? Many contemporary writers and performers certainly embrace that view. An album featuring other artists covering Van Zandt's songs is called *Poet: A Tribute to Townes Van Zandt*. Lyle Lovett has remarked that "Guy's songs are literature." And, as Tamara Saviano relates in her essay, Clark tells the story in several interviews about a standard of excellence he shared with Van Zandt, judging their lyrics by comparing them to Dylan Thomas reading his poetry. Saviano also recounts how Clark wrote "Desperados Waiting for a Train" first as a poem.

Do the lyrics stand alone as poetry without the musical context? Has poetic music been the popular outlet in Texas for the creative use of words? Although there are some admirable poets to come out of Texas, Texas is not known for its poetry the way it's known for its songwriting. Is "the song" an accepted form of or an alternative for poetry in Texas? How significant is the fact that the Texas Legislature has designated two career songwriters—Red Steagall in 2006 and Steven Fromholz in 2007—as Texas poet laureates? Many of the state's poets, as well as a few English professors, were incensed. Steagall and Fromholz are songwriters, not poets, they protested. Were the poets and professors being snooty? Were they erecting artificial barriers?

One of the pitfalls of overemphasizing the lyrics of these finely crafted songs is to shortchange the "structural poetry" of the music. The majority of the music this book focuses on is what many would call folk music, so on the surface the musical format might seem sparse and simple. Kristofferson's "Me and Bobby Magee" only has three chords. Van Zandt's "Rex's Blues" only has two. Conversely, some of the "structural poetry" that provides the musical mechanics of other poetic songs is quite complicated. Michael Murphey's "Song of the South Canadian," co-written with Gary P. Nunn, is truly symphonic in its musical and harmonic structure. Lyrically, it unfolds as a short philosophical treatise that couples the flow of a Southwestern river with the flow of the human journey from birth though salvation. Musically, it features definitive movements, themes, and various chordal textures reminiscent of Aaron Copeland and his American *Gebrauchsmusik* sensibilities. But for all these great songwriters, what is going on musically is just as precise as what is going on lyrically. The melodies, chord structures, precise finger-picking styles, delicate passing notes, and related performance nuances are essential components of the larger work. The perfect marriage of music and lyrics is an essential component of these exceptional songs. You might say that the music expresses musically what the lyrics express lyrically. But even that formulation treats the two as separate entities. Perhaps a better way to say it is that the meaning and impact of the song come from the artistic whole created by the meticulous blend of words and music. And that is no simple task. In these ruthlessly poetic songs, the lyrics are front and center, but the music is an indispensable part of the meaning of the song. Take away the music from Van Zandt's most famous song, "Pancho and Lefty," and it's no longer a song—it's just that simple. The title "Pancho and Lefty" refers to a unique combination of music and words, not just to a collection of words.

Musick and Poetry have ever been acknowledg'd Sisters, which walking hand in hand, support each other; as Poetry is the harmony of Words, so Musick is that of Notes; and as Poetry is a Rise above Prose and Oratory, so is Musick the exaltation of Poetry. Both of them may excell apart, but sure are most excellent when they are join'd, because nothing is then wanting to either of their Perfections: for thus they appear like Wit and Beauty in the same person.

—HENRY PURCELL: PREFACE TO *The History of Dioclesian*

Even if songs are not poems in the strict sense, the literary influences on these ruthlessly poetic songwriters are crucial. Most of these songwriters are extremely well read, in some cases well educated, and they often mention their interest in fine poetry and literature. For example, Clifford's essay "Too Weird for Kerrville" discusses David Rodriguez's comment about studying great poetry and trying to emulate it. Likewise, Guy Clark comments in response to a question about songwriting after an *Austin City Limits* taping that he grew up in a "literate family" that talked about literature at the dinner table. In her essay, Saviano documents the great poets that Clark grew up reading. Jerry Jeff Walker in his autobiography, *Gypsy Songman*, talks about "drifting through" his final years in high school with "lousy study habits" yet being blessed with a love of the written word: "In class, when I wasn't staring out the window, I'd be paging through Thoreau, Camus, Emerson. Planting the seeds." Hillis reports that during his tenure as Michael Martin Murphey's guitar player, "Murph was an avid reader and researcher. In the early 1970s, for example, he was really into Albert Schweitzer and many of his songs reflected the essence of Schweitzer's 'Reverence for Life' themes." Like many great literary writers, these songwriters provide voices for the common people of their homeland, but they are themselves anything but ordinary when it comes to their learnedness.

In assembling our list of ruthlessly poetic songwriters, we have tried to be objective, selective, and inclusive. We have embraced the input and opinions of our fellow writers to establish comprehensive standards for the "ruthlessly poetic" designation. Nonetheless, determining who is "in" and who is "out" is, by nature, an extremely subjective task. With that in mind, we have sought out venerable and informed members of the Texas music community—record executives, producers, studio engineers, artists' managers and agents, and prominent musicians—for input on songwriters who they feel warrant the ruthlessly poetic designation. Inevitably, some of our choices were motivated, at least in part, by personal reasons. To the extent that the two of us have somewhat different perspectives on the subject, we believe that the combination of our individual perspectives has produced a more encompassing view. Still, it is not possible to be exhaustive, so we've done our best to be thoughtful in making these tough decisions.

In discussing how we made our selections, we should reiterate that the seminal Texas songwriters for the tradition this book addresses were "folksingers" in the same sense that early Bob Dylan was a folksinger. This generation of folksingers, in Greenwich Village as well as in Texas, made a profound transition from the performance of traditional folk songs to the creation of highly poetic songs heavily influenced by folk traditions. Woody Guthrie was a pivotal figure for these folksingers, in a sense the model of a "singer-songwriter," penning countless songs to traditional folk melodies. Of course, the tradition of the solo blues artists weighed heavily in the influences behind Texas songwriters like Townes Van Zandt, who played the same venues in Houston as Texas bluesman Lightnin' Hopkins. Even the haunting finger-picking guitar style that so many of these Anglo folksingers employ echoes the style of the blues guitar pickers. It goes without saying that strands of Cajun and Mexican-American music were also liberally woven into this fabric.

Still, although the music this book is about draws from these many Texas musical traditions, this book is not about the broad sweep of Texas music. One of the characteristics of all music, and especially of Texas music, is crossfertilization, but we believe there is still some value to making distinctions and drawing lines. For that reason, we excluded many great Texas performers and songwriters who are just as great at what they do as these ruthlessly poetic singer-songwriters are at what they do because we want to delineate the boundaries, however fuzzy and fluid they may be, of a unique tradition. We're not including Townes Van Zandt and excluding Stevie Ray Vaughan because Vaughan is less important but because these two artists are working in different genres. We're not excluding Los Lonely Boys or the Texas Tornados or Lightnin' Hopkins or Blind Lemon Jefferson or T-Bone Walker because their music isn't as good as the Anglo folksingers we address in this book. They are toiling in different soils, albeit soils that the Anglo folksingers are deeply rooted in.

On a related note, when we initially considered the spectrum of potential ruthlessly poetic songwriters, we both realized the conspicuous absence of women among our potential subjects. There seems to be general agreement, among males and females, that the great songwriters of this tradition have been males. So is this a result of women of equal talent being ignored? Or is it the result of the fact that Texas women who grew up at the same time as the first generation of white folksinger boys were socialized in other directions? On the subject of gender socialization, it's arguable that Texas males of Guy Clark's generation were led to believe that writing poetry is unmanly, so they directed their poetic talents into songwriting. These questions could no doubt lead to contentious debates along the lines of the Modern Language Association's culture wars over the literary canon.

So we asked Kathryn Jones to write an essay answering the question, "Where are the women?" Her answer, "Roots of Steel: The Poetic Grace of Women Texas Singer-Songwriters," directs our attention to the numerous first-rate women songwriters of Texas. In other words, yes, there are women, and we need to pay more attention to them. Should the women songwriters Jones discusses have been addressed in individual essays alongside the essays about the men? Clearly, we decided against that, and, as grouchy old men, we accept the consequences; but Jones's essay certainly raises some important questions that merit further attention.

The poetic talents of one woman songwriter, Lucinda Williams, clearly demanded a full essay. From early on, her poetic talents as a songwriter have received widespread acclaim among songwriters and critics, and, nomadic as her life has been, she spent enough time honing her skills in the coffeehouses of Austin and Houston to merit Texas songwriter status. Her song about Blaze Foley, "Drunken Angel," is a testament to how centrally involved with the tradition of Texas singer-songwriters she has been. Jones's essay, "Lucinda Williams: Poet of Places in the Heart," shows just how clearly she has situated herself in this genre.

Obviously, we can't dedicate comprehensive essays to all the worthy designees, so we have tried to strike a balance between the selective and inclusive components of our equation by including a third category beyond our standard essay format. We have included a series of shorter vignettes that highlight the contributions of various gifted Texas songwriters, songwriters who, for any number of reasons, played an essential role in this unique tradition. These vignettes are tactically laced throughout the larger text to satisfy our inclusive criterion and to provide valuable segues from one major topic to another.

The writing in this book is scholarly when it needs to be, but often it is passionate and personal. It is unapologetically—for everyone concerned—a labor of love. Many of the writers in this book are journalists with a deep and abiding passion for Texas music. Jan Reid's writing on Texas music, for example, has ranged from his classic *The Improbable Rise of Redneck Rock* to a biography of Doug Sahm. Joe Nick Patoski has written the definitive biography about Willie Nelson, *Willie Nelson: An Epic Life*. Some of the contributors are musicians with a bent for thinking and writing about the music they've been a part of. Craig Hillis, for example, recounts his experiences playing lead guitar for Jerry Jeff Walker, Steve Fromholz, and Michael Martin Murphey. All in all, the knowledge in this book is knowledge from the heart.

Who is the audience for this book? Certainly, scholars in the fields of Texas music, Southwestern Studies, American Studies, American Literature, and other disciplines will find this book attractive. Such a publication would serve well as a text for courses in these areas. But we're determined to reach beyond the academic sphere to a broader audience. This book should appeal widely to the devotees of this music, ranging from working musicians, to journalists in the arts, to the die-hard fans looking to delve more deeply into the music they love. Also, given the strong interest in the Texas singer-songwriter tradition, Americana, and roots music in Europe, Australia, and other foreign locales, this book will help to explain why the great Texas songwriters have been welcomed with open arms in music scenes worldwide. As Steve Earle, writing "Fort Worth Blues" in Dublin, Ireland, on the occasion of Townes Van Zandt's death, put it:

> There's a full moon over Galway Bay tonight
> Silver light over green and blue
> And every place I travel to I find
> Some kind of sign that you've been through

One of the reasons for this book to exist is to document a distinctive tradition of music that has had and is still having, albeit in most cases beneath the surface, a profound effect on popular music and culture in America, and, indeed, well beyond our domestic shores.

Another reason for this book to exist is to hold up an alternative to contemporary Texas country music, and, for that matter, contemporary Nashville music—an alternative to what some have recently dubbed "bro country." Mainstream popular culture always has a tendency to exclude the radically independent, the fiercely creative, and the unashamedly intelligent. Mainstream country music—Nashville, Texas, and otherwise—has always had its share of the sentimental, the clichéd, the shallow, and the anti-intellectual. The music industry has a tendency to clone what sells, to create a formula that songwriters are expected to follow. The so-called "outlaw" revolt of Texas songwriters and musicians was in part a reaction to the confining formula of Nashville songwriting.

At a symposium on Texas music at Tarleton State University in 2013 featuring Lloyd Maines, Terri Hendrix, Larry Joe Taylor, and Richard Skanse, one of the central themes was the independent Texas spirit and the role it played in the Texas insurrection against Nashville. Texans don't like to be told what to do. However, another theme that surfaced, although there was some disagreement on this topic, is the way that mainstream contemporary Texas country music has developed its own homogenized formula that is just as confining and banal as the Nashville formula. We think it might even be worse in Texas because there are so many clichés that are readily at hand— Lone Star Beer, bluebonnets, Willie and Waylon, the names of certain Texas rivers or towns, and of course the ever-present American cowboy myth.

In all honesty, however, most of the tropes of mainstream contemporary country are the same in Nashville and Texas. When Grady Smith of *Entertainment Weekly* included Kacey Musgraves's *Same Trailer Different Park* as one of the ten best country albums of 2013, he contrasted her to the male-dominated mainstream:

> Part of what made 2013 a fascinating year for country music was the rise of an outspoken, revolutionary group of female singer-songwriters in the face of "bro country," which saw the mass-market proliferation of dumbed-down lyrics about painted-on jeans, beers, and trucks from generic male artists that earned both eye rolls and platinum sales.

Smith's video *Why Country Music Was Awful in 2013*, a montage of short clips from contemporary country songs, is a tour de force of letting the villains hang themselves. But getting back to Texas, without naming names, it's clear that painted-on jeans, beer, trucks, and other uninspired clichés dominate just as much of contemporary Texas country as it does Nashville country.

What's encouraging is that this holding country music reality up to the light is coming from a young journalist just out of college. If there are not young people protesting this inanity and doing something about it, there's not much hope for the future. It's interesting, however, that only a few months after Smith stirred up a hillbilly hornet's nest, Collin Raye, one of Nashville's old guard, made essentially the same point about contemporary country. Again, he's talking primarily about Nashville country, but everything he says about contemporary Nashville country applies to mainstream Texas country:

> There appears to be not even the slightest attempt to "say" anything other than to repeat the tired, overused mantra of redneck party boy in his truck, partying in said truck, hoping to get lucky in the cab of said truck, and his greatest possible achievement in life is to continue to be physically and emotionally attached to the aforementioned truck as all things in life

should and must take place in his, you guessed it…truck. (http://collin-raye.com/category/collin-raye-news/)

In a Fox News interview in April of 2014, Raye, after quoting from Kris Kristofferson's "Me and Bobby Magee," says this about classic country:

> It was poetry. Country music has never really been about the chord progression or the complexity of the music. It's always been about lyrics and stories and real slices of life. And the one common thread has always been poetry. It's like American Shakespeare in a way. That's what it's supposed to be.

As we indicated above, we're not as willing to paint "classic" country music as poetic across the board. But Raye is right to set that as the ideal. Amidst the sea of Nashville pap, there have indeed been poetic greats, from Hank Williams Sr. to Kris Kristofferson.

We should point out that when Raye mentions that some contemporary songwriters are bucking the I-love-my-truck tide, he names Miranda Lambert, a feisty Texas bad girl who is, if not ruthlessly poetic, certainly independent and happy to satirize truck-loving rednecks who have done her wrong in songs like "Kerosene" and "Gunpowder and Lead."

Perhaps we shouldn't make too much about two examples, but there does seem to be some evidence that the future of this tradition, however male-dominated it might have been in the early days, may well depend on intelligent young women who can navigate the commercial waters and still manage to keep the tradition of ruthlessly poetic songwriting alive. Certainly, one of the chief purposes of this book is to harken back to a great Texas tradition of poetic songwriting, which has informed Nashville's culture, popular American culture, and even international popular culture. These essays are reflections on a great tradition, but we hope that they will also be an inspiration.

The book is organized into three parts:

PART ONE: THE FIRST GENERATION—FOLKSINGERS, TEXAS STYLE

The essays in Part One examine the origins of the ruthlessly poetic songwriting tradition in Texas. Part One begins with Craig Clifford's essay "Too Weird for Kerrville" because that is where the term "ruthlessly poetic" originated. Subsequent essays address the songs and styles of the initial generation of ruthlessly poetic songwriters—Townes Van Zandt, Guy Clark,

Kris Kristofferson, Steven Fromholz, Michael Martin Murphey, Jerry Jeff Walker, Billy Joe Shaver, Vince Bell, and a cadre of creative characters from Lubbock—all of whom framed their careers in the sixties and seventies. The discussion then turns to the role of women in the Texas songwriting scene and weighs their ever-expanding role in the main currents of contemporary songwriting. Jeff Prince then takes us on a full-swing personal odyssey from the Kerrville Folk Festival to the Larry Joe Taylor Texas Music Festival and then back to Kerrville, an exploration of the significance of Texas music festivals in the development and popular dissemination of the Texas singer-songwriter genre. Part One concludes with the editors' reflections on Willie Nelson's essential role in—and transcendence of—this tradition.

PART TWO: THE SECOND GENERATION—GARAGE BANDS, LARGE BANDS, AND OTHER PERMUTATIONS

A number of Texas singer-songwriters in the generation following close on the heels of Townes Van Zandt and company show the influence of that tradition but opted for more commercially viable music. No one is more clearly a protégé of Van Zandt than Steve Earle, as the documentary *Be Here to Love Me* makes clear, not to mention Earle's 2009 album *Townes*, which features fifteen of Van Zandt's songs. Jason Mellard's essay on Steve Earle leads off Part Two. An essay on the "Cosmic Aggies," Robert Earl Keen and Lyle Lovett, follows, and then individual essays on Lucinda Williams, Rodney Crowell, and James McMurtry conclude the section. All of these songwriters were influenced by and carry on the ruthlessly poetic tradition of the seminal songwriters of the first generation who are discussed in Part One.

PART THREE: EPILOGUE—PASSING OF THE TORCH?

Assessing the current scene would certainly involve an examination of the influence of the ruthlessly poetic songwriting tradition in Texas on contemporary songwriters. Many young songwriters list Townes Van Zandt, Guy Clark, and company as influences. Is this tradition having an effect on contemporary popular music? Earlier, we posed the question about what Townes Van Zandt would have done had he been born into the current generation. That's the situation, of course, that young songwriters of today face if they aspire to write the kind of poetic music that Townes Van Zandt wrote.

Rather than provide an overview of the contemporary scene or a catalog of every young Texas songwriter who might be the next Townes Van Zandt or the next Guy Clark, we decided instead to focus on a few young artists who are clearly working in this tradition: Hayes Carll, Terri Hendrix, Ryan

Bingham, Miranda Lambert, and Kacey Musgraves. There are certainly other artists we could have chosen, but these are good examples of how the tradition of ruthlessly poetic songwriting plays out in twenty-first century Texas music and in the ever-evolving trends of American popular music.

The final essay of the book, "Beyond the Rivers," argues that the strongest candidates for carrying forward the torch that the great Texas songwriters lit may be coming out of Oklahoma, and in one case Alabama, not Texas.

PART ONE

THE FIRST GENERATION

Folksingers, Texas Style

Too Weird for Kerrville

The Darker Side of Texas Music[1]

Craig Clifford

As David Rodriguez recounted it to me, Townes Van Zandt was banned for several years from the Kerrville Folk Festival because his music wasn't "family entertainment." And when Blaze Foley punched out Rod Kennedy at Emma Joe's (or got punched out by Rod Kennedy for spitting on him, depending on which version of the story you trust), he too was given the Kerrville boot. According to Rodriguez, a group of Kerrville outcasts and their spiritual brethren started gathering at Taco Flats in Austin each year during the Kerrville Folk Festival to play their brand of Texas music. They called their festival "Too Weird for Kerrville."

Exactly who was or wasn't banned from Kerrville and what the reasons might have been I won't try to pin down. But this story does point to a powerful current that has defined the Texas singer-songwriter tradition of the last few decades. It's an undercurrent for the most part, but it occasionally surfaces; and it pulls and pushes on anyone who wades in the waters of Texas music.

As you can tell already, this essay issues from reflections on my personal engagement with these songwriters, rather than from a scholarly or journalistic interest. I've been trying to make sense of their music for my entire adult life—as a musician playing it, as a songwriter trying to write it, as a writer trying to define it, and as a Texan looking for self-knowledge. From the days of swapping sets with David Rodriguez in Austin coffeehouses in the early 1970s, my identity has always been wrapped up with Texas music.

Who am I talking about, and what about them is "weird"? Texas music intersects with countless currents in American music—currents that come out of Scottish, Irish, and British folk traditions by way of Appalachia and the Deep South; Latino and Cajun cross-pollination; African rhythms and harmonies filtered through American slavery and its aftermath; and many others. The "Too Weird for Kerrville" music comes out of and intersects with all of these traditions, to be sure. But there is also a defining characteristic to the music Rodriguez was talking about. It's not easy to put a label on it—about the best anyone has come up with is "Texas singer-songwriters." But, of course, strictly speaking, any Texan who writes and performs his or her own songs is a Texas singer-songwriter.

For the sake of convenience, I'll limit myself to three Texas singer-song-writers who exemplify the tradition I'm talking about, in part because they are important and in part because of my personal involvement with their music: Townes Van Zandt, Terry Allen, and David Rodriguez. It would be a worthy challenge to catalog everyone who might fit into this tradition, but I'll save that for another venue. In spite of obvious differences, which I'll discuss, the music of these three songwriters shares this defining character-istic: it is ruthlessly poetic in a way that is almost frightening to popular and commercial sensibilities. Unlike, say, Pat Green's feel-good-about-yourself Texas roadhouse music or contemporary I-love-my-truck "bro country," this music takes us to places we're not necessarily comfortable with.

It is ruthlessly poetic in several ways. David Rodriguez once wrote to me that Townes Van Zandt was "a brilliant poet and, like Dylan, he copied or drew from the forms and language usage of old ballads from the British Isles and Ireland. It's as though we were on a common path because I had grown up reading English poets from Sir Walter Scott to Dylan Thomas. So when I came into contact with guys like Townes (because there were others as well) it was like a homecoming."

The vision of these musical poets is Romantic in the full-fledged liter-ary sense. They are driven, even cursed, by the desire for the perfect song. Townes Van Zandt once remarked in an interview: "I want to write songs that are so good nobody understands them, including me." These songwrit-ers are outcasts, too weird for Kerrville, not because they want to be rebels, but because they are devoted first and foremost to their muses.

By contrast, the Willie-and-Waylon outlaw movement was motivated by a conscious desire to buck the Nashville establishment. The indepen-dence this rebellion made possible led to some genuinely poetic work like Willie's *Red Headed Stranger*. But "Luckenbach, Texas," "Don't Let Your Babies Grow Up to Be Cowboys," and countless similar songs were politi-cal anthems for the self-proclaimed Texas outlaw movement. These songs, along with the long hair and rowdy ways, were making a statement, a worthy one to be sure, but they were making a point rather than bringing a vision of things into words.

What is it about most of the music of Townes Van Zandt, Terry Allen, and David Rodriguez that is a little too unsettling to become mainstream? From a personal perspective I can say that as much as I see myself as an ambassador for this music, many of their songs I'm not comfortable singing in any setting, and some I might sing for a few friends but not in a public venue—even though I profoundly admire all of the songs I'm referring to here.

Let's start with the master. Steve Earle said that Townes Van Zandt was the greatest living songwriter and that he'd stand on Bob Dylan's coffee table in his cowboy boots and say it. I'd say Townes Van Zandt is the Texas Bob Dylan, but that makes him sound derivative, and he's not. (By the way, there's a bootleg recording of Dylan singing Van Zandt's "Pancho and Lefty" at the Bonnaroo 2004 Music Festival in Manchester, Tennessee.) In one sense, Van Zandt was doing the same thing that Dylan was doing, except that Van Zandt, unlike Dylan, was always clear about where he was from. In "Fort Worth Blues," Steve Earle says about Van Zandt, "You used to say the highway was your home, but we both know that that ain't true / It's just the only place a man can go when he don't know where he's going to."

When I told a friend a few years ago that I was putting together an entire set of Townes Van Zandt songs for a show, he said he couldn't imagine anyone wanting to listen to that much of him at one sitting. "He's so dark," he said. Not family entertainment, I thought. He is dark. In the 2004 documentary *Be Here to Love Me* there's a clip in which a journalist asks Van Zandt, "Why are so many of your songs so sad?" Van Zandt responds, "Well, many of my songs, they aren't sad, they're hopeless." *Live at the Old Quarter*, recorded in the summer of 1973 in Houston, is the quintessential Townes Van Zandt, a poet singing truth without the protection or veneer of the studio engineers and the record industry. At his best, he was a man and a guitar facing the existential darkness and all of his demons and giving them voice.

Imagine hearing this verse from "Many a Fine Lady" on your local radio station:

> Endlessly sorrow rode high on the north wind
> slashing and slicing to take him his toll
> and endlessly creatures of darkness were cuttin'
> the paths through the walls that sheltered her soul

Or this one from "Our Mother the Mountain":

> So I reach for her hand and her eyes turn to poison
> And her hair turns to splinters, and her flesh turns to brine
> She leaps 'cross the room, she stands in the window
> And she screams that my first born will surely be blind
> Singin' too - ra - loo - ra - li - o

But it's easy to overstate the dark side of Van Zandt. Most of his songs are also about the interplay of darkness and light, and about catching the light. Take this line in "If I Needed You": "If you close your eyes, you'll miss sunrise, and that would break my heart in two." When another friend said that the use of darkness and light images is hardly new, I reminded him of the line in "Rex's Blues": "There ain't no dark till something shines." That's not your run-of-the-mill use of light imagery.

Why do I love to listen to and sing these songs? Strangely, I find them uplifting. They're uplifting for the same reason Faulkner is uplifting. For the same reason that Greek tragedy and Homer are uplifting. They look the darkness and tragedy that we all know are part of life right in the eye, even dwell on the darkness much more than most of us do or should, but they embrace the whole of life nonetheless, with its darkness, its flashing light, its irony. For whatever reason, Townes Van Zandt's life was much more tragic than the lives most of us live, and yet he drank up every drop of it: "If it rained an ocean, I'd drink it dry and lay me down dissatisfied."

Terry Allen is probably better known as a visual artist, but his music, like that of Townes Van Zandt, percolates in the inner recesses of many a Texas songwriter, whether consciously or unconsciously. Robert Earl Keen does a rowdy roadhouse version of Allen's "Amarillo Highway," but there is a significant body of Allen's work that you're not likely to hear on your local country radio station.

I once called Terry Allen's *Lubbock (on everything)* a Yoknapatawpha of the Texas panhandle. A double LP odyssey, it starts with vivid tales of the people Allen grew up with around Lubbock, ordinary people struggling with life's difficulty and unfairness, but somehow salvaging a kind dignity out of it all. It ends in California with a ferocious satire on the dehumanizing shallowness of the hip culture Allen presumably was exposed to while teaching art at California State in Fresno.

While Van Zandt's dark vision is more existential—a look into the abyss that lies beneath the surface of our lives—the dark side of Allen's vision focuses on the fatefulness of human lives and the darker possibilities that reside in all of us. Tom Pilkington, a critic of southwestern and western literature, once remarked that Allen's "Blue Asian Reds (for Roadrunner)" is the saddest song ever written. It opens with these lines:

> Yeah she got them red eyes
> Ahhh from doin' the red pills
> And she says it's for the high times

Yeah she says it's for thrills
So she does reds . . . with her coffee
With her Pepsis and her gin
And she says it really does her out fine
But . . . it's just doin' her in

But Allen also shakes up our everyday complacency with visions of human violence—graphic at times, vivid and strangely alluring, but horrifying precisely to the degree that we find ourselves drawn in. His first album, *Juarez*, is the story of a gruesome murder and of the sheer senseless chance that brings the murderers and the victims together—Cormac McCarthy set to music, you might say. "Ourland" from *Bloodlines* is a symphony of gore, a biting satire on the dangers of nationalism and racism run amok, but it digs deep down into the white-hot hatred that drives that kind of violence, and it pulls us into a place we don't want to know we're capable of finding attractive. It opens with these lines:

Ourland is my land
Her history is calling me
From the shores of another land
To ourland across the sea
Well I fancy a bomb inside my head
Ticking for the men
And I'll put it in a little cafe
And blow 'em to hell again
An I fancy a pistol in my coat
Loaded for the kill
And we'll gun the ones who run outside
I swear by god we will

Some of Allen's satire is non-violent and funny but still just nasty enough, and truthful enough, to make us a bit nervous. Take this poetic assault from "Rendezvous USA":

'Cause sleazy chic haunts the ballrooms
Dancing disco's debonair
An boo-coos of hip medallions
Rub against Frederick's brassieres
An they'll soon get off together
to French tickle some tête-a-tête

Or the rollicking satire on Texas football, "The Great Joe Bob (A Regional Tragedy)," about how the great halfback "goes bad" after he "gives up prayer and grows his hair" and robs a Pinkie's Liquor Store with his girlfriend, the waitress "Loose Ruby Cole." Although I don't think I would have the nerve to sing "Ourland" to myself in the shower, I do perform "The Great Joe Bob" in public venues, but I'm always slightly nervous that someone will take serious offense at this sacrilege against the most sacred of the sacred, Texas football.

But, as frightening as it sometimes is, Terry Allen's music is ultimately ennobling rather than demeaning. Like Townes Van Zandt drinking up the ocean and wanting more, Terry Allen's encompassing vision embraces the broad range of human possibilities. He certainly doesn't approve of everything he writes about, but there's a kind of affirmation in looking at the way things are honestly, ruthlessly, and courageously. Veterans of the Vietnam War have told me that when something really horrible happened, one of the standard expressions was, "Well, there it is." Terry Allen looks at all there is about being human, from the ordinary to the noble and from the goodness to the violence, and says, "well, there it is." And there is a strange admiration in his songs for the ordinary people who deal with the difficult lot that life has given them. "Lubbock Woman" is a sad elegy to a woman who "is destined to lose," complete with the unhappy details of her life, but it ends with the straightforward affirmation that she "has a good heart / she's a Lubbock woman / you got to love that woman."

When Lucinda Williams performed in Amsterdam in 2003, she remarked on David Rodriguez's presence in the audience by saying, "I feel like I'm in the presence of genius because my friend David is here. Do you know him?" In an Austin poll conducted by *Third Coast Music*, David Rodriguez was voted best Texas songwriter for three consecutive years, 1992, 1993, and 1994. Lyle Lovett recorded Rodriguez's "Ballad of the Snow Leopard and the Tanqueray Cowboy" for his tribute to fellow Texas songwriters, *Step Inside This House*. But much of Rodriguez's music, outside of certain circles in Austin and Houston, has never made it onto the popular Texas or American music scene, and in 1994 he abandoned his native Texas soil for good, heading off to Europe in the time-honored tradition of American expatriate artists looking for a home for their poetic spirits. Stories abound about why Rodriguez never returned to his native country, most of them explaining why he *couldn't* come back for various nefarious reasons. The winds of rumor will always blow, but what most defined David Rodriguez was his ruthlessly poetic music.

Like Van Zandt, Rodriguez was steeped in the folk music of the British

Isles, an interest that he developed in high school through his friendship with several girls from southeast Houston whose parents listened to the Weavers, the Kingston Trio, and Pete Seeger. Rodriguez was a member of the Milby High School folk club called the Wayfarers. When I met him in college, he was playing songs like "I Loved a Lass (She's Gone to Be Wed to Another)" and "Rosemary Lane." His finger-picking guitar on those songs—flat pick and two finger picks on his third and fourth fingers—was unequaled by any of the folk guitarists of that generation. Rodriguez's contrapuntal guitar on "Rosemary Lane" made Bert Jansch's version sound uninspired. When I met my future wife during my junior year in college, it turned out that she was one of those southeast Houston girls who had turned Rodriguez toward folk music, something of an irony for me since he introduced me to folk music when I met him during my freshman year of college.

Rodriguez's commentary on Texas—cultural, political, and poetic—is not of the warm and fuzzy variety, and it was inevitable that it would ruffle feathers. In part because of his Hispanic heritage and in part because of the bright light his mind seemed to shine on everything it came in contact with, his relationship to Texas was powerfully ambivalent. His music ranges from romantic lyricism steeped in the Texas of his youth to moving but profoundly disturbing indictments of social injustice, often in the same song. "The Other Texas" starts with a romantic encomium to his homeland:

> She's got lowlands just like Holland
> She's got mountains just like Spain
> And all the sunshine of the summer
> Western winds and eastern rain

Then it turns to "the other Texas":

> But drive your rent car across my hometown
> To the streets the map don't show
> And you'll see children with no future
> That's the Texas that I know

Of the three songwriters I'm discussing here, David Rodriguez, is the most overtly political. In fact, he spent a number of years as a political activist lawyer in Austin. He told me a few years ago that I should be careful about mentioning his name in certain circles in Austin because he still had enemies because of his activism. Whether that's true or not, it tells you something about how Rodriguez understood himself. Occasionally he crosses over from a poetic vision of things political to preachy political accusation, sometimes telling us what we've done wrong rather than getting us to see it by way of the seductive story or perfect turn of phrase. My relation to his songs as a performer has brought that home to me. Some of his songs I can't see myself singing at all, like "Ballad of the Western Colonies," a bit too much of a sermon for my taste: "As if it was something to be proud of, all the killing the cowboy done / How the boundaries were shaped with the barrel of a gun." And some of his songs, like "The Third World" and "The True Cross," I'll put aside for being too much in the white-man-bad vein, then come back to them a few years later because the perspective they present, whether I "agree" with it or not, is so compelling.

This ambivalence in Rodriguez's poetic mind resulted for the most part, not in political propaganda, but in art that forces us to rethink the way we look at ourselves and our place. Not unlike Faulkner's relation to the South, loving it and hating it, Rodriguez's relation to Texas was a beautiful but unsettling challenge. Rodriguez's lyrics are the musical equivalent of what writers like Rolando Hinojosa and Larry McMurtry have done in literature. They may in the end move us to action, but only because they get us to see things from a perspective that we would not ordinarily have.

But it's important to note that Rodriguez's perspective challenges *and* simultaneously strengthens our identity. Although Rodriguez left the United States in 1994 to live in the Netherlands, he never abandoned his Texas identity. Some of his political finger pointing makes an old gringo like me uneasy, occasionally even angry. Still, I continue to find his music attractive because it talks about the same Texas that he and I grew up in during the 1950s and 1960s in Houston. His "Ballad of the Snow Leopard" (the title comes from the fact that he proposed to his first wife in front of the snow leopard cage at the Houston Zoo) is so rich in the images of my own childhood, of *our* own childhood, that the Hispanic and Anglo differences fade away in the vivid poetry of our "native borderland." His music indicts the powerful and extols the powerless, but at the same time it unifies us in our humanness—or at least in our Texan-ness.

On *A Winter Moon,* his 2007 live CD recorded in Dordrecht in the Netherlands, Rodriguez brought back one of his most personal songs about his roots in Houston and Mexico, his family history, and his father's death—"Hurricane." To be sure, it includes a satiric condemnation of the unpoetic lives that most of us live:

> And whatever it was they told him was worth this rat race
> To this day I'm still not sure I understand
> Except to keep your woman happy and the children all in school
> And pay the doctor bills and pay the light bill too

In fact, it's probably that kind of in-your-face condemnation that kept Rodriguez's music from "making it big." But this song also evokes a passionate sense of place—and I recognize it as my place. It's an odd pairing in a way—Rodriguez an activist Hispanic from the southeast side of Houston and me an Anglo philosophy professor from the southwest side, Rodriguez finally leaving Texas after many years of fighting the good fight and me returning to Texas after nine years away. But I identify with this song as much as with any song ever written about Texas. The end of the song recounts the burial of his father:

> And we laid him low in the same old southern grasslands
> In his very own piece of this Texas coastal plain
> Where you can almost smell the ocean
> It's just twenty miles away
> I said, "You'll like it here."
> And I could hear him sayin'

> When the south wind blows in from the Gulf of Mexico
> It makes me think about long ago, up on the bayou again
> Son, you'd do well to live right and watch those ladies at midnight
> When they start comin' on like a hurricane

The only Texas burial scene I can think of with as much poetic power is the one at the end of Larry McMurtry's *Horseman, Pass By*.

The Irish poets know something about inescapable rootedness. In "Gravities," Seamus Heaney talks about James Joyce in exile:

> Blinding in Paris, for his party piece
> Joyce named the shops along O'Connell Street.

In a 2007 email, after living in the Netherlands for over a decade, David Rodriguez could still name his childhood haunts in South Houston:

> At the corner of Old Galveston Road and Winkler Drive—I think it is or
> some other name—was the Winkler Drive-In, but first you have to cross
> the railroad tracks. Then there was Vicky's Drive-In, and then there were
> a couple of old oil pumps, right out of *Giant*, and then was a lounge, I
> think, and then Kenny's store.

Racing Aimless, released almost two decades since Rodriguez had last set foot on Texas soil, leads off with a haunting elegy to his homeland, "Gulf Coast Plain":

> I was born on a Gulf Coast plain,
> You can smell the saltwater in the rain
> Land of the willow and the slow movin' bayou
> And the hurricane

And the album closes with an unedited version of "Yellow Rose of Texas." Childhood roots, positive or negative, run deep. In his deep heart's core, Rodriguez never left Texas.

David Rodriguez died on October 26, 2015, in the Netherlands at the age of sixty-three. I am finishing up this essay a couple of weeks after his death. He was a charismatic personality with an endearingly mischievous smile that I am reminded of every time I see a photograph of his daughter, Carrie Rodriguez. He was also incredibly difficult to deal with at times. Because of that he sometimes sabotaged himself, burned his bridges, and alienated even his admirers. But he was a brilliant songwriter whose best songs stand alongside the best songs of Townes Van Zandt, Guy Clark, and the other great Texas folksingers who came of age in the coffeehouses of Austin and Houston in the late 1960s and early 1970s. As I wonder whether David Rodriguez will be laid low in the Netherlands or in "his very own piece of this Texas coastal plain," I think of the lines from Yeats that Larry McMurtry put to such good use: "Cast a cold eye / On life, on death. / Horseman, pass by!"

The intersection of this darker current in Texas music with the rest of Texas music is a story in its own right. The influence of Townes Van Zandt on Texas music has been well documented, but all three of these songwriters inform the more popular brand of Texas music in untold ways. We can lament the fact that more of their music hasn't made it into the mainstream, that they haven't been given a wider and more popular recognition and the accompanying financial rewards, and that far lesser talents are the ones that tend to make it big. Or we can appreciate the sheer beauty of their songs and thank them for the pathos and healing catharsis that their ruthlessly poetic music offers to those who choose to listen.

Kris Kristofferson once called Townes Van Zandt a "songwriter's songwriter," and the same term has been applied to Terry Allen and David Rodriguez numerous times. These songwriters weren't cut out to be wildly popular—they had a more pressing calling. They made their choices from early on, and they stuck to those choices and paid prices for them. But I see no regret in them, and whatever mistakes they may have made in their lives, they go to their graves with their poetic integrity intact. That single-mindedness of purpose is a bit frightening to the rest of us—and certainly it can be a destructive force for those who get in its way. But in terms of the one thing these three songwriters set out to do well, and a noble thing to do at that, they can say, as Townes Van Zandt did in "Rex's Blues", "Tell my mama I done no wrong."

TOWNES VAN ZANDT

THE ANXIETY, ARTIFICE, AND AUDACITY OF INFLUENCE

Robert Earl Hardy

In an unpublished interview I conducted for *A Deeper Blue: The Life and Music of Townes Van Zandt*, the great Texas songwriter Mickey Newbury (1940–2002) discussed his artistic influences in no uncertain terms, and in fascinating personal detail:

> Townes Van Zandt is the only writer that ever influenced me, on a one-to-one. I got all the influences that we all have, all the influences of people that I've heard on record. But I'm talking about from talking to him, discussing music, discussing the philosophy of music.
>
> I told him, when I went in the Hall of Fame, I called him and I said, Townes, guess what? We went in the Hall of Fame. He laughed, he said what are you talking about? I said, I just want you to know that you're the only writer that ever influenced me. So I said, if you ever see anybody saying, he writes like Mickey Newbury—which about that time I was about the hottest writer in Nashville—I said, you can take solace in knowing that you're my major influence.
>
> I think that I know what my influence was on Kristofferson. He'd be one of the first ones to tell you that. And he was influencing everybody. If you just think about the fact that if I hadn't met Townes—I took Townes and I also took Guy Clark. Guy only had a couple songs, but I took him

to Nashville, signed him with Columbine Music, basically off the strength of one song, a song called "Step Inside This House." If I hadn't taken Townes to Nashville, then there would have been no Guy Clark. Then you think about all the people that said that their major influences were Guy Clark and Townes Van Zandt. Now you're talking about Steve Earle, Lyle Lovett, Nanci Griffith, Joe Ely, all of those people. Townes never realized his influence.

"Why does this happen after the artist has died?" I asked.
Newbury replied, "Well, people love dead artists. Because they're the only ones that are truthful. They've got nothing else to win or lose."[1]

I'd like to write some songs that are so good that nobody understands them, including me.

—Townes Van Zandt[2]

In the years since his death in 1997, Townes Van Zandt has risen to epitomize the "poetic songwriter," at least—and certainly—in the context of the tradition of twentieth-century Texas music. The concept of "poetic songwriter" has been with us for some time. One could argue (and some have, I imagine) for Homer being the first poetic songwriter, the first singer-songwriter. One could trace the medieval European troubadour and minstrel traditions directly up to Woody Guthrie and to the American folk revival of the 1950s and 1960s, and then right up to the latest contemporary commercial manifestation of this globally essential folk-art form in the twenty-first century (Americana?).

The idea of poetic songwriting seemed to come to its zenith in the 1960s, though, in connection with Bob Dylan. The rest is the history we know so well: the list of singer-songwriters in popular music since Dylan emerged is staggeringly long, with only a precious few in Dylan's league in terms of consistency and quality of output. Quality aside, though, the widespread adoption of the Dylan model revolutionized popular music, with a long-lasting cultural impact. But how many singer-songwriters were or are "poets"?

In fact, while Dylan was for a time known to vacillate between identifying himself as a "poet" and as a "mere" songwriter—a mere *performer*—in later years he addressed the question of what poetic songwriting means to him, interestingly, by writing about one of his primary influences, Hank Williams. Dylan writes that he "became aware that in Hank's recorded songs were the archetype rules of poetic songwriting. The architectural forms are like marble pillars and they had to be there. Even his words—all of the syllables are divided up so they make perfect mathematical sense."[3]

Poetic songwriting means different things to different people, and it would certainly miss the point to attempt to define it scientifically, but the concept of architectural form, of a mathematical level of integrity, is central. Mastery of form equates to a high quality of work, and a "mere" song becomes "poetry."

Appreciation of art is subjective, although it typically does not stray from certain cultural standards. It is those standards that we depend on to support arguments about quality. Influence is more objective, but not completely so, as we shall see. For a poetic songwriter then, since quality is at issue, it is pertinent in ruminating on the concept of influence to ask two questions: What are the artist's influences (perhaps meaning at least in part what *poets* are influences)? And what level of quality, or as Dylan put it, of architectural form—of *"poeticism"*—has the artist attained? In fact, the semi-objective question of influence bears in interesting ways on the subjective question of quality.

> Poets and prophets, like magicians, learn their craft from predecessors.
> And just as magicians will invoke the real or supposed source of an illusion
> as part of the patter, or distraction from what his hands are doing, the
> most ambitious poets also take some stance about sources in the past,
> perhaps for an analogous purpose.
>
> —JOHN HOLLANDER[4]

"I studied a lot of Shakespeare and Robert Frost," Townes told an interviewer. "I always considered him, Frost, among my biggest influences. Some people don't know what to think when you tell them your two biggest influences are Lightnin' Hopkins and Robert Frost."[5]

Townes had been writing, performing, and recording his own songs for about twenty-five years when he offered this key summary of his influences. What he was doing when he mapped the Texas bluesman and the New England poet as the poles of his influence—while also throwing in Shakespeare—was to offer guideposts for his audience, to show his audience explicitly where on the map he was located as an artist. This is something that artists—and, by the way, marketers—do: the juxtapositioning of two disparate influences allows a synthesis to occur for the audience (the consumer). This works on various levels, including with the explicit juxtapositioning of the ordinary, the "low" (the blues), and the exalted, the "high" (poetry), a dichotomy Shakespeare mastered on a grand scale in his plays—something that surely did not escape the young Townes Van Zandt as he studied those plays in school.[6]

To a great extent, artists choose their influences consciously. Juxtaposition helps define the artist, both for himself and for his audience. But the juxtaposition, the dialectic—thesis, antithesis, and synthesis—has a deeper purpose.

"The emotion of art is impersonal," T. S. Eliot wrote. "And the poet cannot reach this impersonality without surrendering himself wholly to the work to be done. And he is not likely to know what is to be done unless he lives in what is not merely the present, but the present moment of the past, unless he is conscious, not of what is dead, but of what is already living." Influence was a fundamental part of the arts for Eliot—for one thing, a way for the artist to deflect the gaze of the audience productively from the artist himself to his art; then, more deeply, it was a way for the artist to merge with his traditions. "What happens is a continual surrender of himself as he is at the moment to something which is more valuable," Eliot continued. "The progress of an artist is a continual self-sacrifice, a continual extinction of personality."

So as the artist sets the poles of his influences, he is able to take part in this necessary process of depersonalization; he is triangulated, and he enters into the historic tradition. His influences are not only guideposts that he has set, but conscious decisions he has made about the context of his art, even covert suggestions he is offering about how to interpret his work. They are a mask he wears.[7]

I come from a long line / High, low, and in between.

—TOWNES VAN ZANDT[8]

Talk about "the anxiety of influence": no matter how he might have tried to escape it, or to deflect it to Shakespeare, it was hard for Townes Van Zandt *not* to be influenced by—in fact, to feel rooted in the soil of—his home state, Texas. While he spent years living in other places and traveling endless miles and months on the road—no place, far from any home—Texas *was* his home, and, for better or worse, he returned again and again to Houston and to Fort Worth and to Austin for various kinds of nourishment or infusions of energy, both physical and spiritual, and both negative and positive. Home can be a place where you know too well where to find things you don't need. Townes is addressing himself in the opening verse of his best-known song when he says, "Living on the road, my friend / Was gonna keep you free and clean / Now you wear your skin like iron / And your breath's as hard as kerosene."[9] Overall, he enjoyed—and suffered—a sense of ubiquity in the Lone Star State, as his family roots—and his own legend—were deep and widespread.

Of course, the legend is compelling, taking on the qualities of myth as it moves across time, beginning with the origin story, which is the story of Townes's earliest musical influences. It was as a child riding in the car as his father drove on oil company business across Texas, from oil field to oil field, listening to the radio, that Townes first heard Hank Williams. Listening to those radio stations—KSIJ out of Gladewater, KLEE out of Houston, the powerful WSM out of Nashville—he would have heard Ernest Tubb, Lefty Frizzell, Floyd Tillman, Tex Ritter, Red Foley, Kitty Wells, Webb Pierce—the golden age of country-and-western music unfolding before his young, impressionable ears.

And suddenly one day there was rock 'n' roll—Elvis, Buddy Holly, Chuck Berry, Little Richard. It can hardly be overemphasized how stimulating a time this was in popular music, in popular culture, and all of this gave Townes creative impetus, touched him, and provoked him in a fundamental way. It was just a few years later, once he had learned to play guitar and was honing his own musical approach, in Houston, that he heard Bob Dylan's first album.

"When I heard him," Townes said, "that's the direction I took."[10]

How many aspiring musicians spoke those same words, took that same path? Thousands did. To cite Dylan as an influence for a songwriter in the sixties and seventies was almost a given. Dylan was in the air that artists were breathing, in the water they were drinking. For Townes, as for many others, following Dylan's direction was on the one hand a broad stroke—the seemingly very natural decision to adopt the model of writing his own songs and singing them, songs about serious topics, about pointed emotional issues, in the folk tradition, a minstrel, a humble troubadour, humble but hip, with acoustic guitar accompaniment: "that's the *direction* I took," Townes said. On the other hand, Townes (and so many others) seemed compelled to take a more narrow, more forced approach to Dylan as well—so powerful was his magnetic pull—as demonstrated by the specifically Dylan-influenced songs that he wrote, some of which can be identified as mere imitations and dismissed as youthful indiscretions and a few of which go a step further and have borne closer examination.

But while his *direction*—the form and attitude his work was to take, you might say—was set by Dylan, his *influences* were spread wider and deeper, and had more authenticity—and hence more artistic and spiritual authority—than Dylan. As Townes said, his influences encompassed not only the poetry he read as a young man, in school and at home—Shakespeare, Frost, Dylan Thomas—but also, significantly, the blues he heard on records and later in person, face to face, in the nightclubs of Houston—particularly Lightnin' Hopkins. And, just as the legend has it, those sounds and images began to hold sway with the visceral, plaintive sounds of Hank Williams coming from the car radio in the Texas oil fields—sounds that seemed to emanate from the landscape itself, and words that fell perfectly into place and resonated deeply. And this heady brew of influences gathered like clouds on the horizon of Townes Van Zandt's creative life until it burst forth into his work, a storm of song.

> I said to Hank Williams, "how lonely does it get?"
> Hank Williams hasn't answered yet,
> but I hear him coughing all night long,
> about a hundred floors above me in the Tower of Song
> —LEONARD COHEN[11]

"The difference between Townes and Bob Dylan," according to Townes's acolyte and interpreter Steve Earle, "is Dylan was really heavily influenced by the same kinds of music, but lyrically he was influenced more by modern French poets and the Beats, whereas Townes was much more influenced by old-school, conventional lyric poets like Robert Frost and Walt Whitman."[12]

Lumping Frost and Whitman together as "old-school, conventional lyric poets" is not the question here, fortunately; the point is the broad influence of both popular music and poetry. Townes and Dylan both had Hank Williams in their DNA, and, on top of that, they had "real poetry" as an influence as well—both "old school" and contemporary poetry. Hence, the helix of poetic songwriting: nothing new, nothing novel, but powerful in the context of the juxtaposition of "high" and "low" art and in what that means to the artist's identity and to his audience's sense of identification with him.

Leonard Cohen said "I don't fool myself, I know the game I'm in. When I wrote about Hank Williams 'a hundred floors above me in the tower of song,' it's not some kind of inverse modesty. I know where Hank Williams stands in the history of popular song. 'Your Cheatin' Heart,' songs like that, are sublime, in his own tradition, and I feel myself a very minor writer."[13]

> As I get older and have written a whole bunch of songs, each song has to be perfect. There can't be a wrong anything: a note or a word or a comma or a pause, it's got to be correct. And it's got to be about something that is worth writing about. So, it's like being zeroed in.
> —TOWNES VAN ZANDT[14]

It's like taking a raw diamond and cutting away at it until you get a perfect cut. The only thing you have to be careful of is that you don't cut the diamond so small that you have a perfect cut that can't be seen. Do you understand?

—Mickey Newbury[15]

When we listen to and read their work, respectively, where can we observe that Townes Van Zandt and Robert Frost intersect? What do they share? Without comparing individual pieces of work side by side (Frost's poem "Tree At My Window" and Van Zandt's song "At My Window," for example?)—which inevitably seems like trying to separate the men from the boys, an unfair exercise in this forum ("Vague dream-head lifted out of the ground / And thing next most diffuse to cloud / Not all your tongues talking aloud / Could be profound"[16])—we can make some generalizations. The primary similarity between the two writers is an ease with colloquial American speech, with natural rhythms of conversation. Townes certainly did not *learn* this quality from Frost—this is also a quality of the blues, and a quality that Hank Williams mastered in his best songs. Frost reinforced that and certified it with the stamp of the poet. In simple terms, internal rhyme is another characteristic of Frost's poems—and also of the blues. Again, in Frost, Townes found reinforced a mode of writing—based in patterns of speech—with which he was familiar and comfortable.

It's when we dig a little deeper that we see the more profound influence of Frost on Townes—or at least the more profound similarities between the two. Most broadly, the two share the sense of honesty and seriousness of purpose—the sense of calling, perhaps—of a poet. Deeper down, they share an appreciation for nature as a metaphor, and for metaphysical detail. In Townes's work, the metaphor is given depth and complexity by its thematic connection to his "inner life," specifically to his mental state—essentially, to his bipolar disorder. Whether or not a similar biographical dynamic played out in Frost's work—another question we are not here to pursue—Townes's subject matter is ultimately the same as Frost's: the fundamental questions of existence, of humanity. Townes's take on the connectedness of man and nature is actually not as bleak as Frost's: Townes places humanity directly in nature, an integral part of its cycles, whereas Frost seems to place mankind always outside of and at odds with an indifferent nature. Whereas Frost fears and wants to turn away from a degeneration into madness, Townes accepts it as inevitable, as part of the cycles of nature, like the turning of the earth and the changing of the seasons. But essentially, both poets turn to nature for their metaphors, and both find them there.

Talking about small changes he makes to songs as he's writing them,

Townes said, "That's where my poetic background comes in," again acknowledging the influence of his favorite poets. He explains, "A lot of my best songs are where every single word is where it's supposed to be." He goes on, "Whereas a lot of country songs are more like everyday conversations; it's like a paragraph that rhymes as opposed to words that fit and come to form a big rhyme. I have a lot of songs that are written that way."[17]

As vague as this explication is, it is not difficult to uncover examples of Townes's technical intent in his work. For example, Steve Earle took an interest in "Don't You Take It Too Bad" and noted, "It's so unique. It has no chorus. It's a sentence, basically; a thought."[18] Mickey Newbury also used this piece as an example, offering that the song "is so wonderful because it is so concise. It's like taking a piece of wood and just making a couple of cuts on it and having a beautiful statue. You understand what I'm saying?" He continued:

> Some songwriters . . . if they're going to build something out of clay, they'll squeeze a piece and make a foot, make a leg, and they'll take another piece and they'll squeeze that with their hands and they'll make a leg and they'll make a foot, and they'll make a body and they'll make a head, and they'll stick the two legs on the body. Right? Townes would throw the clay down and pull off pieces of the clay until a song emerged. You follow what I'm saying? Now, that's the same way that Michelangelo worked with marble. He would chip away. Somebody asked him one time, How do you sculpt? What are your ideas when you go in? He said, I take away the marble that's not necessary.[19]

> It's *real*. It's not perverted or thought—it's not a concept. It is a chair, not a design for a chair or a better chair or a bigger chair or a chair with leather or with design. It is the first chair, it's chairs for sitting on, not chairs for looking at or being appreciated. You *sit* on that music.
>   —JOHN LENNON ON THE BLUES[20]

The resonances shared by Townes Van Zandt and Sam "Lightnin'" Hopkins—real Texas resonances, with an aura of American authenticity—are in plain view both musically and lyrically as one holds the work side by side. When the young, middle-class white man covers the older, working-class black man singing "My starter won't start this morning / Something must be wrong with my little machine / Mechanic say your car's alright / You just been burnin' bad gasoline,"[21] we know where he's coming from, and we know what he's learned from his mentor—just as we know where he's coming from when he takes the form to a higher level in his own song, played in straight Lightnin' Hopkins style: "She's got a homespun disposition / Man, she's just as gentle as you please / She's got arms just like two rattlesnakes / Legs like a willow in the breeze."[22] When Townes's girl "chases away those howlin' bottles of wine," she is the same blues archetype as Lightnin's Katie Mae, who "walks just like she got oil wells in her backyard," and who "you can bet your bottom dollar" will "love and treat you right."[23]

Lightnin' Hopkins gave Townes access to and appreciation of natural blues form, with a personal insouciance of musical and lyrical style, approach, manner, and even lifestyle, as well as facility with a spectacular vernacular tradition. Hank Williams and the other country-and-western music that Townes Van Zandt absorbed as a young man—about as roots-oriented and powerful as commercial music can be—provided the basic structural and emotional template for Townes as a singer-songwriter. Bob Dylan provided a fully contemporary model, a *poet*, with serious intent—with *import*—as well as wry humor and hipness. Not only that, Dylan was a catalyst in a broader sense— as his *calling*—actively facilitating the transmutation of low folk songs into high art, and in this he was also a model. From Robert Frost, Dylan Thomas, and the poets Townes read and from whom he drew influence, that influence provided him with a deeper context, a historical positioning—a necessary depersonalization—as well as with specific techniques and refinements that raised his work to a level of quality equated with poetic credibility.

"It's murky territory," Townes once astutely observed, "because you can't say that Hank Williams isn't thoroughly poetical. And Blind Willie McTell, too. And Lightnin' Hopkins, too."[24]

It is, indeed, murky territory.

We could say that Hank Williams and Lightnin' Hopkins were the "chair"; Bob Dylan and the poets were the cushions, the embellishments. If Townes were to sacrifice himself to his work, to allow his personality to be subsumed into his songs and to follow the true dictum of the poetic calling, located in time, but timeless, he needed the tool that his influences provided—also the magician's trick of distraction, of triangulation. And Townes—incredibly? naturally?—became the template that others followed. He became the primary influence among a younger group of songwriters who continued the tradition, expanded on it, and took it to new audiences.

"Townes was right there," Guy Clark emphasized, "and while you couldn't *be* Townes or write *like* Townes, you could come from the same place artistically."[25]

Townes Van Zandt commanded a deft and powerful mixture of influences—high, low, and in between—and that potent brew provided the catalyst by which a unique artist was able to transmute his life, his humanity, into a powerful body of work.

VIGNETTE—THE BALLAD OF WILLIS ALAN RAMSEY

Bob Livingston

I jumped into the deep end. The bar was raised pretty high really quickly!
—WILLIS ALAN RAMSEY

I first met Alan Ramsey (as he was known in 1970) at a folk club in Dallas called the Rubaiyat. He was opening for Frummox, a folk duo featuring Steven Fromholz and Dan McCrimmon, and the tiny, dark room was packed. All of nineteen, Ramsey was standing alone on the small stage, brilliantly finger picking his Martin, singing into a mic on a straight stand, no boom, with one white tennis shoe tapping out rhythm on the base of the stand. Eyes closed, he was delivering the goods with a version of "Suite: Judy Blue Eyes," dead on, a perfect rendition with all of Stephen Stills's licks rendered as if by Stills himself.

"This kid is phenomenal," Bob Johnson, the club owner, whispered. "He's going places."

Johnson was right. Ramsey was mesmerizing and in command of the stage in a shy and endearing way. I was playing bass with Michael Murphey at the time, and I knew I would be hearing a lot more from him.

But no one could have imagined at that time how far this nineteen-year-old *prodigy* who had been playing cover songs in small clubs would go. No one knew that he was on the cusp of writing and recording a monumental debut album for Leon Russell's Shelter Records that would take its place as one of the greatest albums ever to come out of Texas.

What was his process? How did he survive and thrive after "jumping into the deep end"? Where did he get the inspiration and ideas to write such an abundance of material in such a short time? How did he wrangle a major album deal and blast past many of his songwriting contemporaries?

As near as I can figure it, after chasing down Willis between Texas and New Mexico, sometimes by phone, sometimes in person, sometimes listening between the lines to our conversations, and on one occasion, when we shared the stage at Poor David's Pub in Dallas, this is how it happened:

Not long after the Rubaiyat show, Willis met Segle Fry, a godfather of Texas folk music and the proprietor of the Chequered Flag, Austin's popular listening room. Segle was impressed enough to give him a shot playing at "The Flag." Willis's parents were so concerned that their son had dropped out of college *again* that they drove down from Dallas to watch him play and try to talk some sense into the boy. After the show, they spoke with Segle who assured them that their son "had it" and could make a good living in the music business.

Once Segle got his parents on board, he plugged Willis into the college coffeehouse circuit. He hit the road playing and hanging out with like-minded songwriters on the circuit like Keith Sykes and Fred Arger. During this period, he focused on writing his own songs and, according to Willis, "The bar was pretty high," set by Fromholz, Murphey, Sykes, and other folkies whom he respected.

"I knew I had to rise to the occasion to compete with those guys. They were great songwriters and I had a lot of work to do."

A few months into the college circuit, Ramsey met Dickey Betts, Greg Allman, and Leon Russell at a festival they were playing in Austin. Willis approached Leon in the big-show crush and asked if he could bring his guitar up to his hotel room and play him some songs. Leon must have had a premonition or he simply liked the kid's forthrightness and confidence, because he said, "Sure, bring it up." Things like that just don't happen every day.

Willis played Leon "two or three songs" and, though nothing was promised, Leon said if Willis ever got out to California to look him up.

Later that day, Willis hooked up with Allman and Betts for an extended visit. They were so impressed with Willis's voice and delivery that they invited him to a studio in Macon, Georgia, where they recorded three of his new songs.

"It was the first time I'd really heard my own voice on a recording, and I knew my songwriting had to get a lot better. So I kept working on it and wrote whenever I could. I listened to a lot of music, studying how other writers put songs together."

The college circuit was a creative proving ground, and Willis dug deep for ideas. He wrote constantly, he honed his musical and "people-watching" skills, and he road-tested his new material in front of an ever-changing audience. "I spent a good deal of time in and out of Wisconsin," he recalled. "There was a strong college circuit up there."

Willis talked in bits and pieces about some of the songs he wrote on the road . . .

The song "Muskrat Candlelight" "came out of a [special guitar] tuning. . . . Sometimes a new tuning will take you to a whole new area."

"'Spider John' was just an exercise in writing a ballad. I wanted a story song and I wanted to stay away from what was being done by other folkies like train songs. So I made the whole thing up."

Willis took Leon up on his invitation and headed west to Los Angeles for a proper audition with Leon and Denny Cordell, the president of Shelter Records. He passed the audition with flying colors, they signed him to a five-year contract and a publishing deal, and Willis was off and running. And of course, he was still writing.

Although many of the songs came from real-life experiences, Willis didn't shy away from blending a healthy splash of poetic license into the mix. In "Good Bye Old Missoula," there was a line about a girl he met named Rosie. "I sort of manufactured a relationship with her for the song," he said. "Years later, Rosie came backstage at a show, mad as hell! She said all her friends had teased her ever since about the song and she was furious with me. Nothing romantic ever really happened between us. She was real but the relationship wasn't. Don't ever write a song with a girl's name in it unless you can back it up!"

He wrote "Angel Eyes" about a girl he met in Chicago but in that case he wouldn't reveal her name. That song has always been special to me because Willis sang "Angel Eyes" at my wedding 43 years ago.

In a remarkably short period, Willis created a collection of ten to fifteen exceptional songs, and he began recording them two or three at a time in different studios around the country.

"After a while, I had eleven songs in the can, but I felt it was just a bunch of tracks that sounded alike. They didn't seem to fit together."

The secret was in the mix and the man behind the mixing console. Al Schmitt had engineered and mixed many of the greats from Duke Ellington, Frank Sinatra, and Sam Cooke to rockers like Jackson Browne and Jefferson Airplane, and, later on, pop icons like Michael Jackson and Madonna. Denny Cordell hired him to mix Willis's new record.

"When Al got a hold of it," Willis said, "the album came together. It was like magic!"

But there were some bumpy patches.

"I'd bug Al all the time asking him questions about EQ and mixing. I guess I went overboard because Al called Denny Cordell and said, 'This kid is driving me crazy. I'm going to quit the project!' Denny called me into his office and said, 'Shut up and let Al work!' So I kept quiet and if there is any good that came out of this record, it's because of Al Schmitt!"

More than four decades after the album's release, Willis is trying to complete his elusive second album tentatively titled, *Gentilly*. All that remains is the final mix, and this time Al Schmitt isn't around. But there is plenty of magic in the new tracks, and through the years Willis has become an outstanding recording engineer. According to Willis, "I was a week away from finishing the final mix when the Colorado floods of 2013 came through and ruined my studio in Loveland. It's taken me two years and it still isn't back up and running, but it's almost there."

We have a great deal to look forward to in anticipation of the new album. There are a whole lot of folks who have been waiting . . . and waiting. That there is such a strong demand for the new record is a testament to the exceptional quality and staying power of the songs on the original album. I have heard most of the new material; I even sang on a track called "Positively" that rekindles the feel and vibe of where he left off all those years ago.

I kept asking Willis where his songs come from . . . what is his inspiration? The closest I could get to an answer was, "Townes called his songs 'sky songs'." By all indications, Willis's new songs have come in for a landing and await only a few technical tweaks before they find their way into our heads and our hearts. We'll see.

Meanwhile Willis is on the road touring quite a bit, plowing the money back into that final mix. Maybe he'll pass through Wisconsin, Montana, or Chicago again and write one more masterpiece to include on the new record.

As for the road? "I still love it," Willis said with a weary, but truthful smile. And there is a rumor that has Willis moving back to Texas soon, "At least for a little while."

GUY CLARK

OLD SCHOOL POET OF THE WORLD[1]

Tamara Saviano

I n 1976, I heard my first Guy Clark song on my Dad's turntable at our home near Milwaukee, Wisconsin. Dad's friend brought a stack of LPs in, and Guy's debut album, *Old No. 1*, was in the pile. As the two of them debated the worth of Memphis soul versus Southern rock, I sat on the floor and planted my ear against the speaker. The lyric sleeve floated on my lap as I tried to listen and read at the same time. I wanted to know everything about the songs that blared out of the box, the four-minute colorful and vivid short stories about exotic people and locations.

Who is Rita Ballou and what is a slow Uvalde? "She's a rawhide rope and velvet mixture, walkin' talkin' Texas texture" was the best line I'd heard in my fourteen years. And that was just the first song. "Words and Music by Guy Clark" was clearly printed beneath each song title on the white paper sleeve. I know for sure this was the first time I understood that the artist had written the songs. From this beginning, my love for Guy's poetry introduced me to others like him—bold and eloquent songwriters that place the art and poetry of their writing far and away above any profit-making ambitions or having a song cut by the latest pop sensation.

Songwriters and music journalists who admire Guy often comment that his approach to writing lyrics is comparable to his skills as a luthier—that he crafts songs with the same detail and precision of an artisan woodworker. Building on the "master craftsman" theme, in 1995 Rounder Records released a thirty-song, double-CD Guy Clark collection titled *Craftsman*. The title didn't sit well with the esteemed Texas songwriter, who says craftsmanship and songwriting use two different parts of his brain.

"I should have put a stop to that craftsman shit a long time ago," Clark said. "It makes my skin crawl. It's nobody's fault but mine because I didn't step up and say 'No, that's not right.' I consider what I do poetry. I don't need to prove I'm a poet in every line and I'm not afraid to speak plainly in my songs. Not everything needs to be metaphor and I don't need lofty words. But it is my obligation as a poet to be faithful to the verse. I write what I know. I write what I see."

Being a poet is part of Guy's DNA. The English poet John Skelton is an ancestor. Skelton was born about 1460, and at one time he was poet laureate at Cambridge and Oxford. He became a tutor to Prince Henry and rose to court poet when the prince ascended to the throne as Henry VIII. Skelton wrote at a time when English pronunciation was changing, and his peers and the mainstream often misunderstood his wit and satire. His work didn't fit in with the popular poetry of the era.

The same could be said of Skelton's descendant. In 1975 the Captain and Tennille's "Love Will Keep Us Together" and the Bee Gees's "Jive Talkin'" topped the pop charts. C. W. McCall sang about a "Convoy," while Mickey Gilley had a No. 1 hit with "Don't All The Girls Get Prettier at Closing Time" over on the country charts.

Meanwhile, the Monahans native released *Old No. 1*, an album of gritty and dazzling story songs rooted in the culture of the West Texas desert. Guy wrote the songs at a scarred table at his home—a ramshackle bungalow in East Nashville—or in his cubbyhole in a third-floor garret at the publishing company's old house on Music Row. Sparked by real people and events, Guy's vibrant narratives thrust the colorful characters from his life to the page and immediately separated him from the fluffy pop songwriters of the day.

"Most of the songs I write I couldn't make up by any stretch of the imagination. They either happened to me or they happened to someone I know," Guy says. "Like 'LA Freeway.' It was about four in the morning and I was coming back from a club gig sleeping in the backseat of the car. I woke up to see where we were and said, 'If I could just get off of this LA Freeway without getting killed or caught.' Lights started going off in my head with that line, so I got Susanna's eyebrow pencil and a burger sack off the floor and wrote it down. Then I carried that scrap of paper around in my wallet for a couple of years while the song simmered."

Also from the *Old No. 1* album, "Rita Ballou" was inspired by teenage trips to Garner State Park in Uvalde County. "Texas 1947" is a true story of a streamline train speeding through Monahans when Guy was six years old. And perhaps his most vivid song, "Desperados Waiting for a Train," is a remembrance of Guy's earliest male influence, a fascinating wildcatter named Jack Prigg who showed young Guy a world of pool halls and taverns and oil wells that gushed black gold.

"One time I was with Jack when an oil well was blowing out," Guy said. "They struck oil and it blew the racking board right out . . . a real gusher. I remember standing next to that rig watching it happen, oil splattering everywhere and the smell, and Jack's running around in every direction. He did not know what to do. To me, as a kid, Jack was a real desperado, the real deal."

In "Desperados Waiting for a Train" the flesh and bone of Jack Prigg is laid bare on the page, as is the love of his protégé:

> He's a drifter, a driller of oil wells
> He's an old school man of the world
> He taught me how to drive his car when he was too drunk to
> And he'd wink and give me money for the girls
> And our lives was like, some old Western movie
> Like desperados waitin' for a train
> Like desperados waitin' for a train

Because he wrote it as a poem first and song second, it should come as no surprise that cowboy actor Slim Pickens's recitation of "Desperados" is Guy's favorite version.

"That really is my favorite thing anybody has done of one of my songs." Guy says. "It literally, the first time I heard it, to have Slim Pickens recite in his voice 'Well, I'd play the Red River Valley,' you know, it just gives me chills."

"Desperados Waiting for a Train" is not the only song of Clark's that clearly stands alone as a poem. Many of his songs illustrate scenes and people from his life in rich detail—each stanza in perfect balance to the whole. "Texas 1947," "The South Coast of Texas," "LA Freeway," "The Randall Knife," "Stuff That Works," "Baby Took A Limo To Memphis," "Dublin Blues," and "My Favorite Picture of You" are just a few examples of songs lifted elegantly from Clark's history.

"Guy is an oral historian and relevant chronicler of life," Clark's longtime friend and cowriter Rodney Crowell says. "He can sum up a feeling in a word or a phrase. What he doesn't say is as powerful as what he does say. Pronunciation and inflection are as important as the cultural references. He presents worlds and experiences without judgment or comment, and he does it with an evocative style and rhythm."

Old No. 1 was commercially categorized as country music. "Desperados" was famously recorded by paragons of the genre including The Highwaymen (Johnny Cash, Willie Nelson, Waylon Jennings, and Kris Kristofferson), Jerry Jeff Walker, David Allan Coe, Bobby Bare, and Mark Chesnutt. Yet, "Desperados" is truly a folk song, inspired by a poem. Guy was deliberate when he sat down to write the poem in stanzaic form. He wanted to tell the story of Jack Prigg, one of the most important people from his life, and he wanted to write the story as a poem with a simple melody over it. Guy did not write a song to be played on country radio and gave no thought to what might happen to the song after he wrote it.

Guy swears he can't crank out cookie-cutter songs even if there is big money to be made. "I've had people call and say they need a song like 'Heartbroke' for their next album. Well, that's not how it works with me. I have songs I worked on for years and years before they came to fruition. 'Baton Rouge' and 'Ramblin' Jack and Mahan' are two of them. I held on to those songs and tinkered with them because I knew they had good parts but it took me a long time to finish them."

During his childhood, the Clark family read poetry around the kitchen table. Guy was influenced by Robert Frost, who wrote about the life and landscape of New England; Stephen Vincent Benet, whose Pulitzer prize-winning poem "John Brown's Body" knitted historical and fictional characters to chronicle incidents from the Civil War; Robert Service, who illustrated life on the Yukon within his poetry; and Vachel Lindsay, whose dramatic delivery in public readings could be likened to a modern-day troubadour like Guy.

Inspired by his friend Townes Van Zandt, Guy began writing his own poetic yet plainspoken songs around 1964 in Houston. *The Freewheelin' Bob Dylan* had been released a year before. Kennedy was dead, and college students all over America were burning their draft cards. The Montrose neighborhood in Houston was a center for the burgeoning counterculture movement, and folksingers came together at the scene.

"Townes is the first person I heard who was writing his own songs in a way that made me want to do it, too," Guy says. "Not necessarily in his style, but the care and respect he took with writing. He never rhymes moon-June-spoon to make a buck. I've always been inspired by Townes. But even with Townes's songs, I move around verses where I think they are more poetic. 'Days up and down they come like rain on a conga drum' should be the first line in 'To Live Is To Fly' and that's the way I sing it. Steve Earle gets so mad at me for changing Townes's song but I think it works better that way."

For inspiration, they often listened to the poet Dylan Thomas reading his own work. "Townes and I would think we were hot shit and then we'd put on Dylan Thomas and go, 'Goddamn, now I see.'"

From the earliest days Guy wrote in lined, perfect-bound notebooks. He meticulously laid out his verses with No. 2 pencils in practiced handwriting, shaping ordinary words into extraordinary poetry.

"Step Inside This House" is the first song Guy put on paper—an artful peek into his identity and personality. Although Guy never recorded it, the song was shared in and around Houston by his fellow folksingers. "Step Inside This House" was passed around from stage to stage, much in the way Stephen Foster's "Oh Susanna" made its way from Pittsburgh to the California Gold Rush in the nineteenth century:

> That picture hangin' on the wall
> Was painted by a friend
> He gave it to me all down and out
> When he owed me ten
> It doesn't look like much I guess
> But it's all that's left of him
> It sure is nice from right over here
> When the light's a little dim
> Step inside this house girl

> I'll sing for you a song
> I'll tell you 'bout just where I've been
> It shouldn't take too long

The song goes on many more verses that describe items from Guy's house: a book of poetry, prism glass, a guitar, a pair of boots and yellow vest, a leather jacket and bag, a hat.

Lyle Lovett finally recorded the song as the title track to a 1998 album that paid homage to Texas songwriters.

"When we were out on the songwriter tour I'd listen to Lyle sing that song every goddamn night," Guy recalls. "One night I grabbed him backstage and said 'Lyle, will you please change that song, man? Leave out this verse and do this and fix this. It's too cumbersome and people just get bored as shit listening to it.' I would have fixed it before I played it live and that's why I don't play it, because it's not a finished song."

"Guy is a ruthless self-editor," says Rodney Crowell. "I've witnessed him come up with the most inspired and beautiful lines, yet he'd throw them out because they didn't work for the particular song he was writing."

Even lyrics on Guy's albums aren't always ironclad. He often changes lines years after the song has been recorded to make the song more poetic.

"I find better ways to say stuff. To me, the songs are all works in progress," Guy says. "When I wrote 'Better Days' there was a line in it that made my skin crawl. I hated it. I could not think of anything better. Right up to the minute I recorded it, I kept thinking I'd get something better but didn't so I went ahead and recorded anyhow. The line was 'On a ray of sunshine, she goes dancing out the door.' It was just like 'Goddamn, Guy, surely you can come up with something not that goofy.'"

Guy took the song out of his live set because he could not bring himself to sing the line. Years later, at a gig in Australia, the director of a women's shelter approached Guy to tell him that the shelter used "Better Days" as a theme song. Guy said he didn't sing the song anymore because of the one line he hated.

"And then, the damnedest thing, the perfect line finally came to me right that minute, 'She has no fear of flying / Now she's out the door.' It took four years. I knew it was there, but I couldn't get to it."

> See the wings unfolding, that weren't there just before
> She has no fear of flying, now she's out the door
> Out into the morning light where the sky is all ablaze
> This looks like the first of better days

The right words are so important to Guy that when Rosanne Cash recorded "Better Days" for a tribute album, *This One's For Him: A Tribute to Guy Clark*, Guy called three times to make sure Rosanne sang the new line and not the old one.

Like a poet reading his work aloud, Guy believes that the final step of writing a song is to perform it in front of an audience. He says the song is not finished until he learns to deliver the sounds and rhythms, to learn what to leave in, what to leave out, or even whether the song works at all.

"Poems and songs are living and breathing things," Guy says. "I can play something on stage for two weeks or two months to just see how it works. You can sit in a room all day long and sing it to yourself and not know where the flaws are. But when you start to communicate it and see if people get it, then you find out where it needs to be fixed."

Back in the early days in Houston, Townes and Guy practiced their songs at the Jester Lounge, Sand Mountain, and the Old Quarter. They also played for fellow members of the Houston Folklore Society, which included the famous blues musicians Lightnin' Hopkins and Mance Lipscomb. Musicologist Robert "Mack" McCormick once said that Hopkins "is the embodiment of the jazz-and-poetry spirit." Hopkins and Lipscomb's influence on Guy's writing and performance is significant. It laid the groundwork for what was to come in Nashville.

After *Old No. 1*, RCA, and then Warner Bros., did not know what to do with Guy. Folksingers were largely under the radar in the late 1970s and 1980s, and while *Old No. 1* was critically acclaimed, this was a major label; mainstream country radio world and hit records were what mattered most. *Texas Cookin'* in 1976 and *Guy Clark* in 1978 were produced with more instruments and polish as Nashville tried to figure out how to fit the Guy Clark square peg into the round hole of commercial country music.

The style didn't suit him and he thought often about Lightnin' Hopkins, Townes, and the folksingers he had come up with in Houston. Yet, Guy went along with the advice from his label. He figured they knew better than he did how to find an audience and sell records.

If things had gone as originally planned, 1981's *The South Coast of Texas* album would have been titled *Burnin' Daylight* and produced by Craig Leon. Leon had produced eponymous records for Blondie and the Ramones in 1976 and most recently Rodney Crowell's 1980 album *But What Will The Neighbors Think?* Crowell's song "Ashes By Now" had made the pop charts, and the brass at Warner Brothers thought Leon's approach might drive the same commercial success with Guy.

But Guy and Leon didn't hit it off. Guy wanted to give the label what they needed, but his songs, his poetry, were getting lost in the mix. With little budget left and a deadline for the album looming, Guy turned to Crowell.

"Rodney was enamored with Brian Ahern and his mobile truck so we went to Los Angeles to record there," Guy said. "It seemed like as good a thing as any to do at the time. It was Rodney's crew and they were all great players."

Yet, Guy still wasn't happy with the results of *South Coast of Texas* or with his next album, 1983's *Better Days*, also produced by Crowell.

"I just didn't really know what I wanted to do," Guy admits. "I didn't like my records after *Old No. 1*. Some of the songs were badly done and the records didn't sound like I wanted them to sound. I see myself as a folksinger and my songs as poetry. When there is too much instrumentation the songs get lost."

For the next six years, Guy practiced singing his songs in front of a mirror in his basement. He wanted to get back to the basics of putting the lyrics out front. He wanted his poetry to come first.

Guy finally took control of his own recordings with 1989's *Old Friends*, his first record on the noted Americana and bluegrass label Sugar Hill Records. It was a gutsy move at a time when his friend Rodney Crowell was having mega-success in country radio with slickly produced albums. Major label country-pop artists including Reba McEntire, the Judds, Eddie Rabbit, Restless Heart, Alabama, Steve Wariner, and a new guy named Garth Brooks rode the wave of the Urban Cowboy era into the next decade when Guy decided to move in the opposite direction.

Old Friends was the first album where Guy started cowriting with other writers outside of his close circle.

"I really enjoy the nuts and bolts of writing. Probably my weakest link as I've gotten older is dialing up the ideas. It's not that my ideas aren't good; it's just that I don't see them like I see other people's. It's a strange thing. I'll get so far into someone else's three-line idea, when I have probably one hundred times better stuff here and can't focus like that on it."

With *Old Friends*, Guy changed his recording style to complement the verses, parsing sparse musical arrangements to give the words more weight and put the vocals out front.

First, Guy went into the studio with just his guitar and co-producer/engineer Miles Wilkinson. He played his songs one after the other, over and over, and ran through them for several days until he got them recorded in a way that pleased him. It was only then that Guy called in other musicians and overdubbed their parts—guitar, mandolin, bass, and a little percussion, but no big rock 'n' roll drums. With the understated instrumentation, for the first time since *Old No. 1*, the songs took a starring role on the album. Guy felt so strongly about this album that the cover is a self-portrait painting.

"*Old Friends* was the first record where I finally got to make the record I've always wanted to make, with an acoustic approach and no drums," Guy says. "I quit trying to please everyone else in the room and only worried about pleasing myself."

Guy teamed up with Wilkinson again for 1992's *Boats to Build* and 1995's *Dublin Blues* after being courted by Kyle Lehning, who had just opened a Nashville office for the Elektra/Asylum label. On the two albums, the artist made a strong statement about his commitment to poetry. The songs were written with insight and authority and grown-up themes of hardship, risk, and consequences. All of the arrangements and sounds are in service to the song. Guy re-recorded "Randall Knife" because he loved the personal song about his father, but hated the faster tempo arrangement on the *Better Days* album. On *Dublin Blues*, the heartrending ballad is delivered in the slow cadence of a poetry reading as a spoken word song:

> My father died when I was forty
> And I couldn't find a way to cry
> Not because I didn't love him
> Not because we didn't try
> I'd cried for every lesser thing
> Whiskey, pain and beauty
> But he deserved a better tear
> And I was not quite ready
>
> So we took his ashes out to sea
> And poured 'em off the stern
> And threw the roses in the wake
> Of everything we'd learned
> When we got back to the house
> They asked me what I wanted
> Not the law books, not the watch
> I need the things he haunted
>
> My hand burned for the Randall Knife
> There in the bottom drawer
> And I found a tear for my father's life
> And all that it stood for

Along with "Randall Knife," "Stuff That Works," "Dublin Blues," "The Cape," "Boats to Build," and "Baton Rouge" became instant folk classics.

And it's remained the case for Guy's subsequent five studio albums. He returned to Sugar Hill Records for 1999's *Cold Dog Soup*, which introduced "Sis Draper," a true story about a fiddler from Arkansas known by Guy's cowriter Shawn Camp. The folk poetry inspired by "Sis Draper" continued on 2002's *The Dark* with "Magnolia Wind" and "Soldier's Joy, 1864."

After Sugar Hill was bought by Welk Music Group, Guy moved over to the independent Dualtone Music for 2006's *Workbench Songs*, 2009's *Somedays the Song Writes You*, and 2013's *My Favorite Picture of You*. All three albums were nominated for Grammy Awards for Best Folk Album. *My Favorite Picture of You* includes the final songs in the Sis Draper series, "Cornmeal Waltz" and "The Death of Sis Draper." On January 26, 2014, at the Staples Center in Los Angeles, Guy Clark finally won a Grammy, on his seventh nomination. *My Favorite Picture of You* took home the honors for Best Folk Album. Guy was not there to accept the award.

The title track is a profound final tribute for Susanna, Guy's wife of forty years who died in 2012. As it was in the early years with "Desperados Waiting For a Train," Guy's intention when writing "My Favorite Picture of You" was to honor his wife within the framework of a poem.

Bob Allen wrote about Guy in *Country Music* magazine in 1989: "He is, in many ways, what Picasso was to modern art, or what Raymond Carver was to the American short story: a master of expression and conciseness who has often set the benchmark standards for artistry, originality, and integrity in his chosen field."

In 2013, the Academy of Country Music awarded Guy Clark its Poet's Award for outstanding musical and lyrical contributions throughout his career. Guy was honored along with Hank Williams, and they joined a short list of previous recipients that includes Merle Haggard, Tom T. Hall, Roger Miller, Harlan Howard, and Cindy Walker.

Kris Kristofferson

The Silver-Tongued Rhodes Scholar

Peter Cooper

K ris Kristofferson felt the cold Nashville concrete through the sad soles of his boots, and in that moment he began to doubt William Blake.

Perhaps, Kristofferson thought, it was unwise to base the remainder of his existence on something a dead British poet said in some other world, across an ocean and a century.

What Blake said was, "If you, who are organized by divine providence for spiritual communion, refuse, and bury your talent in the earth, even though you should want natural bread, sorrow and desperation pursue you through life, and after death shame and confusion." Kristofferson—who studied Blake back when he was the only future member of the Country Music Hall of Fame in classes at the University of Oxford, via a Rhodes Scholarship—took that to mean that the love of creation can save your ass, and that his externally ratified life as a student, a writer, an athlete, and a soldier was a ticket to writhing, thrashing doom. Music, he had been certain, was spiritual communion.

Kristofferson's talent was buried not in the earth but beneath rudimentary guitar skills and a voice that sounded like a flu-ridden frog, but over time he grew certain that he was meant to convey truth in rhyme. He received nothing approaching ratification on this matter from friends or, especially, family, but he could not expect them to grasp the nature of his calling. His guiding stars were both Williams—Hank Williams and William Blake—and they would have understood, but they were long gone.

Anyway, Kristofferson figured, Blake may have lied. Blake was too bright to be wrong, but not too smart to deceive. The real deal may have been what Hank Williams sang: "You'll curse the day you started rollin' down that lost highway." In 1966, Kristofferson learned that Nashville is colder than advertised in the wintertime. He kept wrecking his little Honda motorcycle on woozy evenings, his marriage was failing, and his mother disowned him upon learning that he had ditched an appointment to teach at West Point in favor of chasing his wretched muse and associating with degenerates and drug addicts like Johnny Cash.

"Pleased to meet you, it's a hairy-legged town," Tom T. Hall told him when they first met. And Hall's words were ringing like melody in Kristofferson's head as he assessed his situation this winter day. He wanted natural bread, and it seemed that sorrow and desperation need not pursue him: he'd chased them down on his own.

"Fuck William Blake," he thought. "Fuck me, running."

"I was selfish," Kristofferson said, forty years later. "If I hadn't been, I never would have been able to put up with the hardship I was causing other people. I had a little girl I wasn't seeing much of. And for my wife, it must have been miserable."

His wife, Fran, married the smartest and most successful man she'd ever encountered. Kristofferson was an Army brat, born in Brownsville, Texas. By the time he turned twenty-nine, he'd been a Golden Gloves boxer and a college football player and wrestler. He'd had two short stories published in *Atlantic Monthly*. He'd graduated summa cum laude from college in California, and the Rhodes Scholar thing was heartening to his family. He made himself into an Army Ranger and a helicopter pilot, and the US Army made him a captain, pleasing his father, an Army man for life. The Army deemed him too valuable to send to Vietnam, and he was on a path to financial security and, more than likely, high political office. He was the smartest, most charismatic, most handsome man in every room he entered. He was also guided by parents who valued duty, honor, and obligation above all else.

"If they deal you down and dirty in a way you don't deserve, you'll feel better if you take it like a man," Kristofferson wrote in "The Heart," setting to verse words his father, Henry, told him. His mother, Mary Ann, inspired in him a sense of social justice.

"When I was growing up down in Brownsville, Texas, the racial issue wasn't between blacks and whites," he said. "It was Mexicans that there was prejudice against, and my mother made sure we knew that was wrong. One example I remember of it is when a Mexican from Brownsville won the Medal of Honor and they had a parade for him, and we were the only Anglos at the parade."

That was the man Fran married. Then came the West Point invitation, and on his visit there Kristofferson was told that cadets would enter his literature classroom and stand at attention until he ordered, "Seat!" That made him uncomfortable. Then he was told that he'd have to provide lesson plans, advising his superiors of what he'd be saying on any given day, months in advance. This sounded far from freedom and made him shudder. Then he started thinking about William Blake and divine providence and how the love of creation can save your ass. And then, in the summer of 1965, he headed down to Nashville for the first time, to visit with an Army friend's cousin, the songwriter and publisher Marijohn Wilkin.

On his first night in Music City, he met Cowboy Jack Clement, who helped invent rock 'n' roll at Sun Records and who would soon desegregate country music by bringing Charley Pride to popularity. Cowboy Jack was prone to reciting Shakespeare, and he was already known for elevating the "artist" component of the "bullshit artist" equation. He was a delight, and he took Kristofferson—still in his Army dress uniform—to a gulch where trains passed by. The Cowboy—so called even though he hated horses and preferred Hawaiian shirts to Western wear—talked of hitching freights, of recording Elvis Presley, and of his best friend, Johnny Cash.

"He had a thing about trains," Kristofferson said of the Cowboy. "He talked about how he'd get onto a train and ride from Nashville to New Orleans and back. Just ride down, come back."

Kristofferson had never met anyone like him. Cowboy seemed to him like a nobler, more interesting version of Shakespeare's Falstaff, and Nashville seemed a town without lesson plans. Kristofferson awoke the next late day with a headache, a molecular unsettling, and thoughts of William Blake.

On that trip, Kristofferson went backstage at the Grand Ole Opry, where he saw Johnny Cash, gaunt and prowling.

"He shook my hand and it was electric," Kristofferson said. "I felt that these people I met in Nashville were so fascinating that if I didn't make it as a writer of songs I could write about them. Backstage at the Opry, breathing the same air that Hank Williams breathed, it all felt enchanted."

Not long after, he resigned his teaching appointment, refused what looked for all the world to be a king's future, moved his family to Nashville, and became what he now, accurately, calls "a songwriting bum." That job involved late nights, drinking, a Honda that often found itself resting dirty side up, the feel of a sidewalk through a filthy and fragile sole, and sorrow and desperation for companionship.

"I went through periods of some despair, when I looked around me and felt like I'd trashed it all," he said. "My wife and I finally split up. The music came to be . . . a wall between us. It brought all these shady people into the house. She didn't want them in the house, let alone have me hanging with them for three days and nights at a time."

Hindsight makes the story glorious, at least to those of us who didn't live it. But at the time, it was a rough show to watch.

"See him wasted on the sidewalk in his jacket and his jeans, wearing yesterday's misfortunes like a smile," he would write, ostensibly about Cash, restlessly creative compadre Chris Gantry, and others, but—later, admittedly—about himself. "Once he had a future full of money, love, and dreams, which he spent like they was going out of style."

That song, "The Pilgrim, Chapter 33," was as compelling a portrait of artistic abandon as had been heard in country music. Its hero was "A pilgrim and a preacher and a prophet when he's stoned / He's a walking contradiction, partly truth and partly fiction, taking every wrong direction on his lonely way back home." In Kristofferson's mind, the wrong direction was the correct one. Artistry was possible through madness, but not through conformity.

"I'll never forget hearing 'The Pilgrim' for the first time," said Todd Snider, a brilliant singer-songwriter who has emerged as a leading light of the scuffling generation that followed Kristofferson's. San Marcos, Texas-based Kent Finlay, who mentored dozens of songwriters, pulled out "The Pilgrim, Chapter 33" at a late-night picking session that turned into a late-night listening session. Moments later, Snider found some semblance of purpose.

"I wanted to live every line of that song, immediately," Snider said. "I wanted to be wasted on the sidewalk in my jacket and my jeans, and I definitely wanted to wear yesterday's misfortunes like a smile."

Kristofferson would also pen a song called "To Beat the Devil," about a guitar swap in a Nashville bar. In the song, an "old man" buys a down-and-out guitar player a beer, borrows his guitar and says, "I've got something you oughta hear."

And then the old man sings: "If you waste your time a'talkin' to the people who don't listen to the things that you are saying, who do you think's gonna hear? / And if you should die explaining how the things that they complain about are things they could be changing, who do you think's gonna care?" That old man haunted Kristofferson's dreams. He mocked the songwriter. He mocked William Blake. His was the voice of reasoned doubt.

"There were other lonely singers in a world turned deaf and blind, who were crucified for what they tried to show / And their voices have been scattered by the swirling winds of time, 'cause the truth remains that no one wants to know."

Kristofferson lived along Music Row, right down the street from a place called the Tally Ho Tavern. At the Tally Ho, the owner would allow patrons to get drunk, but not to arrive drunk. The place was located on a corner, and it had a seating area in the back and a bar up front. A drunk walked in one night and was quickly thrown out. He stumbled around the corner, turned right, saw the back seating area and found his way onto a chair. The owner saw him there and hollered, "I told you to get the hell out of here!" The drunk stammered, "Damn, do you own every bar on this block?"

Kristofferson's Nashville world was such that he witnessed that scene first-hand. As he entered his thirties, he figured total immersion into Nashville's blurry wildlife was the only way to learn to create. He worked as a bartender and, more famously, as a janitor at Columbia Recording Studios, where some of the musicians grumbled about his late arrivals. It seems he seldom got to the studio early enough to make a pot of coffee before the 10:00 a.m. recording sessions began. Some at Columbia also faulted his opportunistic streak: he wasn't shy about talking with artists about his own songs. At one point, Columbia forbade him from cleaning up at a Johnny Cash session, but Cash insisted that the young janitor be present. Cash had a soft spot for Kristofferson. He'd seen the letter that Kristofferson's mother wrote, telling her son that his irresponsible decision to become a songwriting bum meant he was no longer a part of the family.

Cash's support provided for some measure of hope, as did Dave Dudley's 1966 decision to record Kristofferson's "Viet Nam Blues." The winter of '66 became the spring of '67, and Kristofferson was on no one's idea of a fast track. Billy Sherrill produced "The Golden Idol," a Kristofferson single, in 1967, but it failed to connect. Betrayed by William Blake, Kristofferson took jobs flying helicopters around the oil rigs in the Gulf of Mexico.

"When I was working in the Gulf, I wrote songs all the time," he said. "I was flying for hours without anything to think about except for the songs. I'm surprised they didn't all come out with the same rhythm of the blades."

Some of them did come out to that rhythm, and most of them came out in perfect iambic pentameter, and people began to take notice. Billy Walker recorded Kristofferson's "From the Bottle to the Bottom," and Tom T. Hall thought enough of that version to praise the song out loud one night at Tootsie's Orchid Lounge—Hall's words provided for the finest honor of Kristofferson's career to date. Publisher and record mogul Fred Foster signed Kristofferson on the condition that the songwriter would record for Foster's Monument Records. This seemed crazy to Kristofferson, who was painfully aware of his singing voice's limitations, but Foster found Kristofferson's songs all the more compelling when delivered by their author.

All these developments are indicators of genre-shaking, culture-tweaking successes that would soon come. At the time, they were merely straws at which to grasp. Kristofferson would walk an empty Music Row on Sunday mornings, impatient for bars to open at noon, and know that his artistic aspirations were causing the dissolutions of relationships with his mother and his wife. In a lonely moment, he wrote lines that spoke to his condition and would later be received by millions: "On a Sunday morning sidewalk, wishing, Lord, that I was stoned / 'Cause there's something in a Sunday, makes a body feel alone."

In another instance, depleted by his efforts to pay his humble bills and at the same time remain creative, he confessed to Foster that he had run out of songs. Foster offered some dough to ease the financial distress and offered an idea to combat Kristofferson's writer's block: "Write a song called 'Me and Bobby McKee,'" Foster advised. McKee was a secretary for songwriter Boudleaux Bryant, and the repeating hard E sounds made for a good title.

In a helicopter above Baton Rouge, Kristofferson's blades recalled the rhythm of a Mickey Newbury song, "Why You Been Gone So Long," and his mind recalled Foster's song suggestion. Later, he drove a car through heavy rain, thought of a Fellini film called *La Strada* and of a woman he'd known, and he turned a corner.

"When it came together was when the lines finally came about, 'With them windshield wipers slapping time and Bobby clapping hands we finally sang up every song that driver knew,'" Kristofferson said, remembering the creation of a now-classic, "Me and Bobby McGee." The windshield wipers line was the glue, but it was another line that made the song indelible: "Freedom's just another word for nothing left to lose." Kristofferson was not only familiar with sorrow and desperation, he gave voice and reason to sorrow and desperation.

Haphazard genius Roger Miller recorded "Me and Bobby McGee" in 1969, and it landed at No. 12 on the *Billboard* country singles chart. Bob Neuwirth, a musician and pal of Bob Dylan who was, and is, something of a professional free spirit, taught the song to Port Arthur, Texas, native Janis Joplin, and she wound up recording it for her *Pearl* album, released not long after her 1970 overdose. Kristofferson, who'd shared a brief love affair with Joplin, heard her version just after she'd died. It wound up as Joplin's only chart-topping single, snapping Kristofferson's heart every time he heard it on the radio. Forty years removed, he still called her name at every show: "Brother, that was good enough for me . . . and Janis," he'd sing.

By the time "Me and Bobby McGee" hit the airwaves, Kristofferson was already American roots music's next big deal. Everything changed in 1970, when he won an Academy of Country Music song of the year award for penning the Ray Price smash, "For the Good Times," and a Country Music Association top song honor for writing "Sunday Morning Coming Down," which Johnny Cash brought to popularity.

In 1970, he also released his Monument Records' debut, *Kristofferson*, a commercial dud in spite of its staggering content. Kristofferson classics "Me and Bobby McGee," "Help Me Make It Through The Night," "Just the Other Side of Nowhere," "Sunday Morning Coming Down," and "To Beat the Devil" are all there, the latter selection featuring Kristofferson's wry answer to the old man in the barroom who haunted his dreams, questioned his purpose, and defied that sage, William Blake. The man had hectored, "If you waste your time a'talking to the people who don't listen to the things that you are saying, who do you think's gonna hear?" Kristofferson answered, "You still can hear me singing to the people who don't listen to the things that I am saying, praying someone's going to hear." And in the final chorus, he sings, "I was born a lonely singer and I'm bound to die the same, but I've got to feed the hunger in my soul / And if I never have a nickel I won't ever die ashamed, 'cause I don't believe that no one wants to know."

Born a lonely singer. Organized by divine providence for spiritual communion. Wrecked and bent and righteous as a boxer's bloody nose.

Kristofferson's songs changed things. Some people point to the way he brought sex into the poetic mainstream, singing, "Take the ribbon from your hair, shake it loose and let it fall." That was part of it, but mostly it was that he fused poetry, melody, and reality in a way that no one before him had done. He was among a small group of writers that included Hall, Newbury, and John Hartford, men who transformed the language of country songwriting in the way that Bob Dylan transformed rock 'n' roll song craft. Nashville-based country songs became literate, layered, and credible to people who had cared nothing for the stuff about honky-tonks and little darlin's.

In spite of the debut album's poor sales (it did better when reissued in 1971 as *Me and Bobby McGee*), Kristofferson's solo career soon took off. Cash touted him at every opportunity, and Kristofferson put together a band of songwriting buddies to play gigs at The Troubadour in Los Angeles and at a hastily arranged festival performance at the Isle of Wight. There, he was less than enthusiastically received.

"They were throwing shit at me, but I kept singing," he said. "I told 'em, 'I brought this band over here at my own expense. They told me to do an hour, and I'm going to do an hour, in spite of anything but rifle fire'."

Band member Billy Swan—whose "I Can Help" would become a national hit—quickly reprimanded, "Don't say 'rifle fire!'"

But they survived, and then they thrived, and they toured big halls, and Kristofferson made movies and wrote big songs, played sheds and arenas, scored a No. 1 country album with 1972's *Jesus Was a Capricorn* and scored a No. 1 country hit with "Why Me" in 1973, backed by Larry Gatlin and new love Rita Coolidge. His and Rita's marriage lasted seven years. They were beautiful people surrounded by what seemed to be beautiful circumstances, and they moved to Malibu and Kris became a bona fide movie star.

One casually and improperly accepted version of the story is that his acting came at the expense of his songs. Hand in hand with this version comes the notion that Kristofferson sold out and traded talent for natural bread, fuck William Blake-style. In truth, a lot of his acting gigs were of the art film variety: people don't sell out to do *Bring Me The Head of Alfredo Garcia* and *Alice Doesn't Live Here Anymore*. He did some blockbusters as well (*A Star Is Born* among them), but his acting career is distinguished, and his musical output after moving from Nashville is uncompromising.

His finest album might be 1974's *Spooky Lady's Sideshow*. That album's "Broken Freedom Song" finds a wounded soldier on a train, lying out loud about how he hated going home, and then Kristofferson's omniscient narrator chimes in a chorus: "Just a simple song of freedom, he was never fighting for / No one's listenin' when you need 'em, ain't no fun to sing that song no more." Then there's a woman, pregnant and thwarted and hopeless. And then a verse about Christ on the cross: "And he's sadder than he's wiser, and a longer way from home / And he wonders why his father left him bleeding and alone." That one is set alongside the questioning "Star-Spangled Bummer (Whores Die Hard)" and the morality play "Shandy (The Perfect Disguise)," and all this adds up to nothing approaching a sellout.

"Nightmares are somebody's daydreams," he sings in "Shandy." "Daydreams are somebody's lies / Lies ain't no harder than telling the truth / truth is the perfect disguise."

On 1975's "Who's To Bless and Who's To Blame," he conjures a laughing deity who ponders earth: "Who says that He can't take a dirty joke?"

The marriage to Coolidge didn't last. As often happens, friends chose sides. Much is made of Kristofferson's political stances, of his attention to justice and compassion and fairness. Nowhere is that devotion to fairness better exemplified than in a song he wrote in the wake of his dissolved marriage, "Maybe You Heard."

"Don't turn away there, hey, goddamn you, you used to love her," he sang, to those who would side with him after the breakup. "Turn on your father, sister, mother, mister she was your friend / Don't you condemn her, leave it to strangers."

After the breakup, Kristofferson recorded in a supergroup with Cash, Willie Nelson, and Waylon Jennings, and a fine-selling 1985 album was more of a success than any of those much-vaunted troubadours could conjure on his own. Kristofferson could have used that supergroup's brief commercial triumphs to reinvent himself as a market-ready singer. Instead, he released an album called *Repossessed*, with songs that found him wrestling with how to live honorably in times of dishonor.

"They Killed Him" was about Ghandi, Martin Luther King, and Jesus Christ. In "The Heart," he recalled his father's advice in ratifying Blake's ideas of artists and artistry in the face of criticism: "They say every song is sweeter when you sing it from the heart / I won't know it 'cause I've tried it and it's true / I may never get to heaven but I've seen a lot of stars, and I'm here to bring the same advice to you." Then, in 1990, he returned with *Third World Warrior*, singing about America's lost ideals in "Don't Let the Bastards (Get You Down)," about Nicaragua, about freeing Nelson Mandela, about the Sandinistas, and about Jesse Jackson. You know, typical sellout country music fare. One reviewer noted that Kristofferson was now "irrelevant," a word that still riles Kristofferson.

"I was trying, and I'm still trying, to live up to my responsibilities as a human being," he said. "If you're given the tools to be a creative person, would you use them right?"

In 1992, Irish songwriter Sinead O'Connor tore up a picture of the pope—I forget which pope—on an American comedy show called *Saturday Night Live*. Mayhem ensued. A couple of weeks later, O'Connor performed at a Bob Dylan tribute show at Madison Square Garden. As she went onstage, she was booed. She attempted and failed to wear misfortune like a smile. Kristofferson whispered into her ear, "Don't let the bastards get you down." She ditched her planned performance and sang some of Bob Marley's "War" without accompaniment. She was castigated by a ticket-holding mob. She walked off the stage, and the only one there to comfort her was Kristofferson. In the moment, he remembered the ache of cold Nashville concrete through the soles of his boots. He embraced her as she cried. Later, he wrote about her, and he sang about her in a song called "Sister Sinead."

"And maybe she's crazy and maybe she ain't / But so was Picasso and so were the saints."

This was sellout, money-grab era Kristofferson: hugging a disconsolate, bald, unflinching, lost young Irish woman while the boos rang through "The World's Most Famous Arena," then writing a song about her that he knew the radio would never play.

In the new century, Kristofferson collects awards and adulation. He enters the Country Music Hall of Fame. He releases a purposeful album to rave reviews. He gets a lifetime achievement prize from the Grammy people and performs at the Grammy Awards with fellow icons Merle Haggard and Willie Nelson. His wife, Lisa, is a constant and a joy. His children shine even in darkness: they are lit from the inside out. Audiences stand for him and applaud before he sings a note. This is all as it should be.

"All alone all the way on your own / Who's to say that you've thrown it away for a song?" he sings.

Plenty of people said that about him, and there was a time when he did toss everything he'd accomplished, for a song. It was a song yet unsung: Kristofferson did not have "Me and Bobby McGee" or "For the Good

Times" or "Help Me Make It Through the Night" or "Sunday Morning Coming Down" or "The Pilgrim, Chapter 33" in his back pocket when he rejected his West Point commission. He came to the songwriting life out of faith in himself, faith in creativity, and faith in dead poets. He came for the love of creation. He came out of artistic obligation. He came because he surmised he was supposed to. He stayed out of belief in revolution, in art, in justice, in words, in actions, in love, in mercy, in excellence, in sorrow, and in redemption. He believed in belief, though he doubted it at times.

"Sometimes I laugh about it today, thinking how audacious I was," he said. "It makes you feel like there's some kind of divine guidance going along there. I know there were mistakes. I know there were things I did that were stupid, and that I probably would rather I didn't do. But I'd hate to change anything because of the way it's turned out."

Beginning with 2006's *This Old Road*, Kristofferson released a triumvirate of stripped-down, minimalist, acoustic albums: *This Old Road*, *Closer to the Bone*, and *Feeling Mortal*. Some of the material was taken from his Hollywood-era works that were commercially ignored, and the bare-bones soundscapes allow for a textural immediacy that was lacking in the initial recordings. The new songs tended towards reflection and gratitude, and there are moments that sound like the beginning of a long goodbye of the sort that his friends Waylon Jennings, Shel Silverstein, Stephen Bruton, and Mickey Newbury were never able to offer.

"Wide awake and feeling mortal, at this moment in the dream," he sang in 2013, soberly facing "that old man there in the mirror." Other song titles offer an indication of his mindset: "Thank You for a Life," "Final Attraction," "From Here to Forever."

Today, Kristofferson is cheered for the same things that once brought him scorn. What was selfish is heroic. What was offensive is brave. He has shouldered the burden of freedom.

"It's a brief time we've got here," he said in 2013, at age seventy-six. "The thing that's surprising to me is actually how good I feel. I'm not depressed that it's going to be over, I'm grateful for how wonderful it's been."

Sorrow and desperation did not follow him through a life that did the Williams proud. Yesterday's misfortunes are a smile.

VIGNETTE—DON HENLEY

LITERATURE, LAND, AND LEGACY

Kathryn Jones

Don Henley, singer-songwriter of one of the most popular and respected rock bands of all time, the Eagles, entered the music business through another door—literature. He discovered the writings of Henry David Thoreau and Ralph Waldo Emerson while in high school and college at North Texas State University (now the University of North Texas). Their words never left him and planted the seeds of environmental activism.

Inspired by Thoreau's and Emerson's works, Henley founded the Walden Woods Project in Massachusetts to preserve Thoreau's beloved Walden Pond and his legacy. In 1992 he created the Caddo Lake Institute to safeguard the ecology of Caddo Lake in northeast Texas near where he grew up in Linden.

After the Eagles split up in 1980, Henley went solo and remained a successful singer-songwriter, cowriting biting social commentaries in slickly produced numbers such as "Dirty Laundry" and "Inside Job" and wistful love songs like "The Boys of Summer." Strangely enough, though, until recently Henley didn't write many songs about his native Texas. One stands out—the elegiac "Goodbye to a River," based on the classic Texas book by John Graves. Cowritten with Stan Lynch, Jai Winding, and Frank Simes, Henley's inner outrage and poetic lyrics dovetailed in a plaintive lament for a once-wild river.

Goodbye to a River, of course, is one of the must-reads of Texas literature about Graves's canoe trip down the Brazos in the late 1950s before a string of dams changed it forever. The song, featured on Henley's album *Inside Job* (Warner Bros., 2000), combines bongos, violins, piano, and tambourines to create a haunting, mournful sound and captured the book's message in four long stanzas and a chorus:

> Lakes and levees, dams and locks
> They put that river in a box

Well, it was running wild
Men must have control
We live our lives in starts and fits
We lose our wonder bit by bit
We condescend and in the end
We lose our very souls
Goodbye to a river
Goodbye to a river
So long

Henley has said he believes he is doing the most important work of his life with his environmental projects, but "Goodbye to a River," as a line in the song goes, crosses "generational fences." Graves died in 2013 and didn't even get to see his namesake stretch of the river, the John Graves Scenic Riverway, extended to his hometown of Glen Rose—lobbyists for quarries made sure to line the pockets of Texas legislators to keep a bill from passing. The song isn't just about the Brazos and never mentions it by name. It's a collective, universal cry against "killing everything divine" and the corrupting power of industry on nature. Ruthless? Hell, yes—and rightfully so.

Finally, in 2015, Henley rediscovered his Texas roots on *Cass County*, his first solo record in 15 years. The title refers to his home county in northeastern Texas, and Henley lined up some of the musicians he admires most to perform on the album, including Merle Haggard, Mick Jagger, Alison Krauss, Miranda Lambert, Martina McBride, Ashley Monroe, Dolly Parton, Lucinda Williams, and Trisha Yearwood. Henley described the album to *Rolling Stone* magazine as a "natural progression. It's not me trying to do the 'Don Henley country album.'" He again collaborated with Lynch, the original drummer for Tom Petty and the Heartbreakers, and included one of his most autobiographical songs, "Train in the Distance," with Williams contributing her evocative harmony. The lyrics paint a wistful picture of a boy putting pennies on the railroad tracks for trains to run over, lying in bed in his grandmother's house, and wondering what life would be like far from his hometown.

Henley said the album is about "who I am and where I come from." Write more songs about Texas, Don.

STEVEN FROMHOLZ, MICHAEL MARTIN MURPHEY, AND JERRY JEFF WALKER

POETIC IN LYRIC, MESSAGE, AND MUSICAL METHOD

Craig D. Hillis

Fromholz, Murphey, and Walker—three defining figures in the history of Texas songwriting, three songwriters instrumental in ushering Texas music into the national spotlight, and three talented musicians largely responsible for the trajectory of my professional musical career. I began playing with Fromholz, Murphey, and Walker in the early '70s and have enjoyed their friendship and support for almost forty-five years.

Fromholz, Murphey, and Walker build their songs on enduring foundations of lyric and message while blending chord and melody to create what we have chosen to call "ruthlessly poetic" songs. Being razor-focused on their aesthetic challenge, they sometimes ignore other pressing aspects of their day-to-day lives. In this hyper-focused state, this state of *passive ruthlessness*, Fromholz, Murphey, Walker, and other writers featured in this book go about their work wearing "nothing-but-my-art" blinders for the sake of their songs.

My first meaningful encounter with songs of this caliber came in 1970. I experienced what might be called an aesthetic conversion when I heard the folk duo Frummox at a small nightclub in Austin and met Steven Fromholz.

Frummox was Steven Fromholz and Dan McCrimmon, and their 1969 album release, *Here to There* on ABC Records, had created a notable stir in the national folk music scene. The Chequered Flag was Austin's premier folk venue and routinely booked many of the artists featured in this study. The room's ambiance lent itself to listening, and the audiences came for that specific purpose. My initial encounter with Frummox at the Chequered Flag was an aesthetic wake-up call that had a profound effect on my musical sensibilities. Fromholz and McCrimmon presented melodies that were both delicate and dynamic, well-balanced harmonies, and lyrics that painted a vivid picture of the story. I was particularly impressed with *Texas Trilogy*. This three-song suite blended history and insight with words and music that transcended the normal parameters of the "folk song." The *Trilogy* guided the audience through the *bigness* of growing up in a *small* Texas town while reifying the *bigness* of the experience in the lives of the song's characters.

My friend Segle Fry, co-owner of the "The Flag," introduced me to Steven and Dan after the show. As is often the case with touring musicians, the end of the last set signaled a retreat to a hotel or a friendly living room for some serious song swapping and party pickin'. That night was no exception. Steven was even more of a character off stage than on, and as we passed the guitars around a spark grew that kindled a lifelong friendship. He liked my guitar playing, and I was bowled over by his writing and performance talents. We hit it off, and I became the official Frummox sidekick and was happy to have Steven bunk at my place when he was in Austin for a show. During the winter of 1970–71, I was a regular visitor at Steven and Janey Lake's homestead in the Rockies high above Boulder. Gold Hill was a rustic community of artists, university types, pine-huggers, and hippies. There were no paved roads, no flushing toilets, no stores or related commercial blemishes. It was a bohemian heaven tailor-made for an aspiring songwriter from Kopperl, Texas, and an energized rock 'n' roller from Austin. Our wooden guitars came alive in the high, dry air, and Steven's big baritone filled up every corner of Janey's front room. The isolated mountain environment, the warmth of Steven and Janey's hospitality, and the smoky song sessions around the pot-bellied stove linger as magic moments in my musical upbringing. I learned a great deal about songs, how they came to be, and, thanks to Steven's patience, I developed some guitar skills that, in a very small way, contributed to his extensive store of original works.

Since those early days in Gold Hill, Steven and I have played innumerable gigs together and registered more than our share of road miles. After all the gigs and miles, I am more convinced than ever that Fromholz is one of the greatest songsmiths ever to pick up a guitar. Further, I'm far better equipped as a sixty-five-year-old-guitar-playing academic to offer some insights into the enduring magic of *Texas Trilogy* and the merit of Fromholz's songwriting than the twenty-year-old college kid at a small Texas folk club.

STEVEN FROMHOLZ

Texas Trilogy is one of the best works ever written about life in rural Texas. Fundamentally, it is an epic poem set to music that describes Fromholz's experiences growing up in the Bosque (pronounced "boss-key") County town of Kopperl on the northwestern end of Lake Whitney in Central Texas. These three songs—"Daybreak," "Trainride," and "Bosque County Romance"—portray the people in their daily routines as they navigate relationships, jobs, and families and try to transform youthful dreams into durable realities. The songs map out the lay of the land, the structure of the towns, the course of the rivers, and the railroad tracks that slice through the county. The songs depict what those tracks take away from the community and what they bring back from the curious world beyond Bosque's borders. Like other epic compositions, these songs stand the test of time and the perpetual recycling of popular culture. They are tough old tunes, not unlike their author, and seem to take on greater meaning as the decades slip by and Americans log more and more miles on urban freeways far removed from the dusty roads of small towns and rural settings.

"Daybreak," the first song of the *Trilogy*, begins with an A-minor chord accented by a single-note run that sets up a D-major chord, a musical combination that implies the subtle gray shift from night's darkness to morning's light. Then the lyrics begin: "Six o'clock silence of a new day beginning, is heard in the small Texas town. Like a signal from nowhere, the people who live there, are up and moving around." And, like countless other American mornings, the work starts early "'cause there's bacon to fry," and there are "biscuits to bake," on the old stove "that the Salvation Army won't take." And as the sun appears in the east, folks open their "windows and turn on their fans, 'cause it's hotter than hell when the sun hits the land."

After the new day begins, Fromholz introduces Walter and Fanny who "own the grocery that sells most all that you need." The elderly couple has been "up and working since early this morning" because "they've got the whole village to feed." These life-long residents "put out fresh eggs and throw bad ones away that rotted because of the heat yesterday." They take special care to keep the store "all dark so you can't see the flies" that "settle on round steak and last Monday's pies."

A few doors down from Walter & Fanny's grocery is "Sleepy Hill's Drugstore where the café is open and the coffee is bubbling hot." There you will find "all the folks who ain't working" sitting "there 'till sundown and" talking "about what they ain't got." There's talk about some ol' boy who "just threw a clutch in" his "old pickup truck" whose family has been "riding on a streak of bad luck" because the "doctor bills came and" their "well has gone dry," and "their grown kids don't care whether they live or die."

Having set the scene in Kopperl, Fromholz returns to the song's signature A-minor-to-D riff to create a musical bed for the following monologue:

Hell, I can remember when Kopperl, Texas, was a good place for a man
to live and raise a family. 'Course that was before they closed down the
cotton gin. Has it been that long ago? Seems like only yesterday that ole
Steve Hughes lost his arm in the infernal machine and walked all the way
home bleedin' to death.

New highway helped some when they dammed up the Brazos to build
Lake Whitney. Brought some fishermen down from Dallas and Fort
Worth. Town sure has been quiet, though, since they closed down the
depot and built that new trestle out west of town. You know, the train
don't stop here anymore. No, the train just don't stop here anymore.

The underlying chord structure then moves from A-minor to D and
takes off on a crisp, upbeat tempo that suggests the rhythmic feel of steel
wheels on rails as the second song begins. In "Trainride," Fromholz describes
a train stop in Clifton and the subsequent ride into the tiny town of Kopperl,
where his mom was there to meet Steven and his brother John. The song
then moves to a chorus supported by a series of rapidly changing chords as
Fromholz takes the listener from his childhood memory of an exciting train
ride to the present where:

> kids at night break window lights and the sound of trains only remains
> in the memories of the ones like me; who have turned their backs on the
> splintered cracks in the walls that stand on the railroad's land.

The Kopperl Depot is now a fractured shell with a fading Santa Fe logo
on weathered wood, but the song moves back in time when the depot was
the nexus of the small town's commerce and the visiting trains were the link
to the excitement of a world of possibility beyond the Bosque County line:

> I remember me and brother used to run down to the depot
> Just to listen to the whistle blow when the train pulled into Kopperl
> And the engine's big and shiny, black as coal that fed the fire
> And the engineer he'd smile and say, "Howdy, how you fellas?"
> And the people by the windows, playing cards and reading papers
> Seemed as far away to us as next summer's school vacation.

"Trainride" closes with a final chorus recalling "the sound of trains only
remains in the memories of the ones like me." Then Fromholz makes a
smooth transition from the key of D to the sister key of G to introduce the
third song of the *Trilogy*.

"Bosque County Romance" is a blue-collar agrarian chronicle of a young couple making its way on a small farm outside of Kopperl. The characters are real. Fromholz knew the protagonists, Billy Archer and Mary Martin, who graduated several years before him at Kopperl High School. The author begins his tale by recalling that "Mary Martin was a schoolgirl, just seventeen or so, when she married Billy Archer about fourteen years ago." They were just a couple of young kids, "not even out of high school" and all the folks in Kopperl "said it wouldn't last," but "when you grow up in the country, you grow up mighty fast." Fromholz recounts that "they married in a hurry, in March before school was out," and many of the locals "said that she was pregnant, while others said, 'Just wait and you'll find out.'" The gossip proved to be true: "It came about that winter one gray November morn, the first of many more to come a baby boy was born."

In the chorus, Fromholz describes the challenges of making a living from the land, and by extension, the challenges that confront countless American agrarians who embrace the Jeffersonian dream of the yeoman farmer:

> And cattle is their game, and Archer is the name
> They give to the acres that they own
> If the Brazos don't run dry, and the newborn calves don't die,
> Another year from Mary will have flown.

In 1957, there was a tremendous drought, "a curse upon the land," and no one in Bosque County "could give Bill a helping hand. The ground was cracked and broken and the truck was out of gas," and cattle "can't feed on prickly pear instead of growing grass." In the final lines of the last verse, Fromholz describes the ongoing challenges that faced the Archer family:

> The weather got the water and snakebite took a child
> And a fire in the old barn took the hay that Bill had piled
> The mortgage got the money and the screwworm got the cows
> The years have come for Mary, she's waiting for them now.

After the final chorus, Fromholz shifts from the key of G back to the initial A-minor chord of the *Trilogy* accentuated by the melodic signature riff that defines the beginning of "Daybreak." *Texas Trilogy* ends as it began, with a fresh sunrise and another day with the town folk embracing the habits and routines that mirror the cycles of nature.

Over the last forty-five years, *Texas Trilogy* has carved out an indelible niche in the hierarchy of Lone Star creative works. Fromholz described the circumstances surrounding the genesis of *Texas Trilogy* in an interview I conducted with him in 1994:

I got my draft notice for the Army in 1965. I didn't want to go to Fort Hood or Fort Polk or *Fort Anything*, so I signed up with the Navy. After basic training in San Diego, they sent me to Electronic Technician's School at Treasure Island up in San Francisco. That was in late September of 1965. There I was, a fledgling musician and songwriter who loved to get out and play, right in the middle of the biggest damned hippie scene of the sixties. I experienced what a lot of young folks experienced back then: I had Uncle Sam yelling in one ear and my "artistic urges" whispering in the other. Thank God I'm a Gemini!

I played a lot of music in San Francisco and that's when I wrote *Texas Trilogy*. I wrote the *Trilogy* in one setting. Once I got started, it just seemed to flow along, like it had been hiding in my head for years. And actually, I guess that's really true. After a few hours of working on it, I had the chord changes in my head and all the lyrics written down. I learned it that afternoon and sang it that night at the Drinking Gourd to a packed house. I thought I sang it very well but when I finished, the room was total quiet and I thought, "Oh Jesus, I really screwed up this time!" But then, after about fifteen seconds, the room exploded and everybody just went nuts! I figured at that point that I might be on to something good. That was a great night for me. I'd never written a song, much less three songs, in such a short time, and I'd never experienced such immediate approval for my work. It's very rare in this business to have that happen.

Fromholz, like other ruthlessly poetic songwriters, has a definitive "one-two" punch in his songwriting. First, his unique poetic talent reduces complicated real-life situations into simple, accessible lyrics. He then blends idea and lyric with chord and melody into a synergistic musical whole. All songs have words and music, but you might say that great songs have poetry and sinfoniettas. These songs become larger than the sum of their parts—powerful lyrics bolster the effect of the music, and innovative music bolsters the effect of the lyrics. This is certainly evident in *Texas Trilogy*. Fromholz's words and phrases are crisp and concise, and the musical accompaniment moves beyond the standard three-chord country formula to add spice to the melody and flow of the song.

Fromholz provided my initial gateway into the world of songs and songwriting. In the spring of 1971, I moved to Colorado on his invitation to start a band and make a serious run at fame and fortune. When I arrived in Denver, Fromholz told me that he had just taken a job offer from Stephen Stills to play rhythm guitar and sing second voice in his new band that would later be known as Manassas. The "Fromholz Band" was on hold until he returned from the upcoming Stephen Stills tour. In his absence, I was able to secure a temporary residence in Boulder at the home of fellow musician, Marty Javors, an excellent guitar player who was away for the summer and fall.

After several months of picking up gigs in the Boulder–Denver area and giving guitar lessons at a local music shop, I had a couple of unexpected visitors. One evening two bearded characters in cowboy hats showed up at Marty's house. Michael Murphey and Bob Livingston introduced themselves and said that Marty had invited them to stay at his place during their four-day booking at the Cafe York in Denver. The guitars came out, and we spent the afternoon sharing songs, guitar licks, and stories. When they opened at the Cafe York the following evening, I was in the band.

MICHAEL MARTIN MURPHEY

Murphey is only writer in this Texas triumvirate who pursued a serious academic path and studied literature, poetry, creative writing, and classical Greek. He began college at North Texas State in 1963 where he excelled in his studies and assumed a leading role in the vibrant music scene in Denton. Although his tenure at North Texas State (now called the University of North Texas) was brief, it was certainly not void of long-term music business developments and connections. At North Texas State, he befriended the venerable professor and folklorist Stan Alexander and was an active participant in the campus folk music club. There he met a variety of future Texas music dignitaries like Eddie Wilson, later of Armadillo World Headquarters fame, and swapped songs and hot licks with musicians like Steven Fromholz, Travis Holland, Ray Wylie Hubbard, Johnny Vandiver, and Spencer Perskin, who later founded Shiva's Headband.

After three semesters, Murphey transferred to UCLA to participate in its highly acclaimed undergraduate writing program. By the time he settled into the Los Angeles scene and hit the musical streets of Westwood and Hollywood, he had a stage-tested repertoire of original songs, a slightly raspy, high-tenor voice that radiated authenticity, and an endearing stage presence. Then, as now, Murphey was an inventive guitar player, a tremendous fingerpicker, and a master of innovative chord progressions.

While studying at UCLA, he had one eye on his books and the other on the business of songwriting. He got married, decided to focus on his music rather than college, and took a "day gig" as a staff writer with the massive publishing house Screen Gems. After the birth of his son, Ryan, he supplemented the family income by playing in a country-music copy band at night while maintaining his nine-to-five songwriting routine at Screen Gems. In an email Murphey sent me in March 2011, he described his tenure in Los

Angeles during the late 1960s leading up to his move back to Texas in 1972. In the narrative, he mentions a photograph he attached to the message. It features four aspiring young actors, all clad in late-nineteenth-century Western dress, in a staged publicity shot. A very young Michael Murphey sits, staring into the camera, with long blonde hair, his right hand tucked into his shirt, and a weathered cowboy hat in his lap.

> The attached picture was taken [in 1969] on the set of a television pilot when I was writing songs, playing twang-infested hillbilly music in Southern California nightclubs (read honky-tonks), and acting in California. Well, at least I thought I was acting. This photo was made for a television series pilot called "The Kowboys," which was supposed to be a country-and-western version of *The Monkees*, "Western style." The pilot was rejected by the network, and as a television film, it flopped.
>
> Back then, I wanted "The Kowboys" to make it so badly it hurt. But it failed, and miserably, I might add. Critics said it was really bad, and they were right! So I dug in as a songwriter in my A-frame cabin in Wrightwood, California, in the piney forests of the San Gabriel Mountains, and there I pursued my own vision.

In that cabin Murphey started writing "Wildfire," the song that brought him the most broadcast airplay of any song he had written. There, in the San Gabriel forest and kicking around in the Mojave Desert below, he developed his eclectic mix of rock, country, folk, gospel, and Aaron Copland-esque Western music. As he described it in his email to me,

> It was quirky, but it was My Quirky. Every student of poetry from the UCLA English Department (two of my classmates at UCLA were Ray Manzarek and Jim Morrison, founders of the Doors—I was overshadowed to say the least!) had their special influences and my lyrics were inspired by American poets like Edgar Lee Masters' *Spoon River Anthology*, Vachel Lindsay (the father of American "singing poetry"), Walt Whitman, William Carlos Williams, Wallace Stevens, Marianne Moore, and Carl Sandburg. And, Oh Yeah! . . . Let's not leave out those "not-so-much-like" UCLA English Department writers like Hank Williams, Woody Guthrie, Peter LaFarge, John G. Niehardt, and Harlan Howard!

One of the most ambitious undertakings of Murphey's California years was inspired by the mountain-desert environment, his penchant for history of the American West, and his active and romantic imagination. When I met Murphey and Livingston in Boulder, Colorado, in early October 1971,

Murphey was in the final stages of a recording project with the country-rock group Kenny Rogers and The First Edition. Rogers and company had embraced a project presented to them by Murphey and Larry Cansler, one of his fellow writers at Screen Gems in Los Angeles, called *The Ballad of Calico*. This recording effort involved producing a double-disc concept album that portrayed the colorful past of Calico, a late-nineteenth-century silver mining town in the Mojave Desert several miles east of Barstow, California. During the late 1960s, "concept albums" were hardly the norm and *The Ballad of Calico* marked a creative leap in Rogers's already successful music career.

Rogers was a native Texan, born in Houston in 1938, and had experimented with several musical styles from doo-wop to folk music before forming The First Edition in 1967. The five-piece ensemble went on to release eight hit singles, most notably "Just Dropped In (To See What Condition My Condition Was In)" in 1967 and "Ruby, Don't Take Your Love to Town" in 1969. By the time *The Ballad of Calico* took shape in late 1971, they had nine previous albums to their credit. Rogers also was attracted to the culture of the American West, and *The Ballad of Calico* offered a focus for his affinity. According to a February 1972 article in *Billboard* magazine, Murphey had "researched the town and its most well-known inhabitants thoroughly and all the stories in the album are true. It was originally 23 songs long, but was cut to 18. 'We picked the most important ones and ones that would make the album flow well,' says Rogers."

Shortly after the town was founded in 1881, Calico had a population of 1,200 people, over 500 silver mines, a booming economy, and the typical assortment of bars, brothels, and gambling halls counterbalanced by several churches, a frontier school house, and the *Calico Print*, the local newspaper. The town's name comes from the geological formation of the "strange mountains" that surround the town "which are every color of the rainbow," as the *Billboard* article pointed out. In the mid-1890s when the price of silver plummeted, the silver mines closed, and by 1907 Calico was completely abandoned. Theme-park entrepreneur Walter Knott, creator of Knott's Berry Farm in Buena Park, California, bought the ghost town in 1951 and refurbished the tiny settlement as a tourist attraction just off Interstate 15 in San Bernardino County.

Murphey reasoned that Calico and its quixotic history would provide an ideal landscape for a series of stories that tapped into the popular American imagination.

Murphey's writing partner, Larry Cansler, shared this vision, and they were soon immersed in the task of creating a musical portrait of Calico. Murphey focused on the history, the lyrics, and fundamental song structures while Cansler oversaw the orchestral components for the project. Like

Murphey, Cansler began his musical career at North Texas State, where he majored in composition. After graduating and a hitch in the US Army, he moved to Los Angeles, signed on at Screen Gems in 1967, and began writing with Murphey. Their combined *Calico* effort yielded a collection of songs and symphonic interludes that reified the romantic life and times of the silver miners, their families, their singular lifestyles, and their local institutions. It was a composition that Cansler called an "eighteen-song rock opera."

The title track, "Calico Silver," recorded in two parts, serves as the introduction and the conclusion of the Calico story. The first half of the song introduces the migrant farmer heading west seeking a new future and describes the initial success of the mining enterprise and the ensuing prosperity.

> No rain and the weather got warm
> Broke down and sold my farm
> Headed for the silver strike,
> I took my wife
> Calico silver gave us life.

As the small town at the foot of these colorful mountains exploded in an abundance of newfound wealth, the inhabitants reported that "you could hear the miners sing when they made their hammers ring," rejoicing, day after day "when they found, Calico silver underground." The introduction concludes as our protagonist brings us up to date having worked a decade and a half as a miner:

> Fifteen years down in the mines
> I watched the silver shine
> Listened to the big wheels churn
> They were turned
> By Calico silver that we earned.

The journey through the town's dusty history continues with a haunting ballad that captures the voice of one of the many inhabitants resting beneath the unmarked headstones of Calico's version of "Boot Hill." "Write Me Down (Don't Forget My Name)" is a plea to live on in the public memory. The following tune, "The Way It Used to Be," is a romantic litany of turn-of-the-century memories and social mores: "Strawberry, fire engine, ice cream party, May Day festival, too. Wooden sidewalk, work a full day, love your neighbor, blacksmith wearing big boots . . . That's the way it used to be." Murphey then moves to Main Street with the story of "Madame De Lil and Diabolical Bill." Every mining town has a saloon, its epicenter of coarse culture and entertainment. Calico's popular establishment is owned by the intrepid Madame De Lil, "a lady of wealth," who "didn't run a saloon for her health."

The next song, "School Teacher," is a tale about the lonely yet productive life of Virginia, the frontier schoolmarm, a dedicated woman willing to sacrifice her youth for her students. Unfortunately, Virginia will "soon be an old maid," as her "red hair [turns to] gray." "Road Agent" chronicles the short, violent life of the regional outlaw—a "quick money, catch penny, fly by night" character, he terrorized the local populace, all of whom were "equal in his sight." He now lies "dead on a hill," accompanied only by the ethereal blue song of the whip-poor-will. On another somber note, "Sally Grey's Epitaph" is a song about a young lady who came to Calico chasing a dream, but it "wasn't long 'till she went astray." Now the sound of graveside farewells echo through the valley as "she leaves this town today, for a better place we pray." The first disc concludes on a lighter tone with "Dorsey, the Mail-Carrying Dog." Like other characters in *The Ballad of Calico*, Dorsey was a historical figure, an actual mail-carrying canine who delivered the letters to Calico, to the neighboring town of Yermo, and to mines and settlements in the outlying area.

Disc two opens with "Harbor for My Soul," an upbeat gospel message that stands in sharp contrast to the carnal message of Madame De Lil and her saloon. If "you've worked all your life in the Waterloo mine and [you're] gettin' old," or "if your ship did not come in," then there's "one thing [you] can believe in friend!" You need a "harbor for your soul." Murphey then moves to a classic country format with "Trigger Happy Kid," a song about a young man who idolizes gunfighters and witnesses the misguided antics of a "crazy cowboy" who "can't find his enemies" so "he guns down [his] friends." The song's narrator addresses the brash cowboy: "When your six-guns are empty, empty just like your eyes, your friends they won't speak then, they won't tell no more lies." The narrator finally warns the gunslinger: "But a little boy who hid, he saw what you did, and he's a trigger-happy kid." The next selection, "Vachel Carling's Rubilator," touches on science and technology. Calico's resident inventor, Vachel Carling, created the Rubilator, a gizmo with no specific purpose that nonetheless reigned as the technological darling of the town. The cult of the consumer (*and* the con man) was in full swing: "All God's children got to have a Rubilator; All God's children can't be wrong. Yes, all God's children got to have a Rubilator; listen to the Rubilator singing its song." Murphey then addresses a prevailing theme in Western boomtowns—most of the silver seekers never realized their dreams. "Empty-Handed Compadres" is their song. And when those silver seekers grappled with the harsh reality of their "empty-handed" quest, they often retired to a small desert shotgun shack to address their bleak prospects in "One Lonely Room."

"Old Mojave Highway" describes the road that ran through the desert, then wound through the mountains up to the silver mines. It was a path of hope and adventure for those coming to Calico. But for many of those leaving, the highway was a sad trail of defeat. As *The Ballad of Calico* draws to a close, Murphey embraces a philosophical approach. "Man Came Up From Town" is an allegorical composition that contemplates the relationship between humans and civilization—towns are built on the bones of the earth and, eventually, towns rise from the bones of man. Finally, "Calico Silver (Reprise)," deals with the death of the town and the demise of the dream. This final installment begins during the peak of Calico's prosperity when "days were short and the laughter was long," and the "nails in the pine were strong." No one believed that anything "could go wrong." Certainly no one was "counting on Calico silver to be gone." In conclusion, Murphey revisits our original protagonist as he prepares to close the book on Calico:

> Got my wagon ready to go
> Been a hundred years or more
> Since we hitched up our team
> And it seems Calico silver
> Was a dream.

As mentioned, my first encounter with *The Ballad of Calico* was in 1971, shortly before its public release, when I signed on as Murphey's lead-guitar player. I was stunned at the project's enormity and sophistication. I listened to the preliminary mixes and charted out several songs Murphey was incorporating into his show. While a particular song might sound familiar and accessible, the structure was laced with subtle twists and turns that set it apart from its companion recordings. Of course, it was precisely these delicate chord variations and innovative passing notes that yielded an enduring melody in support of the lyrical message. It was recognizable, it was comfortable, yet it somehow seemed different, memorable. Or, as Fromholz would say, "It stuck to the ribs of your mind!" Each song had a purpose, each song told its own story, each operated as a historical instrument to reinforce the musical ethnography, and each song left ample room for the listener's imagination. The lyrical content of *The Ballad of Calico* illustrated another valuable characteristic of a successful song: the ability to shape a complicated thought, emotion, or message into a concise and simple passage or phrase.

The Ballad of Calico also exemplified the importance of research in creating songs and building valuable song catalogues. Many songwriters claim that certain songs are the product of dreams or that they are powerful mental impressions waiting to be transposed to lyric and melody. Fromholz reports that the three songs that comprise *Texas Trilogy* were "imbedded messages" that simply needed to be drawn out and documented. Similarly, Murphey reports that "Wildfire" was largely the product of a dream sequence. *The Ballad of Calico*, however, was the product of extended research. Murphey made many trips to the small town, consulted various reference books, and based the work on actual characters identified in these sources. Imagination certainly played an integral role, but the bare bones of the tunes were built from the ground up and informed by research and fieldwork.

The Ballad of Calico was released on Reprise Records in 1972. It reached No. 118 on the *Billboard* Album Charts and produced one single, "School Teacher," that topped out at No. 91 on the *Billboard* charts. By contemporary standards, it was a moderate success and featured exceptional songs, but it slipped into the mass category of before-its-time, art-based albums.

With *Calico* under his belt, Murphey was ready to leave California. "After some occasional hits with my songs on the *Billboard* charts and a lot of disappointment, rejection, and unreturned phone calls in the Southern California's 'Valley of Smoke' and the 1970 Lytle Creek earthquake, I took my three-soul M. M. Murphey family, whippet dogs, bagful of songs, Granddaddy Spud's Martin Guitar, and camper-topped pickup truck and moved back to Texas," Murphey told me in his 2011 email. "Had it not been for a failed attempt at being a professional songwriter with his own cubicle at Screen Gems, I might not have ended up in the artistic refuge which ultimately became the music Mecca of Austin, Texas." He added, "When you're aiming for success, it's important to get the timing of your failures right!"

And your successes, one might add. Murphey finally caught a break when producer Bob Johnston came to the Rubaiyat nightclub in Dallas where Murphey was playing. He had heard about the quality of Murphey's songs, and Johnston was an extremely "song-oriented" producer. His top-line clients included Bob Dylan, Simon & Garfunkel, Leonard Cohen, Johnny Cash, Marty Robbins, Hoyt Axton, and Willie Nelson. Murphey's ability to create a steady stream of high-quality material, his eclectic subject matter, his ability to shape songs around specific themes, and the intellectual depth of his compositions piqued Johnston's interest. He signed Murphey on the spot, and in the ensuing weeks, Murphey and Livingston were in Nashville laying down tracks for what would become his debut album, *Geronimo's Cadillac*.

Geronimo's Cadillac was released in 1972 and outperformed the Kenny Roger's *Calico* release by reaching No. 160 on the album charts with the single of the same name reaching No. 37 on the singles charts. Shortly before the release of the album, Murphey had moved to Austin. He was actively involved with Austin musician Gary P. Nunn and with Bob Livingston, who had come home to Texas with Murphey. At this time I returned from Colorado to rejoin Murphey and tour in support of *Geronimo's Cadillac* and prepare for the recording of Murphey's second album, *Cosmic Cowboy Souvenirs*, with Nunn, Livingston, steel guitar player Herb Steiner, and drummer Michael McGeary. The band lived in a 1950s-era motor court in north Austin with Murphey and Nunn in the main house and the band members and road crew in the adjoining bungalows.

A freestanding building behind the main residence served as a rehearsal studio. One evening after a few hours in the studio running over potential tunes for the new album, the band had gathered in the living room of the main house. We heard a car pull up and make a sliding stop in the gravel outside. A few moments later came a loud knock on the front door. Nunn got up and opened the door to find a tall, dark-haired fellow with six-packs in hand and a lovely woman with a collection of backup booze. "Is Murphey here?" he asked. It was Jerry Jeff Walker and his lady-friend on their way from Key West to Los Angeles where he planned to begin work on a new album. Walker never made it to LA on that trip, and after forty-two years, he still lives in Austin.

JERRY JEFF WALKER

In the early 1970s Guy Clark wrote a song called "She Ain't Goin' Nowhere." The song describes a young woman leaving a relationship, determined to escape to anywhere beyond the "there" of her current situation. With a simple gender switch, the initial verse of this song may well have been written about a young man named Ronald Clyde Crosby who was similarly determined to escape to anywhere beyond the "there" of his current situation:

> Standin' on the gone side of leavin'
> [He] found a thumb and stuck it in the breeze.
> [He'll] take anything that's goin' close to somewhere
> [He] can lay it down and live it like [he'd] please.

Ronald Clyde was born on March 16, 1942, in Oneonta, a small town in central New York. Like legions of other young men, he wanted to quit the familiar streets of his hometown and all the predetermined avenues to maturity that they implied. Crosby, who would later be known as Jerry Jeff Walker, had been "standin' on the gone side of leavin'" since his Grandma Jesse bought him a Harmony guitar for Christmas when he was in high school. As he drifted through his final years of school, the Harmony six-string became a constant companion and, eventually, his ticket out of town. In his 1999 autobiography *Gypsy Songman*, Walker describes himself as "popular and athletic" with "lousy study habits."[1] Still, he loved to read and think big thoughts. "In class, when I wasn't staring out the window, I'd be paging through Thoreau, Camus, Emerson. Planting the seeds." He knew that those seeds would never take root in Oneonta. They had to be sewn elsewhere.

Three years out of high school, he was ready. He had a leather satchel packed with clothes and travel gear, his guitar, and a few bucks in his pocket.

> I picked up the satchel, tossed it out the door into the snow and stared at it there on the ground for the longest time. Then I stepped out the door and picked it up. Numbly, I walked down West End Avenue. Toward Route Seven south. I was trembling as I stuck my thumb out. Right away a car picked me up, took me ten or twelve miles south of town.

When his first ride dropped him off, he stood beside the highway, looked north to the glow of the Oneonta lights, then looked south and put the hometown image in his rear-view mirror. Before he stuck his thumb out again, he pulled out his wallet.

> I threw away all my identification except for the Jerry Ferris draft card [a fake ID he had acquired for underage drinking]. Ron Crosby no longer existed. It was Jerry Ferris who climbed into the next car headed down the highway. This was not a road trip. This was the road.

Walker's new life began as Jerry Ferris that winter in 1963, and it would be a decade before he planted new seeds in Austin and let the roots take hold. That decade yielded a road harvest that shaped the rest of his life. He initially hitched down the East Coast and crossed over to Tampa, "but the Gulf Coast was grey and joyless" and he "knew there had to be laughter and music out there somewhere," so it was west to New Orleans. The Crescent City became his base of operations. He learned how to survive as a street musician; he sat at the feet of the venerable Southern songster Babe Stovall and bathed in the Bohemian culture of the French Quarter. He made new friends, had new lovers, heard new stories, wrote new songs, and adopted a new name.

During his New Orleans residency, he took road trips to neighboring states and scattered seeds as he traveled. He made extended forays to Dallas, Austin, and Houston. In Houston, a rock band took shape and, with

Walker's coaxing, they traveled northeast to Greenwich Village. The band settled on the name Circus Maximus, landed a recording deal with Vanguard Records, released their eponymous first album in 1967, and a second album, *Neverland Revisited*, in 1968. Although the band didn't last, it was during this period that Walker befriended an exceptional New York City guitar player, David Bromberg. As Circus Maximus wound down, Walker and Bromberg retreated to the listening rooms and folk salons of Greenwich Village.

Late one night after an extended picking session in the Village, Bromberg suggested that they drop in on Bob Fass, the "midnight-till-dawn" disc jockey at WBAI, New York City's Pacifica "listener-supported communist" radio station. According to Walker, Fass's all-night program featured "live music, new music, poetry, Pacifica's 'lively left-of-left' political harangues," and served as "the musical reference point for the entire city." Walker recalls that "David and I were pretty loose that night" and remembers carrying in a "big 7-Up bottle, half soft drink, probably a little more than half Seagram's 7."

> David and I began to play for [Fass], live radio. We probably played from two in the morning until about five. Talked a lot with Bob, played some music, had a good time. David and I sat on the edge of cheap old chairs, leaning into the mikes. The room swelled with strings coaxing out a six-eight waltz. And I began to sing . . .

> > Knew a man, Bojangles and
> > He danced for you, in worn-out shoes . . .

Bob Fass recorded the radio show, and not surprisingly, he was quite impressed with Walker's new tune, "Mr. Bojangles." Walker had written the song some months before while playing at a small club in Austin. "Mr. Bojangles" told the story of a character Walker had met in a New Orleans jail, sitting out a holiday weekend at the First Precinct drunk tank in 1966. In the days after the Walker–Bromberg visit, Fass played the live recording of "Mr. Bojangles" on his nightly program. Soon, people were visiting record stores wanting to buy a copy of a record that didn't exist, and in a matter of weeks, the song was a regional hit. According to Walker, "Here was listener-supported, leftie-babble WBAI snatching a sound from the winds and playing it over and over to New York City, the nation's largest radio market." Within a year, "Mr. Bojangles" was well on its way to becoming one of the most popular American songs in the last half of the twentieth century.

"Mr. Bojangles" was the apogee of Walker's "Ramblin'-Scramblin'-Troubadour" decade. The song's success took him around the country, provided an enduring financial base, opened doors in the music industry, and was a direct product of his self-styled "Gypsy Songman" identity. "Mr. Bojangles" and other titles penned during the post-Oneonta decade were adventure vignettes, road chronicles—certainly not an uncommon theme in songwriting circles then and now—but in Walker's case, they were not just *about* the road, they *were* the road. In modern musicological terms, Walker graduated with honors as an "American songster," an itinerate troubadour playing and singing what the folks wanted to hear. As he later wrote:

> I've always felt that my years in New Orleans were the equivalent of a college education in life and the world. All those highway confessions were a Master's degree in human nature.

 When Walker rolled into Austin in 1972, he brought his Southern songster sensibilities, a recently negotiated recording contract with MCA Records, and a collection of ideas about how he wanted to proceed with his new album. He was looking for a band, or more accurately, he wanted to find a few "pickin' buddies" and make some music. Walker felt that his story-style songs would be better served through the accompaniment of friends and fellow travelers. His songs required co-conspirators, not slick studio cats. He found that contingent the night he pulled into the old motor court on North Lamar Boulevard in Austin in search of his friend and fellow songwriter Michael Murphey. Not long after Walker's arrival, the band—Gary P. Nunn (keyboards), Bob Livingston (bass), Michael McGeary (drums), and me, on lead guitar—was jamming with Walker and kicking around song arrangements for his debut album for MCA. Murphey graciously agreed to loan Walker his band, and the ensuing loose and lively Austin recording sessions yielded a successful commercial recording, *Jerry Jeff Walker*, released in late 1972. Album sales satisfied the brass at MCA, the band toured with Walker in support of the album, and by the summer of 1973, Walker began to focus on his next recording adventure.

The term "ragged but right" was the operative phrase during the recording sessions for the *Jerry Jeff Walker* album. The playing didn't have to be perfect as long as the core emotions of the composition and the upbeat ambiance of the performances were successfully captured on tape. Another way of saying this is the tracks had to *feel* right. Beyond the predictable quip, "you know it when you hear it," to say a track *feels* right means that the listening experience doesn't require excessive concentration—the message and mood are readily available. The track has a comfortable groove with a steady cadence and moves in sync with the listener's internal rhythm. A recording, therefore, can be loose, friendly, and engaging and, as evidenced by the *Jerry Jeff Walker* album, still be commercially successful. Ragged but right worked; it had been road tested and would chart the course for Walker's next recording.

In late summer 1973, Walker and his band of co-conspirators invaded Luckenbach, a tiny Texas Hill Country town seventy miles west of Austin that would be the venue for the new recording adventure. The logistics involved using the town's dance hall as a large sound stage with a mobile recording truck set alongside to serve as the control room. The Luckenbach Dance Hall was a typical late nineteenth-century affair with waist-high windows on three sides and wooden shutters that swung up and latched to create an open-air pavilion. The musicians were positioned in a circle using hay bales for sound baffles with microphone lines running out to the truck. The sessions ran daily for slightly more than a week. They began in the early afternoon and ran well into the night. The songs were recorded live, a point that warrants clarification.

To describe the tracks as "live" does not necessarily mean that they were performed in front of a live audience. In this case, it simply meant that when the full band assembled and the engineers punched "record," all of the component parts of the song were captured in a single pass. There was no stacking rhythm tracks and no overdubs. Only two songs on *¡Viva Terlingua!* were recorded in front of a live audience—"Up Against the Wall, Redneck Mother" and "London Homesick Blues"—both products of the final night when the dance hall was opened to the public for what was billed as a "Live Recording Concert."

Like other popular musical adventures, a certain mythology has grown up around the making of *¡Viva Terlingua!*. One myth suggests that many of the songs for the album were written on the spot. Actually, Walker arrived with a strong selection of songs he wanted to record. A couple of tunes required some attention, but the laissez faire production structure was designed for just that type of challenge. The first song we recorded in Luckenbach is a good example.

After the band was set up, the mics properly set, and the input levels checked, chief engineer Dale Ashby said through his talk-back microphone, "If you want to roll one, let's see what happens." As we were setting up that afternoon, we had run through the chord structure of a song Walker had in mind. He had the melody and the chords for the verses, some of lyrics in place, and a chorus he was comfortable with. When we heard "We're rollin'" through the talk-back speakers, we counted off the tune and Walker sang a message to the boys on the other end of the mic lines, as he recalled in his book: "Hey, in the truck. It's Camp Walker time again. Going to try and

slide one by you once more." And after a few more ad-lib lines, the chorus
kicked in and the band sang along.

> Just gettin' by on gettin' by's my stock in trade
> Livin' it day to day, pickin' up the pieces wherever they fall.
> Just lettin' it roll, lettin' the high times carry the low
> I'm livin' my life easy come, easy go.

Walker then tossed out other phrases and lyric segments and started to
blend them into coherent passages. As the story took shape, I realized that
he was describing what was going on right then and there—he was documenting the genesis of the recording as the tape rolled. He mentioned the
boss at MCA Records "pacing the floor," worried about Walker delivering
the album finished on schedule, so he sent him a message in the song: "Ah,
Mike don't you worry; something's bound to come out," and finished the
verse by assuring the executive that, "We've been down this road once or
twice before."

After listening to the playback of this initial pass, Walker felt that the
song had "a real flippant feel, but fun." As he notes in his autobiography, he
changed the opening line to "Hi, Buckaroos, Scamp Walker time again," we
ironed out a few musical details, ran over the harmonies, cut it again, and
after the last notes rang out and the boys in the truck announced, "We got
it!" Walker barked, "OK, we're off!" Walker may not have had all the material
lined up for the album, but he knew how to frame the challenge. He cleverly
set out the mission and the methodology in the first song we recorded. This
illustrates Walker's unique talents as a musical storyteller, a communicator,
and a non-domineering bandleader. He had the patience and the belief in
himself to let us join him in the effort. He was practicing what he had been
preaching since leaving home ten years before . . . "Just lettin' it roll, lettin'
the high times carry the low" and "living [his] life easy come, easy go."

Walker brought other original compositions to the Luckenbach sessions.
"Little Bird," a delicate love song initially featured on his 1968 ATCO release,
Mr. Bojangles, was edited for length and arranged in a crisp, accessible format. "Get It Out," a new upbeat composition about uninhibited emotional
expression as a healthy tonic for a relationship, took shape through a series
of afternoon jam sessions. Then there was "Sangria Wine," a song Walker
described as "a recipe for homemade sangria tied into a recipe for a party as
you drink the wine." Unfortunately, the band's initial approach to the tune
hardly reflected a party atmosphere. "Sangria Wine" was a simple one-four-
five format in C that allowed plenty of room for instrumental spice, but as

we ran through it, there was little spark or sparkle. At one point, drummer Michael McGeary walked out from behind his kit and said, "Man, this is a reggae tune! It's got Caribbean written all over it!" He suggested that I play some sort of defining figure on the guitar and then have the bass answer it as was common in reggae arrangements. I played a quick five-stroke staccato chord strum over the first and second beats, then Livingston answered that figure with a bass line over the third and fourth beats to complete the first measure. We continued in this fashion, moving through the progression, other instruments slipped into the pattern until a bright little groove began bubbling up and Walker began to sing. The song popped, and the sangria party came to life.

Other songs came to life through similar exchanges. The band treated the taping process like a live performance, which, in essence, it was. Situated in a circle, we were looking at one other, communicating through body language and subtle signs we commonly used on stage. Steel player Herb Steiner and I were comfortable trading guitar fills and were careful not to get in each other's way, and similar connections linked the entire band together in a type of melodic matrix. Many of the arrangements came about by "just lettin' it roll," which in turn created a ragged but right recording that let the songs, the feel, and the lyrical message shine.

Another essential aspect of *¡Viva Terlingua!* was the inclusion of songs from other songwriters. As Walker reported in his autobiography, "I loved Guy Clark's 'Desperados Waiting for a Train.' I thought it was the most solid song I had heard in a long time, about a kid following his grandpa around, learning at his side how to be a 'big man.'" Walker also embraced Michael Murphey's "Backslider's Wine," a song about falling off the wagon and struggling to regain sobriety and emotional equilibrium. As Walker explains, the song was a good fit: "I felt I could sing this and mean it 'cause I had the reputation, which convinced people I was singing the truth."

Two more songs by other writers found their way onto the album. Late one afternoon during a beer break, Livingston was clowning around with a song and chanting an odd sequence of lyrics: "Up against the wall, redneck mother; mother who has raised a son so well. . . . He's thirty-four and drinkin' in a honky tonk, kickin' hippies' asses and raisin' hell." This immediately caught Walker's attention and he asked Livingston about the song. "It's some weird thing of [Ray Wylie] Hubbard's up in Red River," he said, "but I don't know all of the words!" Walker recognized a gem of a party song when he heard one and suggested that Livingston call Hubbard in New Mexico and get the rest of the lyrics. Within an hour, we were back in the dance hall working it up for the weekend concert. "Redneck Mother" was a big hit at the Saturday night show, particularly when Livingston spelled out the word "mother" during the song. Hubbard only had two verses, and we decided the tune needed a little more "depth." Spoken over the music of the verse, Livingston began, "'M' is for the mud flaps on my pickup truck, 'O' is for the oil on my hair, 'T' is for 'Tammy,' 'H' is for 'Haggard,' 'E' is for enema, and 'R' is for *REDNECK*!" The audience joined in with a thunderous reinforcement of the word "redneck!" Thereafter, *¡Viva Terlingua!* had an official "redneck anthem," Hubbard had a song recorded on a hit album, and although he welcomed the periodic royalty checks, he also inherited a self-described "curse" by having to play the song at his gigs for years to come!

The final track on the album, written by Nunn, surfaced during an afternoon pickin' session the day before the concert. Walker liked it; we worked it up and closed the Saturday-night show with "London Homesick Blues." Gary P. sang the lead vocals, the crowd loved it, and it became one of the most requested cuts on the album. Just as "Redneck Mother" provided a "redneck anthem," the identifying line of the chorus, "I want to go home with the armadillo," became a global anthem for the singular nature of Texas culture.

These four cover tunes—"Desperados Waiting for a Train," "Backslider's Wine," "Up Against the Wall, Redneck Mother," and "London Homesick Blues"—were essential components of the *¡Viva Terlingua!* legacy. Their popularity illustrates the benefits of interpreting a song by another writer and "making it your own." In the tradition of "song covers," Walker had established a high bar with "Mr. Bojangles," one of the most popular and most commonly covered songs of the late twentieth century. "Mr. Bojangles" has been recorded by Sammy Davis Jr., Bob Dylan, George Burns, Harry Belafonte, Frank Sinatra, Chet Atkins, Elton John, Nina Simone, Neil Diamond, the Nitty Gritty Dirt Band, and the list goes on. Walker's efforts in recording the songs of his contemporaries—both on *Jerry Jeff Walker* and on *¡Viva Terlingua!*—illustrate the potential of ruthlessly poetic songs (and, in the case of "Redneck Mother," a ruthlessly entertaining song) in the hands of a talented stylist.

The *¡Viva Terlingua!* recording adventure ended on a very personal note for Walker. The Saturday night concert had gone well; we had two new songs on tape with a great audience reaction. Considering the extended length of the live cuts, this was enough material for an album. Sunday, Monday, and Tuesday had been set aside in case we hadn't gotten everything we needed. We spent Sunday listening to the various tracks and on Monday when "all the boys met by the trees," Walker mentioned that there was a song he had been thinking about that he rarely played. The working title of the tune was "Rolling Wheels." It had been written for a movie project that never materialized and described "how we're rushed to the hospital in an ambulance at birth, the wheels carry us through life, then the hearse carries us to the grave." The notion of rolling wheels carried a strong personal significance for Walker:

> I still had memories of my grandfather's death beneath the overturned tractor. I remembered pictures of my dad standing by a jeep in WWII. I rode motorcycles. I made up a brother who drives stock cars to an early grave. "Rollin' Wheels." I played it for the band and they were spellbound. When I finished, Herb Steiner, the steel player, was crying. I looked around and everyone said, "We gotta cut it. Now!"

The song moved gently between major and minor keys. It developed with a relaxed cadence that slowed down considerably at the end of each verse as it moved into the chorus, and the chorus spun in relaxed orbits before it circled back into the narrative of the next verse. The song didn't operate in a static groove. It was the antithesis of a strong pocket-rhythm track. It was a cut that came together entirely on *feel*. After we recorded the song, the engineers played it back for us on the speaker stacks in the dance hall and Walker said, "It was just as I had imagined it." He described the track as "flowing, breathing, up and down like a tipped-over wagon with a bent wheel spinning lazily in the air." After listening, reports Walker, "the band smiled."

> Then they told me, they'd thought that this was an "off day," that they were only going to listen to the tapes of the week's work. So just before they got to Luckenbach that morning, they all gobbled some mescaline. And there they were, some of them grinning at me with scary vacancy, some with tear-streaked faces.

Walker had been genuinely touched by the band's reaction to this very personal song, which was ultimately titled "Wheel." "All along," Walker remarks, "I thought these guys [were] really into this song. But they were just stoned!" Indeed, they were, but as the self-designated straight man in this pack of "Gonzo Cosmonauts," I can report that their emotional investment in this special song and their inspired performances were genuine. They far outlived the psychedelic nuances of that afternoon. With the recording of "Wheel," *¡Viva Terlingua!* was in the can and moved to the mixing and mastering phase.

Drawing on a decade of ramblin' exploits as a Southern songster, this album marked a crossroad of new paths in Walker's career—new roots in Austin that included a large house he called home, the creation of his first "support" band, and a new-found freedom to make music and to record on his own terms. Pairing up a state-of-the-art mobile recording truck from New York with a state-of-the-art honky-tonk dance hall in the Texas Hill Country, ¡Viva Terlingua! showed that importing the sincerity, spontaneity, and spark of the live performance into the recording environment could lead to commercial success. Ragged but right worked!

Finally, ¡Viva Terlingua! signified the power of the song. At bottom, Walker is a student of and an advocate for the song. Even after writing one of the most popular and commonly covered songs of the last half of the twentieth century, Walker has continually sought out the songs of friends and fellow travelers to complement his compositions in a career that includes over thirty major album releases. His songwriting approach is personally poetic, imbued with rambling adventures, road stories, and street biographies. His song catalogue, particularly the songs of his post-Oneonta decade, is a lyrical and melodic journal of his life, a diary in song, the ethnography of a white, middle-class songster who went to school on the authentic and colorful characters he encountered along the way. Since the winter of 1963, he has welcomed the risks of a young peripatetic provocateur, he's rolled with the good times, and when necessary, he's taken the tough licks, dusted off the bumps and bruises, and moved on to the next escapade. And, more often than not, he emerges with a story that will find its way into a song.

VIGNETTE—KINKY FRIEDMAN: THE MEL BROOKS OF TEXAS MUSIC

Craig Clifford

What do we do with Kinky Friedman? If he was a young songwriter today, "They Ain't Makin' Jews Like Jesus Anymore" would get him banned from every university campus in America. You have to wonder, along those lines, what would happen if a young, unknown Mel Brooks pitched Blazing Saddles today.

But does the Mel Brooks of Texas Music deserve to stand alongside Guy Clark as a songwriter? Better known nowadays as the author of detective novels and as a tongue-in-cheek candidate for governor, in his younger days

Kinky Friedman was a prolific songwriter who made an art form of irreverence. He had a knack for giving the bad guys a voice that is even smarter than they would ever come up with themselves, which, paradoxically, seems to diffuse their power. Like a Texas Archie Bunker, the redneck in "They Ain't Makin' Jews Like Jesus Anymore" finishes off a string of racist epithets with this gem: "And there's one little hebe from the heart of Texas. Is there anyone I missed?" You can't help but like the line, even as you abhor the racism. The song's Jewish protagonist is as zany as a Mel Brooks character, and his response is disarmingly nonsensical:

> Well, I hits him with everything I had right square between the eyes.
> I says, I'm gonna gitcha, you son of a bitch, for spoutin' that pack of lies.
> If there's one thing I can't abide, it's an ethnocentric racist;
> Now you take back that thing you said about Aris-tittle Onassis.

As I go back and review Kinky Friedman's music from the 1970s, I keep thinking, not just of Mel Brooks, but of Sarah Silverman always stepping slightly over the line in her satiric treatments of racism.

So certainly Kinky Friedman deserves sidebar-mention as a brilliant satirist. A lot of this book is about intelligent rebellion, so intelligent satiric rebellion fits in. But Kinky Friedman has also written some dead-serious songs that are absolutely stunning.

"Sold American" is pure poetry. I've been performing this song for probably thirty years. It's hard to sing it because it's so profoundly sad. I should mention that Lyle Lovett does it on *Pearls in the Snow*, a Kinky Friedman tribute album. That in itself tells you Friedman's importance as a songwriter. The same irreverent mind that wrote the raunchy satirical lines of "They Ain't Makin' Jews Like Jesus Anymore" put together these beautifully poetic lines in "Sold American":

> Writing down your memoirs on some window in the frost
> Roulette eyes reflecting another morning lost
> Hauled in by the metro for killing time and pain
> With a singing brakeman screaming through your veins.

One more example of the serious side of Kinky Friedman is worthy of mention: "Ride 'Em, Jewboy." Willie Nelson recorded this song for *Pearls in the Snow*. On an episode of Charlie LeDuff's television show *The Americans*, Friedman tells the story of finding out that Nelson Mandela had listened to this song repeatedly when he was in prison. "Ride 'Em Jewboy" initially made me feel uncomfortable. Is this somehow disrespectful to the victims

of the Holocaust? But I finally realized that my discomfort came from trying to see this song as an example of Friedman's irreverence, when in fact
it is a thoroughly serious song of haunting reverence. Now I cannot listen
to this song without being deeply moved. You can write it off as a clever
but inappropriate translation of disparate cultural symbols, but I don't. It's
a profound reflection of a thoroughly Texas Jew on the experience of the
Holocaust.

It turns out that there's a new chapter to this story. The past tense of this
retrospective on Kinky Friedman's music will have to be abandoned. I just
saw an announcement on Friedman's website for the release of a new album,
The Loneliest Man I Ever Met, the first studio album by Friedman in thirty-
two years. By all accounts, it draws primarily from Friedman's serious side.
It would have been interesting to have Kinky Friedman as governor, but I'm
glad to hear he's back to making music.

BILLY JOE SHAVER

Sɪɴ ᴀɴᴅ Sᴀʟᴠᴀᴛɪᴏɴ Pᴏᴇᴛ

Joe Holley

The first time I saw Billy Joe Shaver perform, my wife and I were at
the old German dance hall in Luckenbach, Texas, the laid-back little
burg that Willie Nelson and Waylon Jennings immortalized in the late
1970s. Sharing a cold Lone Star at a table on the edge of the crowded dance
floor, the wooden shutters propped open for any hint of a Hill Country
breeze, we lost sight of our son Pete, who was three at the time.

Seconds later we spotted him out on the hardwood floor. Barely knee-
high in a thicket of boot-wearing two-steppers, his blond head bobbing and
feet flashing, Pete was lost in his own Billy Joe Shaver bliss.

That was more than twenty-five years ago, but even now the silver-haired
singer with the lived-in face and soul-stressed voice can have that effect on
a person, young or old. Willie Nelson once said that Shaver "may be the best
songwriter alive today." Bob Dylan, Elvis Presley, Johnny Cash, the Allman

Brothers, Kris Kristofferson, and, of course, Waylon and Willie have all covered his songs.

It was Shaver who wrote nine of the cuts on *Honky Tonk Heroes*, Jennings's breakthrough album. Among his many hits are "Georgia on a Fast Train," "When the Fallen Angels Fly," "Black Rose," "Wild Cowboy Gravy," and "I'm Just an Old Chunk of Coal (but I'm Going to be a Diamond Someday)."

Shaver's songs, secular and sacred, are earthy and unadorned. To my mind they hearken back to original country music—music from the Appalachian backwoods villages and country hollows settled by Scots-Irish immigrants more than three centuries ago.

Old friend Kinky Friedman got it right when he focused on the simplicity of Shaver's songs, noting that he writes "with an economy of words; he's ruthless about that. It's never flowery. To take something simple and make it complex, we call that an intellectual. That's what I do. But to take something complex and make it simple, that's an artist. And he's that in every sense of the word." (Andrew Dansby, *Houston Chronicle*, Sept. 23, 2007)

> I've spent a lifetime, making up my mind to be
> More than the measure of what I thought others could see
> Good luck and fast bucks are too far and too few between
> There's Cadillac buyers and old five-and-dimers like me.
> —FROM "OLD FIVE AND DIMERS LIKE ME," 1973

I'm familiar with the "five-and-dime" origins of that music, since Shaver and I are both old Waco boys. Actually we're from Bellmead, a working-class suburb whose residents back then toiled at either the rubber plant (making tires) or at the Katy shops (repairing locomotives).

Shaver was born in Corsicana, thirty miles east of Waco, on Aug. 16, 1939. His teenaged single mother, Victory, who went by Tincie, was a waitress at Leslie's Chicken Shack, a legend in its own right among Southern-style fried-chicken fanciers. His father, Virgil, known as Buddy, was a bootlegger and bare-knuckle fighter who left home when Billy Joe was a baby.

According to his autobiography, *Billy Joe Shaver: Honky Tonk Hero* (with Brad Reagan, 2005, University of Texas Press), Buddy tried to kill Billy Joe even before he was born: "It was June and the evening light had started to fade, but it was still hotter than nine kinds of hell. We were outside of Corsicana, a little cotton town in northeast Texas, and I was in my mother's belly, two months from entering the world."

He goes on to explain how his father nearly beat his mother to death that evening before tossing her into a stock tank and leaving for good.

Put snow on the mountain, raised hell on the hill
Locked horns with the Devil himself
Been a rodeo bum, a son of a gun
And a hobo, with stars in my crown
—FROM "RIDE ME DOWN EASY," 1982

Tincie wasn't much more inclined to raise a child, so the youngster lived in Corsicana with his grandmother, Birdie Lee Watson. She died when he was twelve, and Tincie took him back.

The family didn't have a radio, so Billy Joe would wander across the railroad tracks to listen to music with black families who worked picking cotton on the blackland prairie around Corsicana. One of the families had a standup piano on the front porch, and that's where the youngster learned to sing.

In 1951, he and his mother moved to Waco, where he became familiar with the honky-tonks around town. He also got to know a young singer-songwriter from nearby Abbott named Willie Nelson.

"I met Willie in 1953," Shaver recalled in a 2012 magazine interview. "This DJ introduced me to Willie. He was playing clubs out on the Dallas Highway, all up down the highway there in Waco, he was all over the place. I loved to listen to him 'cause his lyrics were so great. I was inspired by him. I won't say I was influenced, but he lit a fire under me." (Terry Paul Roland, "Billy Joe Shaver and His Maker," *Turnstyled, Junkpiled*, July 30, 2012)

Shaver and I both went to a school called La Vega, and though Shaver is a few years older than I am, we both had Mabel Legg, an English teacher of the old-school variety who died in 2003 at the age of 102. Ageless in her sensible shoes and rimless glasses, she was notorious for requiring that her senior-year students memorize and recite the first twenty lines of the Prologue to Chaucer's *Canterbury Tales*, in a Texas-drawl version of Middle English.

Shaver didn't tarry long at La Vega, so he missed "Whan that Aprill with his shoures soote," but he credits Miss Legg with encouraging him to write. Suspicious that a poem he turned in was too good to be his own, she had the skinny little hood write another, about outer space. He did, she was impressed, and with her support he kept on writing, even after he dropped out of school at age fourteen when the football coach insisted that he shave his Mohawk haircut.

It wasn't long before he was focused on topics more down-to-earth than outer space. He learned to trust himself to write about what he knew—hard times and trouble, mostly.

"Got a good Christian raisin' and an eighth-grade education / Ain't no need in y'all a treatin' me this way," he would write in years to come ("Georgia on a Fast Train").

That "good Christian raisin' and an eighth-grade education" would nurture in later years what anthropologist Aaron A. Fox characterizes as "the prideful figure of 'redneck' identity." (*Real Country: Music and Language in Working-Class Culture*, 2004, Duke University Press)

As Fox points out, the term "redneck" can be derogatory when it's used by someone who doesn't claim the identity, but it's also worn with a sense of pride. In addition, the appellation is race- and class-connected:

> It names, in both senses, an identity that is canonically bound up with a defensive articulation of whiteness—a particularly class-positioned way of being 'white.' . . . It is specifically working-class whiteness, an identity sometimes even polemically framed as 'white trash' by its claimants and critics. The embodiment of this identify entails a stereotypical range of class-marked attitudes and ideologies, including parochialism, nationalism, patriarchy, inscrutability, a penchant for violence and an ingrained racism. (*Real Country*, p. 25)

Shaver, the quintessential "redneck" musician, joined the Navy on his seventeenth birthday, got married, and had a son. Honorably discharged after getting into a fight with an out-of-uniform officer, he then worked a series of dead-end jobs. Working in a lumber mill, he got his right hand caught in machinery and lost nearly all of his index and middle fingers and part of the other fingers on his right hand. Once he recovered, he dedicated his life to music and taught himself to play the guitar, minus the missing fingers.

Hitchhiking cross-country in 1966, he caught a ride on a cantaloupe truck to Nashville, Tennessee, where he found a job as a songwriter for fifty dollars a week. Waylon Jennings heard his songs and was so impressed that he filled most of his 1973 album *Honky Tonk Heroes* with the newcomer's songs. Once Elvis, Kris Kristofferson, and other big names began to record his music, he got a record deal of his own and was soon a key figure in the outlaw country music revolt that roiled 1970s-era Nashville.

In 2012, Shaver recalled for *Rolling Stone* how he got together with Jennings:

> [Backstage at a gig] he let me play a song. He said, 'If I stop you now, you're going to get that guitar out and get out of here and I'm never going to see you again.' So I went ahead and sang, 'Ain't No God in Mexico.' Then I sang 'Honky Tonk Heroes' and 'You Asked Me To.' Then he slapped his knee and said, 'You know what I gotta do?' and he went in

there and ran the [studio] musicians off and brought his own band in and recorded those songs right away.

Culture critic Dave Hickey has written that Jennings found Shaver's music appealing because it rejected the "decorative bric-a-brac that had plagued the Nashville product for decades and created contemporary roots music in the minimalist tradition—music that was not really *simpler*, just stronger, better organized and more totally focused than anything that came before it. . . . Abandoning the pop-hillbilly flummery of contemporary country songs, he [Jennings] embraced the poetic license of lyrics like Billy Joe Shaver's. In the end, he made a new music that, like the singer of Billy Joe's song, 'left a long string of friends, some sheets in the wind and some satisfied women behind.'" (*Texas Monthly*, June 2004)

Nashville wasn't pleased, Shaver recalled in the *Rolling Stone* article:

The label fought about it, trying to stop it. Chet Atkins was afraid it would hurt the business the way we were coming out, you know, saying 'God' and 'damn' and things like that in the songs. But it just couldn't be stopped. It was too good. I'm pretty sure it's the first country album that sold a million.

The success of *Honky Tonk Heroes* changed everything, Shaver told the *Austin Chronicle* in 2012:

All those sequins and things kinda went out the door, and we'd go in places with our blue jeans on. I caught all kinds of hell from old songwriters, claimed I hadn't paid my dues. I'd just say, "Look [holding up his maimed right hand], where you have to pay your dues at anyway? Tennessee have a corner on that or something?"

And I stepped on a lot of toes, rubbed people the wrong way. I was my own worst enemy. And like Townes [Van Zandt] and all these guys, we'd get messed up in a deal where they'd say these guys are unmanageable. So that hurt all of us. I guess I was kinda the ambassador of ill will there for a while, because I was causing trouble for everybody. I did a lot of it by just being me.

"Without Billy Joe, there wouldn't have been a Waylon, at least not a Waylon as an outlaw," songwriter, mystery writer, and occasional politician Kinky Friedman has observed. Shaver, he said, "was the Che Guevara and Waylon was the Fidel Castro who got all the money and the power." (Brad Reagan, "Ode to Billy Joe," *Salon*, May 15, 2004)

Shaver's debut album, *Old Five and Dimers Like Me*, was released in 1973 and was the first of many hits the Texan would record throughout the next three decades. Perhaps most notable was the critically acclaimed *Tramp On Your Street*, released in 1993 and featuring the guitar playing of Shaver's son, Eddy.

His personal life was another story. Reeling from drink and drugs, he got to a point where he didn't care whether he lived or died. "I was in terrible shape," he told the *Houston Press* in 2011, "and that was when I went up on the mountain out there and got right with God. I was comin' down this big cliff in the middle of the night, and He just gave me half of that song 'Old Chunk of Coal.'"

> I went up on the mountain and looked down upon my life
> I had squandered all my money, and lost my son and wife
> —from "Try and Try Again," 1998

Despite his personal difficulties—or perhaps because of them—he continued turning out hits, most of them autobiographical. "I don't fish or hunt or anything anymore," he told Brad Reagan in 2004. "I just write songs."

Reagan, who helped Shaver with his autobiography, wrote that Shaver has thousands of songs, jotted on notepads or sung into a microcassette, stuffed into a box in a back room of the modest Waco home he shares with his wife and dogs.

"He's been writing since he was eight, and he'd be doing it even if the dogs were the sum total of his audience," Reagan wrote. "The process is cathartic, as if by documenting his traumas they will somehow start to make sense."

Everybody's Brother, his 2007 album of gospel-style country music, was nominated for a Grammy. Two years later, the old rebel was in a familiar place—in trouble again. The trouble began on a Saturday night in March 2009, when the longtime Waco resident drove to nearby Lorena and dropped in at Papa Joe's Texas Saloon, an unpretentious little beer joint in a gray metal prefab building on Interstate 35. While he was there, he shot a man in the cheek.

Exactly what happened was difficult to determine, although the story Papa Joe patrons told police and reporters would seem to have the makings of a country-western chartbuster for the songwriting legend, who by then had become a hyper-patriotic, born-again Bible believer. ("If you don't love Jesus, you can go to Hell.")

At Papa Joe's he was sitting at a table on the back patio with several other patrons, including a fifty-year-old man named Billy B. Coker. The two men had never met. Coker told Lorena police that in the course of the conversation, he and Shaver discovered that Shaver's wife, Wanda, had been married to Coker's cousin, who had died some years earlier.

Something apparently annoyed Shaver—some patrons thought it was Coker stirring his drink with a hunting knife—but whatever it was, the two men stepped out back to settle their differences. Moments later, Coker staggered back inside, his face a wet smear of red, a bullet from Shaver's .22 pistol lodged in his mouth. Shaver and his wife were long gone.

Another patron said Shaver posed something of an existential question just before the shot. "Where do you want it?" he asked Coker.

Coker got out of the hospital a few weeks later, and Shaver was charged with aggravated assault with a deadly weapon and unlawfully carrying a handgun. Jailed briefly after turning himself in, he got out on bail and began touring the country promoting the latest of his more than twenty albums, *Billy Joe Shaver's Greatest Hits.*

Predictably, he wrote about the incident in a song called "Wacko from Waco."

> I'm a wacko from Waco, ain't no doubt about it,
> Shot a man there in the head but can't talk much about it.
> He was trying to shoot me, but he took too long to aim.
> Anybody in my place woulda done the same.

Shaver's attorney, Joe "Mad Dog" Turner of Austin, was known for having represented Willie Nelson on a marijuana-possession charge and the actor Matthew McConaughey on a nude-bongo-playing charge. In April 2010, Shaver was acquitted in a Waco court after testifying that he acted in self-defense.

"I am very sorry about the incident," Shaver said outside the courtroom. "Hopefully, things will work out where we become friends enough so that he gives me back my bullet." Shooting a man was a first for the usually mild-mannered Shaver, although jail was nothing new. American jails, Mexican jails, he had known a few.

"When you get right down to it, country music is essentially the blues," he writes in the autobiography. "I've lost parts of three fingers, broke my back, suffered a heart attack and a quadruple bypass, had a steel plate put in my neck and 136 stitches in my head, fought drugs and booze, spent the money I had and buried my wife, son and mother in the span of one year."

That particular wife was his childhood sweetheart, Brenda, who married him three times and who died of cancer in 1999. His son Eddy died of a heroin overdose in 2000. A number of Shaver's songs since then are efforts to reconcile losing his son with his core Christian faith.

Those searingly personal experiences are what he always has written about, just as Miss Legg urged him to do. He sings in a ragged voice planed down by years of hard living, a voice that, to me, is the aural equivalent of an old, neglected rent house in a little country town.

The sadness he's known—the sadness and the solace—are at the heart of "Day by Day," a song on *Freedom's Child*, released in 2002: "Day by day his heart kept on breaking / And aching to fly to his home in the sky / But now he's arisen from the flames of the forest / With songs from the family that will never die."

"They're just little poems about my life," he writes in his autobiography, "and I've never pretended they were anything more. Despite all the ups and downs, I've never been to therapy or rehab or any of that stuff. The songs are my therapy."

ONE MAN'S MUSIC

VINCE BELL

Joe Nick Patoski

I t starts with a song.
It always does.
From there, it usually turns into a passion, a commitment, then an all-encompassing mission, and, ultimately, it becomes your entire life.

In the case of one Vince Bell, that was just the start, which he traces all the way back to hearing the compositions of John Lennon, the so-called smart Beatle. Singing and playing music was great. Singing and playing your own songs became the goal, the big prize he had his eyes on.

"I was actually only intending to be in the fickle game of show business until I had wildly succeeded, or for a couple of years, whichever came first," Vince explained to me not too long ago. "In the real world, it took a decade of gigs between the Red and the Rio Grande rivers to find out I couldn't live well without my work getting ever so better, lyric by bleeding lyric. So, I became a writer."

That serendipitous moment came at the right place and at the right time. He had grown up in the Memorial suburb of Houston, outside the loop. When he took the leap to play music in front of an audience, he headed inside the loop, to the clubs scattered around the bohemian Montrose neighborhood, the *other* Houston.

The experience would prove transformative. "Writing transcended my age, the jobs I had, or the situations in which I found myself, and outlasted most every relationship and circumstance in my life. Music was ingenious and inspiring. And, it was a challenge. I trusted the music when I felt I couldn't trust much of anything else. I wrote about how I could live, and I lived to grow up, so it was nobody else's work but mine. The themes were by heart."

He learned to play music conventionally, by the book, on a cornet, as a kid. Writing music was a different animal, "a freedom equal to my ambition," as Bell put it. "I relied on my own ideas, my own judgment to call it like I saw it. And make it as good as anything I had heard."

"Judgment sometimes took a few Shiners," he admitted, "But I had storms of ideas that came from listening to a youth's worth of popular music on an AM radio. I stood on the shoulders of lyrical giants, and came to know the constellation of those songwriters in Texas."

Ready to put his work to the test, he showed up one afternoon at Sand Mountain, a coffeehouse on Richmond in the Montrose, to audition for the owner. "Mrs. Carrick was kind, but dry as toast," Vince recalled. "'Ya know, you're just not good enough to play here to a weekend crowd. But,' she said, with just the trace of a smile, 'If you come back, you can play any Monday through Thursday night, for tips, 'till you are . . . good enough.'" She had thrown down the gauntlet.

"It was 1970 and I was living out of a bag on a BMW motorcycle somewhere between dear ol' Texas and upstate New York on the St. Lawrence River," Vince recalled. "I was nineteen and had just graduated from high school. I couldn't tell from moment to moment whether I was heading to a university, marrying my sweetheart, or starting a music career inspired by that audition at Sand Mountain. And, I just couldn't get enough of traveling to new and unknown places to play. Nothing made much sense other than keeping up my rehearsals. Everything was in such boyish disarray it was hard to trust anything but the discipline of music. I was getting better at playing the guitar thanks to the never-ending scales and brute strength exercises. But I still had a voice like a high school quarterback."

Writing prose came easy. He kept a black book to catalogue his thoughts and ideas. But, in the songwriting game, the prose had to have meter and rhyme and still tell a good story. Fortunately, he was hanging around some exceptional mentors. Early on, he was shown how to play an A-minor chord by a pretty fair composer named Townes Van Zandt.

His first song, "Coley," came out of nowhere when he was in a faraway place. It was a decent enough composition, it told a story, as good songs should do, about a friend and a place.

Coley

Coley would always be there on Sundays and in the morn'.
When steamers would blast their horns
There was danger in the fog to warn of.

Standing in the stars at night,
Toking on a corn cob pipe.
Coley, so blonde, so meek, and always in the right.
Days and weeks did pass so fleetly
Like woodchucks and rabbits on the ground.
The sun gave up to nighttime more than thirty times the
    sound of evening.

Jim and Larry came around,
We huddled to the warming sound of
Coley and friendship, the common bond we found.

"Coley," as he would later explain, marked his beginning as "a sorcerer's apprentice, casting the first spells of my art in hamburger joints."

Doors did not magically open. Once he decided he was going to devote himself to music, he immediately followed in the footsteps of the vast majority of his envisioned peers and set about doing anything he could to support his singer-songwriter habit—construction jobs, driving cabs, temp work, you name it.

The paying gigs, much like the songs, came from wherever, and soon gelled into a repertoire of their own. Vince earned the trust of Mrs. Carrick and graduated to the weekend "play-for-pay" bracket at Sand Mountain. He soon landed dates at The Old Quarter, navigated a sprinkling of hamburger joints and college coffeehouses, and began opening for bigger acts at concert venues like Liberty Hall. Ultimately, he became a regular performer at Anderson Fair in the Montrose. Vince's "sorcerer's apprenticeship" was in full swing.

One of the best parts of committing to the singing troubadour life was having others to look to for road maps for your ambitions. The Houston singer-songwriter community was teeming with talent. Guy and Susanna Clark, Townes Van Zandt, Don Sanders, Frank Davis, Steven Fromholz, and Jerry Jeff Walker were among the visionary old guard. Lightnin' Hopkins and Mance Lipscomb were the wizened elder guideposts for the American songster tradition. Clubs like Anderson Fair now fostered a new generation of songsters that included Vince Bell, Nanci Griffith, Lucinda Williams, David Rodriguez, Eric Taylor, Shake Russell, and more. "Those were the ambitious days. The energy itself was the inspiration." He was constantly writing and road-testing his new material and slowly but surely, Vince built a viable body of work.

By the mid-1970s Austin was already the best place for Houston singer-songwriters to showcase their music with a built-in audience that seemed as primed to listen to the lyrics as much as be swayed by melodies. It's where Townes lived, and where others were congregating to compare, compete, and commune. Its singer-songwriter community had eclipsed Houston's in no small part due to locals like Willie Nelson and Jerry Jeff Walker.

"Craig Hillis was working with Moon Hill Management in Austin, and I was interested in getting signed there and making a run of it," Vince said. "I was only IN Houston to get the hell OUT of Houston, and the ride down Highway 71 to Austin was like a driveway with a couple of bends in it. Like Houston, with Liberty Hall and the Texas Opry House, Austin had its own scenes with the Armadillo and Soap Creek. And, of course, it became the clearinghouse for bands and songwriters from all the Texas towns. Those of us who lived there stirred the musical melting pot of the Lone Star State. Black Coffee Publishing signed me to a publishing agreement, and Moon Hill Management put me on the road as a solo with an acoustic guitar in front of bands like Michael Murphey and David Crosby."

Vince was no longer a Houston songwriter. He was a Texas songwriter. Embracing his new environment, and interacting with top-tier musicians, he created a new stream of songs and began putting together the first Vince Bell bands. "I wasn't interested in 'folk music,' as much I was in what people like Lennon were doing with poetry and electric guitars."

In 1980, he coauthored the score for a ballet based on his song, "Bermuda Triangle." This bold undertaking was commissioned by the City of Houston, underwritten by the Moody Foundation, and performed at the Miller Out-door Theatre with the Space Dance Theater and Vince, accompanied by the jazz band Passenger.

In late 1982, Vince had been in the studio recording a three-song demo with full band accompaniment featuring guitar players Stevie Ray Vaughan, Eric Johnson, and Chris Holzhaus. On the night of December 21, he had just finished a late-night session and was on his way home when his 1964 Ford Fairlane was broadsided by a drunk driver going sixty mph along the frontage road of Interstate 35 in South Austin. The impact threw Vince fifty feet from his vehicle. His suffered severe lacerations to his liver, an array of broken bones, shattered glass embedded all over his body, and a traumatic brain injury. In the emergency room, his arm was almost amputated before a nurse in the operating room recognized him as a musician and convinced the doctor not to do the deed. Having been erroneously pronounced dead at the scene, his obituary ran in the daily newspaper.

He remained in a coma for a month. His hand and arm had to be completely rebuilt. It would be almost a decade of determined rehabilitation before he could perform again. He had to first relearn how to put thoughts together, use his hands and feet, walk, talk, make a guitar chord, and strum and sing at the same time.

Vince 2.0 had a steep hill to climb.

"They charged the poor fellow that ran into me six hundred dollars for ending my career in music and taking my life for about twenty minutes, but I didn't have time for resentments," he said. "I couldn't write my name, taste, remember who anyone was, or walk a straight line. It's one long climb from there to an encore."

Writing songs and singing them was the previous Vince. With this Vince, every single word, every note, every breath mattered.

As he likes to say, "Learning the guitar the first time was a bitch. Learning the guitar the second time was cruel."

Seven years of rehab later, a musical using eleven of Vince's songs and titled for his composition, "Sun & Moon & Stars," was performed at Austin's Dougherty Theater. A recording of the same name was released shortly thereafter. In 1991, Nanci Griffith, who touted Vince as the best writer of the Houston folk circuit, covered "Sun & Moon & Stars" on her landmark album, *Late Night Grande Hotel*. In 2009, Lyle Lovett recorded the song and featured it as the opening number of his show during the *Natural Forces* album tour.

> *Sun & Moon & Stars*
> The sun and moon and stars make the wind blow.
> Took me twenty years to understand.
> Lost to me is how the lives of friends go.
> Like autumn leaves in Oklahoma wind.

It made me strong,
To be on my own.
It never did me no harm,
To live all alone.
But now and then
In the color of the evening,
Drunken in a barroom,
With the fan turning,
I've come to miss a few.

This afternoon was cloudy and the rains came.
Third day of my first stay, San Miguel.
Seems lately as I'm doubling as storm bait,
Been followed like a shadow since the Dells.

REFRAIN (It made me strong . . .)

Dear friendships and relations see what I have done
I've gathered all my fingers in one place
They breathe a breath that's deathly stale since they
    tooled a song for me
Seems mechanics never really set the pace.

REFRAIN (It made me strong . . .)

Clearly, "Sun & Moon & Stars" is a poetic, insightful creation of the highest order and confirms that Vince's literary musings translate smoothly into strong "meter and rhyme [that] still tell a good story." This delicate paean to "friendships and relations" is one of many examples that Vince's work is always "getting ever so better, lyric by bleeding lyric."

Twelve years after the wreck, Vince Bell released his next album, *Phoenix*. Produced by Bob Neuwirth and supported by a phalanx of fine musicians including legendary Geoff Muldaur, Dylan sideman David Mansfield, Willie Nelson sideman Mickey Raphael, and auteur John Cale, with Lyle Lovett and Victoria Williams adding support vocals, it was everything he could have wanted in a recorded rendition of his music.

"Bob Neuwirth gave me an identity in sound unlike anything I had ever enjoyed," Vince explained. "In the studio you're surrounded by all kinds of tech equipment to help you do just what you would like to do. But, having such a kaleidoscope of choice can be confusing. In addition, every studio is different sounding from every other studio. So, when it's the voice you're gonna use to relate your words, song after song, finding the right fit is so important. Bob had the savvy to put a Shure 58 heavy on the mids in my way, and it sounded great. If it ain't simple, it ain't solved."

Four albums and a DVD of his earlier compositions have followed.

So has an autobiography, detailing his life in music and the aftermath of the wreck, titled *One Man's Music*. Drawing from his book, Vince has written an hour-long, one-man theatrical performance, *One Man's Music: A Monologue with Song*.

Vince Bell 2.0 is not the same person as Vince 1.0. The hair is shorter and grayer. A partially paralyzed left vocal chord added a husky rasp to his singing and speaking voice, lending a weary wisdom to whatever he's singing about. "People often ask, 'Where'd you get that smoky sounding voice?' You really don't wanna' know," he usually tells them. "But I don't sound like that high school quarterback I mentioned earlier."

He continues writing, a process that he describes as "Music School":

Music School was a glimmer of an idea I came up with in the wake of the wreck to find any way that I could to rise the hell up out of my sick bed and get back into the world of capability again. In my high school football days I had learned how to take a lick and come back stronger. But this brain injury fellow was one overpowering dude. He was taller than the sky and bigger than a boat, but he had no business fucking with me. And I aimed to prove it. So Music School began early in my recovery on Providence Street in Austin. A typewriter under a pale yellow table lamp and a parlor piano over in the corner staged my setting in a small, shudderingly quiet room at the back of my tiny frame house. These dear old pieces of my writer's home helped me kick back at the darkness of the brain injury.

Over the years, and from town to town, Music School has gone from that garage-sale-cheery but desperate back room to other cheery, but a little less desperate back rooms, getting less desperate all the time. I took Music School to Berkeley in the nineties along with those black-book journals I filled with the latest tune or musing, scales, phone numbers, poems, guitar tunings, set lists, chord progressions, EQ settings for guitars and vocals, to-do lists, and lyric after failed lyric that I went to war with. With those journals and Bob Neuwirth's incalculable help with *Phoenix*, I reinvented a Vince that had been way out of the loop for a long time. I then took Music School to Fredericksburg, Texas, where I wrote the first draft of my book on a nine-inch, black-and-white, bit-mapped computer screen. Then it was on to Nashville to write and record *Texas Plates* for my friend and producer Robin Eaton.

And now, Santa Fe.

Here, thirty-odd years from that back room on Providence Street, Music School is a seventy-six-year-old adobe on a wooded hilltop a few miles down the highway from Santa Fe, New Mexico. There's a courtyard and a barn. There's an "idea morgue," a decades-old repository computer file for the prospects that never quite found their way into an ambitious writer's repertoire. Guitars and computers are in a wing of the old house off the kitchen. So, like Texas, this Music School has been a real companion, a well-traveled state of mind.

I try to write a song as clear as sunlight through glass. Just tell the story. When I was a young writer, I used the language of sixties rock music. But I honestly couldn't guess where the tune would end up lyrically, or otherwise. So I closely followed each new tune to find out what it was going to teach me about myself. Today I have a mine of lyrical suggestions in various states of together—in my head, in my heart, in a journal, on the computer, or on an iPhone. The books, the plays, the prose, the poems, or the songs come from those sources. Forty years after beginning this "repository" or "idea morgue," I find that if I come up with a novel chord change or a word tumble that comes on like an avalanche, I can write most everything at will. I used to write whatever I could catch, wherever, whenever. Now I fish from my own well.

And, recently, twenty years after *Phoenix*, I went to New York to record a new project with Bob Neuwirth and Dave Soldier. I didn't take a guitar. Bob chose lyrics, poetry, and prose from my "idea morgue," and I read from my isolated sound booth while the music was improvised by a group of musicians ranging from jazz flautists and flamenco guitarists to the percussionist from Saturday Night Live, David [Mansfield], and my old pal Mickey [Raphael] on harmonica.

If Bob gave me an identity in sound with *Phoenix*, this time he liberated my words.

The words still flow melodiously, but I can no longer listen to Vince casually, knowing what he went through, what he had to do to claw his way back to who he is now, knowing how much more everything matters now. Just compare the video clip of "Sun & Moon & Stars" from a local Austin television appearance before the wreck that's on YouTube to any of the versions performed after the wreck. . . . It's no contest. Vince 2.0 is one soulful cat, not that the earlier Vince was not. It took me twenty years to understand.

Had he died in that wreck all those years ago, it would have made for a tragic, albeit compellingly classic music story, pegged on the "Died-Too-Soon" theme. But Vince didn't die. Still, it's hard to ignore what happened, and there's always something to remind you that it did—the limp in his gait, the pause before answering a question as he organizes his thoughts, the feel of pain and sadness when he sings about such matters, and the pure sweetness that manages to come through.

Which merely raises the level of respect for this particular ruthlessly poetic songwriter. Pursuing the craft is hard enough. To continue to chase the muse, after staring death in the face, well, that is the mark of a very special human being, never mind his music-making tendencies.

Poetry, Texas

Dallas in the mirror.
Winter morning, cold as hell.
Me, and my six string,
no one else.

Collar to the wind,
Future in the breeze.
Hardly seems that faraway,
you know what I mean.

Highway 59
drove just like a dream.
Asphalt tops, yellow lines
still call me. . . .

Post Office Box, Poetry, Texas

Wandering and working,
living off the cuff.
Some things never change
I can't get enough.

The train's in Kansas City.
New York's a parking lot.
You can tell where I am
by where I'm not.

Post Office Box, Poetry, Texas.

VIGNETTE—RAY WYLIE HUBBARD

GRIFTER, RUFFIAN, MESSENGER

Jenni Finlay

"Why would they call me the godfather of Red Dirt music?" he asked, clearly perplexed. We were sitting at Cheatham Street Warehouse immediately after the radio interview, reliving battle stories from the road. I grinned broadly, looked straight at him, and recited the familiar lyrics: "Well, he was born in Oklahoma / And his wife's name is Betty Lou Thelma Liz / He's not responsible for what he's doing / His mother made him what he is." My eyes stayed fixed on his. "That's why, Ray," I said. "That's why."

Ray Wylie Hubbard rolled his eyes dramatically. He sighed. Shrugged his shoulders.

Cosmic Cowboy fans worldwide know and love Hubbard's classic anthem, "Up Against the Wall, Redneck Mother." The song helped launch Jerry Jeff Walker on his landmark ¡Viva Terlingua! (MCA Nashville, 1973). The same fans today still hoot and holler along with the chorus no matter who sings it. The song also became an albatross for Hubbard, a Cowboy Twinkie early on who later grew into a serious songwriter, a man deeply concerned with earthly meaning and curiosity beyond this life. Still, a performer must deliver the goods for his crowd.

"I had 'Redneck Mother' and that's it," Hubbard says. "I'd go to these places and I'd walk out and they'd say play 'Redneck Mother' and I'd play 'Redneck Mother.' I'd go, here's another song I wrote. They'd go, play 'Redneck Mother' again. Now, I have 'Wanna Rock and Roll,' 'Snake Farm,' 'Drunken Poet's Dream,' songs that are equal in entertainment value."[1]

Over the past quarter century, Hubbard has delved deeply into blues, honing his songwriting style and crafting a personal catalog rich with both wit ("Rabbit") and wisdom ("Count My Blessings"). Just listen to albums such as *Delirium Tremolos* (2005), *Snake Farm* (2010), and *The Grifter's Hymnal* (2012). Each highlights a songwriter owing a deep debt to Texas tunesmiths such as Lightnin' Hopkins and Mance Lipscomb with turns of phrase often as dense as celebrated lyricist Mickey Newbury. The good disciple never fails to mention those who guided his seismic shift. "I say that Muddy Waters is as deep as William Blake," he croons in "Down Home Country Blues," and nods toward his favorite poet, Rainer Maria Rilke, in the inspirational "Messenger": "The message I give is from this old poet Rilke / He said 'Our fears are like dragons guarding our most precious treasures.'"

Hubbard's also passionate about spotlighting the next generation. He's championed and cowritten with favorites such as Hayes Carll ("Chickens," "Drunken Poet's Dream"), unflinchingly tending the talents of our next generation of ruthlessly poetic songwriters. His version of "Drunken Poet's Dream" intermingles the grit and groove of their two worlds: "Now I'll never pay back my student loan / Smellin' like Coors and cheap cologne," he sings. "She tells me not to worry about Judgment Day / She says dyin' to get to heaven just ain't our way."

Hubbard's a guru, mentor, teacher, always reverential about those who offered him the same guidance. "In my opinion, there's Guy Clark, Townes Van Zandt, Billy Joe Shaver, Robert Earl Keen, Jerry Jeff Walker, and Willie Nelson as songwriters," he says. "That's the level that you aspire to if you're going to be a songwriter in Texas. You have to be aware of those guys and the caliber of their songwriting."[2]

Hubbard might well add himself to the list. Consider his most seamless one-liners: "Some get spiritual, 'cause they see the light / And some, 'cause they feel the heat" ("Conversation with the Devil"); or the darker, "I'm standin' just south of fate / There ain't no exit from the interstate / There's one way in, it's a long, dirty road / Only one way our Robert Johnson knows" ("Last Train to Amsterdam").

Despite his sly reservations about the iconic (and frankly tremendously clever) "Up Against the Wall, Redneck Mother," Hubbard still loves word-play (and audience-play) with tunes like "Wanna Rock and Roll," "Snake Farm," and, of course, "Screw You, We're From Texas." Fans now look to him for enlightenment. He's our Mecca, the Buddha, the spiritual lynchpin that encourages, inspires, and motivates many Texas singer-songwriters, the healer who creatively encourages and motivates us all. His workaday mantra serves as a lesson in blissful minimalism: "The days that I keep my gratitude higher than my expectations," he sings in "Mother Blues," "Well, I have really good days."

THE GREAT PROGRESSIVE COUNTRY SCARE OF THE 1970S

Craig D. Hillis (interview with Gary P. Nunn)

G ary P. Nunn is perhaps best known because of his song "London Homesick Blues," the theme song of *Austin City Limits* for three decades, a song that is often referred to as the Texas national anthem. But he was also one of the driving forces behind the early days of the shifting Austin music scene, a scene that Fromholz affectionately referred to as "The Great Progressive Country Scare of the 1970s."

CDH: When you and I met Fromholz in the early 1970s, we were both playing in Austin rock 'n' roll bands. How would you describe your segue from the Austin rock scene to this new world of "folkie songwriters"?

GPN: During that time I had been playing in a band called "Genesee" that contained the remnants of the Lavender Hill Express. We were starting to lean toward the acoustic-based, vocal-harmony rock style of Buffalo Springfield, Neil Young, and Crosby, Stills & Nash. Not only was this a departure from our usual "top-rock" dance format, we had hired a great singer-songwriter from Denver, Richard Dean, rather than a local rocker to round out that version of Genesee. Richard ran in the same circles as Fromholz and other folk artists. . . . In fact, it was Richard who corralled us one evening and took the band to the Chequered Flag to hear Frummox, the folk duo featuring Steven and Dan McCrimmon. That was where I initially met Fromholz.

Genesee had been tinkering with some of our own songs, but doing original material seemed like a scary and daunting transition at that time. But Richard had been writing some really great songs so we worked them up and performed them. With that new format, Genesee had a pretty good run for a while, but toward the end of 1971, the band parted company. I can't recall the exact reason, but as you know, bands are hard to keep together even when you're on a good roll!

After Genesee, I had decided to leave Austin and move to our family ranch in Oklahoma to do some soul searching and physical work to try and get my head and heart straightened out. Frankly, I was in a bad emotional state with no direction, little confidence or self-esteem, and I felt the need for a change. I had my things packed for the move when someone mentioned that Michael Murphey was going to be in town the first week in January. In that world of folksingers, Michael was always recognized as "the man" when it came to first-rate songs. I know that you had spent some time playing with Michael in Colorado and had great things to say about him. Also, many of the folk-music acts were performing his songs in their sets, and he was always described in the most glowing terms. So I delayed my move for a few days in order to see Michael when he came to town.

It was a Monday, the first night of a one-week run at the "original" Saxon Pub at Thirty-Eighth-and-a-half Street and I-35. The place was packed and I was totally blown away with his songs, his singing and obvious talent. He was in a different category all together! I was caught totally by surprise when he came off the stage after the first set, walked directly to me and said, "Hey man, I've heard a lot about you. How would you like to play bass in my band?" I had no idea that he knew anything about me. I'll bet it was you who had put a bug in his ear.

CDH: Yes, that's right. Not long before Michael got to Austin to play the Pub, I'd done some dates with him and Bob (Livingston) in Colorado and told him that he should look you up when he got to town. Also, Bob knew you from the Sparkles back when he was going to Texas Tech and he had great things to say about you as well.

GPN: Well, Murphey approaching me like that certainly got my attention. There I was, my pickup was packed up and ready to go after that show, and this man who had just blown me away was offering me a job! It was not just another band gig playing the college bars and fraternity houses around the UT campus. It was a step into the professional world of the music business, something I had been dreaming of and wanting to do for years. So my plans to move to our ranch in Oklahoma were jettisoned in an instant. Michael stayed at my house, and we went to work on bringing me up to speed on his material. I had turned the page on a brand new chapter in my life.

CDH: What was it about these guys—Fromholz, Murphey, and later, Walker—that triggered this "new chapter"? What were the factors and circumstances that sparked your rebirth as a songwriter?

GPN: Well, there were several reasons. Some of it had to do with my personal outlook. As I mentioned, I wasn't in a particularly good place regarding my musical career. That post-Genesee period was a major transition. It started when Richard Dean joined the band, then really kicked into high gear when I morphed into the songwriting scene with Murphey.

Murphey had a tremendous influence on me, not only musically, but personally. He really encouraged me. He basically said, "Just go ahead and do it! What you're writing is good." And that was a far cry from what I'd been hearing in the bands I'd been playing in. Plus, Murphey, Fromholz, and of course Richard Dean were actually out there doing it. They had the courage to write a song, perform it, see if it worked with an audience, then own that experience and move forward from there. It struck me as a great template for success. They demonstrated that there was the possibility of a response. You've got to throw your work out there or nobody will see it. They might like it. They might not like it, but if they never saw it, they wouldn't have a chance to like it. It was just that gateway that gave me the courage to keep writing, and when things did come my way, I knew I would have a chance to bring my songs into the real world.

CDH: So what I'm hearing here is that your approach to music changed when you realized the power of the song.

GPN: Yes! That's a good way of saying it. It was the power of the song and the realization that those songs were within my grasp. In meeting Murphey, it was all about writing and we came together in a very creative way. Michael is so easy to write songs with. He was a constant source of ideas, he was a very disciplined writer, and he was very open to the ideas I had, particularly the ideas I had about chord structures and arrangements. I had always been a "band guy." I naturally heard things with bass, drums, guitars, keys, and other instruments, and Michael was in a place where he wanted to expand his songs into an ensemble format.

That reminds me . . . I did end up going up to Oklahoma, but it wasn't to get out of Austin. As things turned out, it was to supplement the work I was doing in Austin. After Michael and I had been working together for a few months, we went up to my family's ranch on the South Canadian to hang out, ride horses, and write songs. That's where "South Canadian River Song" came from.

CDH: And that reminds me, "South Canadian River Song" is an excellent example of the merging of two musical camps in Austin during the period we're discussing; specifically, you from the "rockers" and Michael from the "folkies." The music for "South Canadian," which you wrote, is like a rock symphony with various movements and moods, and Murphey's esoteric lyrics are essentially an ode to a great river, "a free-flowing stream to a tidal wave" and a metaphor for the larger cycle of life.

GPN: That particular piece of music that became "South Canadian" had been rolling around in my head for quite some time, but I hadn't really considered a lyrical theme or message. As you know, that chord structure is a pretty intricate affair. . . . There are quite a few twists and turns, or as you say, a number of "movements and moods." But it all came together when we were hanging out on the river: Michael began to layer the lyrics over the chord structure, and by the time we got back to Austin, we were well on the way to completing the song.

Like I said, writing with Murphey is a very positive experience, and in the case of the "South Canadian River Song," Michael took the sounds and structures I'd been kicking around and combined them with a story and message to shape a unique and powerful composition. Again, it was his encouragement and professional discipline that brought my creativity to the surface.

CDH: I'd like to inject a quick history to bring us to the point of your affiliation with Willie Nelson. As I remember, after meeting Murphey at the Pub, you fellows kick-started a lifelong relationship. At that point, it was just the two of you. Livingston had gone to Red River, New Mexico, on a short-lived junket to play bass with Three Faces West, a very popular trio featuring Ray Wylie Hubbard, Rick Fowler, and Wayne Kidd. When Livingston left, you and Murphey went to Nashville to wrap up the *Geronimo's Cadillac* album. Murphey was working with mega-producer Bob Johnston who had called in a bunch of slick "Nashville cats" to do overdubs and button up the recording project. *Geronimo's Cadillac* was released in May of 1972, and you and Murphey put together the band that included me on lead guitar and Michael McGeary on drums. By that time Livingston had returned from Red River and rejoined the band, and you and Bob switched out on bass and keyboards as needed.

GPN: Yeah, that sounds about right. Right after the album was released, A&M Records brought us to Hollywood for a record debut at the Whisky a Go-Go of all places! In LA Murphey brought Herb Steiner on board. Herb was his pal and band mate from the Southern California honky-tonk scene, and Herb joined the band on steel guitar. This really rounded out our sound and moved it in a country direction.

After playing the Whisky, the record company sent us out to the East Coast to Boston, Philadelphia, and New York. We finally returned to Austin during the summer of 1972, and that's where Eddie Wilson came into the picture. Eddie was the visionary behind the Armadillo World Headquarters, and he sensed the momentum behind Murphey's music and the new scene that was developing in Austin. I believe he wanted to expand the Armadillo brand statewide, because Eddie, along with one of his primary sponsors, Lone Star Beer, put together a concert tour of West Texas. It was called

"Armadillo Country" with Michael Murphey headlining and Willie Nelson opening.

Willie had recently moved to Austin from Nashville, he was making a few appearances around town, but he had yet to play the Armadillo. Eddie booked us in Abilene, Lubbock, Wichita Falls, and some other West Texas venues, and we were supposed to finish the weeklong tour with a grand finale at the Armadillo.

I remember that the "Armadillo Country" tour kicked off in Abilene in a big auditorium. When we arrived that afternoon for the sound check, someone told me that Willie Nelson wanted to talk to me. He and Paul English were traveling in that old beat up Winnebago that had "Remember Me" painted across the back. When I climbed into the Winnebago, he and Paul were playing chess. Willie said, "Hey man, can you play bass for me on this tour?" Well, I knew "Night Life" as I had done it since I was in high school—the Ray Price version—but other than that, I didn't have a clue about his repertoire, but I said, "Sure!" He said, "Great, I'll pay you $50 a night." That was it. No rehearsal, no nothing.

That night we went on stage in an auditorium that probably held three thousand, and I swear there couldn't have been more than fifty people in the place! It was just Willie, Paul, and me, and I didn't have a clue! He did a medley of his songs and changed keys between every song. When he played his famous guitar, "Trigger," he would always turn to his left. Well, I was on his right so I couldn't see his left hand to know what chords he was playing. For me, it was a disaster. I probably didn't hit two right notes all night.

Willie, no doubt sensing my misery, came over and said to me, "Don't worry about it! It don't mean a thing." I was somewhat relieved, but still supremely aware of my inadequacy.

We played the other towns on the tour and by Saturday we were back in Austin for the finale at the Armadillo. By that time I had a handle on what he was doing as he did exactly the same show every night. It was Willie's debut at the Armadillo World Headquarters and it's just Willie and Paul with me on bass! We opened for Michael to a packed house and all the hippies at the Armadillo loved it! Then we went on with Michael and brought the house down! From that night, Willie's career was off like a rocket and the rest is history.

After the show, backstage, Chet Flippo, a stringer for *Rolling Stone* magazine, asked me, "Gary P., do you think country music will go over at the Armadillo?" And I said, "The place is packed. The proof is in the pudding."

CDH: What was your take away from that tour as Willie's bass player? What was your impression of his songwriting?

GPN: Well, as I look back on that experience and as I consider what I've learned about Willie's songwriting style since then, there are several things that come to mind. One of the things that I noticed on that tour was his economy of lyrics. Once I got the chord changes down and got comfortable with the tunes, I was able to focus on the lyrics. I felt that each word had a place in the story line. There wasn't any wasted lyrical effort—no "wasted" words, no theatrical metaphors or overused figures of speech—just clean, accessible language.

I also developed a deep appreciation for the sophisticated nature of Willie's chord structures. I realize that many of Willie's songs are essentially one-four-five affairs. Willie himself has said that a country song is "three chords and the truth!" But many of his tunes have really progressive chord patterns and delicate changes. "Night Life" is a great example. It's put together so seamlessly that it comes off sounding like a simple progression, but once you get into it, it's much more than that. There are a number of subtle passing chords that can be interpreted in a number of ways, and that is a hallmark of a great song. Many of Willie's songs have this great "inside-chord," jazz approach.

Then there's Willie's sincere style in presenting his songs. He is very much in his own world when he's on that stage. It's like there's nothing else in the world at that moment beyond Willie, his audience, and the song. To be up there with Willie when he's performing, to be part of that, is a lesson in concentration and connection.

CDH: I can certainly relate to that "front-man" focus! I'm sure you would agree that Murphey had a similar concentration and connection.

GPN: Definitely, yes. In fact, I sensed a number of parallels in Willie and Murphey. I learned a great deal from both of them, particularly from Michael because we spent so much time together in the early years. That was truly a magical time for me.

PLENTY ELSE TO DO

Andy Wilkinson

et me begin by getting something off my chest. I have no clue as to what is meant by being ruthlessly poetic. Not that I don't like the phrase. I like it. I really do. I like it not because I understand it, but because I am drawn to it. *Ruthless* means cruel, means without mercy, means without compassion. Those are all things that poetry exists to defeat, all things to which poetry stands in opposition, each of those things being anti-poetic. So if I like the phrase, *ruthlessly poetic*, it is because I am drawn to a conundrum like a moth is drawn to a flame. For the same reason that I am enraptured by the birthing of Yeats's *terrible beauty*, or by Mick singing "Good-bye, Ruby Tuesday, who could hang a name on you?" all the while hanging such a beautiful name on such a beautiful mystery, or by Butch singing "Life is a cyclone, death is but a breeze." For the same reason that I wish the Texas highway signs instructing us to *Drive Friendly* would appear in a series, Burma-Shave-style, their seventy-five-mile-an-hour slogan admonitions followed with a second, *Wave When You Go Past*, then with a third, *Drive Friendly, Neighbor*, and finishing up with *Or I'll Stop and Kick Your Ass*. Ruthlessly friendly. Ruthlessly poetic.

My confession and wish notwithstanding, if there be such thing as a ruthlessly poetic songwriter then such musical scribe would come from my home country, the Llano Estacado, the southern tip of the Great Plains, the twenty-five-odd county area around the Hub City of Lubbock, the flattest spot in the flatlands. A place where drivers really do give a friendly wave as they go past and expect one in return. A place where there are more creative people *per capita* than anywhere in the known universe.

You may quibble with me on that last point, but you can't disprove me. For starters, I offer you Buddy Holly, who was a four-year-old tyke when the nation's census-takers concluded that only a quarter-million souls inhabited the vast tablelands that stretch south from Running Water Draw on the high side to Monument Draw on the nether side, all the while spreading west from the steep wall of the Cap Rock to the imperceptible New Mexico state line. What city or county or country of that size has produced even one Buddy Holly, much less a second? A third?

And it's not just Buddy. Though that would be enough. Before Buddy it was Hoyle Nix with his "Big Ball's in Cowtown" and before Hoyle it was Floyd Tillman "Slippin' Around" and before Floyd and even before the First War to End All Wars it was Jack Thorp, riding the range west of Lubbock while writing "Little Joe, the Wrangler." Ruthlessly poetic songwriters? I reckon. "Working on the railroad, sleeping on the ground / We just have to slip around and live in constant fear / Beneath his horse, smashed to a pulp, his spurs had rung the knell."

That not enough? There's lots more. Along with Buddy in the burst of singing songwriters in the last half of the fifties came Buddy's buddies J. I. Allison and Sonny Curtis and Waylon Jennings and David Box, as well as the other buddy, Buddy Knox. Plus Roy Orbison. There followed the briefest of respites as the fifties ended early in early February of '59 in a frozen Iowegian cornfield near Clear Lake. But a scant few years later—just as the Brits were bringing the First Buddy back to the Colonials by naming their combos in his honor and by imitating his singing and singing his songs—other songwriters like Dow Patterson and John Deutschendorf Denver were coming to Lubbock to study at Texas Tech and play music for frat parties. It was also in the sixties when the Llano Estacado sent forth the first big wave of its own songwriters to practice their craft elsewhere: Waylon, first to Phoenix and then to Lubbock East—what the Volunteers of the Volunteer State call Nashville—then Terry Allen to Lubbock West—what the Californios call Los Angeles—and Mac Davis, close behind Terry, after a short detour through Atlanta. By the seventies the ruthlessly poetic Llanero songwriters were back at work, first in their home country before their mass relocation to Lubbock South—what the uninformed Texans call Austin—the Lubbock ex-pats including, just to hit a few highlights, Joe Ely, Jimmie Dale Gilmore, David Halley, Butch Hancock, Bob Livingston, and Jo Carol Pierce. All these years later and they are still pouring out of the Hub City Kingdom like ants from an ant hill on a hot day—if there ever was anything like a hill even of formicidic proportions on the Staked Plains—now marching among their ranks the Gatlins and Natalie Maines and Amanda Shires and Cary Swinney and many, many others.

Pardon a pause for clarification. You've likely noticed that I've not addressed one of the cardinal points. What is Lubbock North, you might wonder? The answer is simple. There is nothing of consequence between Lubbock and the North Pole. Except Amarillo, which is of great consequence, especially when it comes to songwriting and ruthlessness and poetics, being as it is the native land to such songwriting worthies as Susan Gibson, Jimmy Gilmer, Buck Ramsey, Eddie Reeves, and J. D. Souther. But Amarillo is also a special case. Anyone who's gone to the Golden Spread knows that it's its own animal, its own unique spot in the galaxy, much more than just a Route 66 rest-stop that made the song; instead, it's the home of an extraordinary ethos of cultural contradictions, those conundrums that I love. As one example, you might ponder that its east-west axis is drawn through Stanley Marsh 3's *Cadillac Ranch* on one end of town and The Big Texan's "Free 72 Oz Steak" on the other, while its north–south axis is marked by the stunning grandeur of the Palo Duro Canyon below and the secretive horrors of the Pantex nuclear weapons factory above. All this being evidence of why Amarillo can't be Lubbock North, for the plain fact is that the two largest cities on the Great Plains are spiritually inseparable, each one being one side of the same Möbius band, the pair making a duality of Taoist proportions, between them a continuum of Heraclitean dimensions. Or, we could say else-wise, they are but altered states of one another, Amarillo being what Lubbock is when it dreams and Lubbock being what Amarillo is when it works.

Now that that's settled, and now that I've convinced you about the phenomenal *per capita* count of ruthlessly poetic songwriters from our end of the world—or at least cowed you into keeping your quibbling with my assertion to yourself—let's get to the real meat of the matter. Why? Why do so many great songwriters come from this place? Is it the flatness? Or the openness? Or the sky? Or the wind? Or the fact that, as has been often offered, there is nothing else to do? The answer is yes, and partly, and not completely.

I began this essay with a confession. Another is required here. I have no answers, only suggestions to present as answers, well-reasoned though such suggestions may be and even though such suggestions might, on a good day, rise to the grandeur of theory. So it's time to put your quibbler back to work.

Theories—and their little cousins, guesses, and their little siblings, suggestions—of every kind begin with one or more assumptions. I'll make one now. Art is a fundamental fact of being human. It may be the only thing that truly distinguishes us from the rest of the animal kingdom, other members of which do almost everything that we do, to include tool-making and the making of tools to make tools (meaning abstract thought), to include oral communications of all kinds (implying language), to include mating for life (though we as a species may be losing that one), to include organizing in groups (hinting at self-governance), and on and on. Yet no other animal—at least to our knowledge—writes poems or songs or plays or novels or symphonies, or dances for pleasure, or paints for self-expression (and, no, I won't accept YouTube videos of trained elephants slapping paint on canvases as evidence of their art, though I might be persuaded if someone can present me with the discovery of a proboscidean-owned art gallery hidden in the deep, dark reaches of the African savanna).

A corollary of this assumption is that, even though within human populations there will be variability in individual capacities for art—some people being more artistic than others, just as some run faster or jump higher—there will be no significant differences between human populations. People are people, or they aren't, and if they are then they have all the characteristics of being human. Which leads to my first suggestion. If differences are found—say, a substantially high *per capita* number of ruthlessly poetic songwriters hailing from the Llano Estacado—then the cause must be something environmental, with environment inclusive of both the physical and the cultural worlds.

The Llano Estacado is a remnant plateau, rising from its surroundings on all sides, and a particularly large one, some 250 miles long and 200 miles wide. Owing to its having been geologically stable for roughly the past million years its surface is remarkably flat, something you've likely noticed if you've traveled it. Taken together, it's commonly reported that the Llano Estacado is the world's largest flat landmass.

Over his ninety-three-year life, Charlie Goodnight, nineteenth-century trailblazer and rancher and self-made naturalist, had time a-plenty to spend on the Plains, the Llano in particular. In an interesting, wide-ranging interview late in the century-before-last, he asserted that the people of the Plains will have to solve the problems of the people of the East, because on the Plains the eye must see a great long distance and such seeing makes the mind active. He went on to describe how noble were the cowboys on the open range, and how devious and of what low moral character were the cowboys of the brush country where such long-distance seeing could not be had. I, for one, am willing to give brush-poppers the benefit of the doubt, but there is indeed something unmistakable about how open spaces open the mind as well as the heart, and how closed-in spaces have the opposite impact. In open country, one turns outward, not inward.

Then there is the wind. On the Llano, there is always the wind. As children growing up on the Flatlands we learned as early as elementary school that our wind was special when Christina Rossetti—a poet not only from another century but obviously from another place—asked who'd seen the wind and assured us that neither she nor I had seen it and then made no bones about it being visible unless it pushed around the grass or the trees. Pshaw, as my granny would have said, we don't even have trees out here and the grass in our parts is too short to be seen moving. Besides, we Llaneritos didn't need to infer the wind from something else 'cause we could see the wind its ownself, and oftentimes a day or more away in the distance, pushing ahead of it a low wall of blue norther in the winter, carrying aloft a high-roller dust storm in the spring, walking about on thunderhead legs in the summer, hustling along herds of tumbleweeds in the fall.

The wind on the Llano Estacado has substance and consequence. And it has merit. We might even say that it is both ruthless and poetic. It keeps an unreasonable number of city folk from emigrating to our pristine flatness. It pumps our water. Nowadays it generates your electricity. It wipes away the smog and scrubs the skies to a bright cerulean blue. It is a constant refresher of our storehouse of humility. And—most importantly—wind is Nature at her most metaphysical, a physical manifestation in which the past and the future both exist simultaneously in the present, for the wind comes, the wind is, and the wind goes. All at once. Which is the grown-up part of Rossetti's children's poem. And which is also the perfect analogue to music. For the note that occupies the present moment arises from or implies the existence of the note before it, predicates or implies the note that follows it, yet exists fully and completely in the moment. As John Denver might have said during his sojourn on the Llano Estacado, "far out!"

Your quibbler should be beeping and buzzing right now, little lights blinking furiously. If all it takes is big, open horizons with plenty of wind and sky (I hear you murmuring) then we should find a treasure-trove of ruthlessly poetic songwriters anywhere we can find those things. And there is some agreeable evidence—the songs of sailors, for example—but, for the most part, we don't find such songwriting riches everywhere we find flatness and horizon and sky and wind. When you're down in Texas, Bob Wills is still the King of Swing, but the Llano remains the Realm of the Ruthlessly Poetic.

So far, I've only outlined the physical environment, just one part of the story. Now is the time to Paul-Harvey-it by unfolding the rest of the story, which is the cultural environment. Our late and much admired poet-songwriter-philosopher from the Golden Spread, Buck Ramsey, famously and simply defined a cowboy as anyone who is in the right place at the right time ahorse-back. Not that I'm suggesting that our Llanero songwriters are all cowboys or that all cowboys are songwriters—though some certainly are—for there are far more of Terry Allen's flatland farmers inhabiting our remnant plateau than there are members of Buck Ramsey's cowpunch tribe. But Buck went on to define the frontier outlands in which the cowboy could be found as a place where a person is measured by what they can do, not by who they are or where they came from, and pointed out that personal skill and ability are at a premium on the frontier, where neighboring—the culture of standing ready to help your neighbor at any time, regardless of whether or not you like or dislike or know or don't know the neighbor—is the cultural law of the land, a land in which, Buck always finished up by saying, everyone is your neighbor. Buck's observations help to explain why this place that is so far to the right when it comes to politics and religion is at the same time so far to the left when it comes to friendliness and helpfulness.

And let me be emphatic that Lubbock and the Llano Estacado are still the frontier. We know from the archaeological evidence—much of it gleaned from the famous digs at Lubbock Lake Landmark—that people have been traversing this land for twelve thousand years, principally because there has always been water available in the series of small lakes and springs along the trail that runs from present-day Yellowhouse Canyon on the east of Lubbock to Portales, New Mexico, on the west, a stretch that the Spanish named *La Pista de Vida Agua*, which we loosely translate as "the trail of living waters."

That same archaeological work also shows, however, that no one lived here year-round until a few *transhumante* New Mexican shepherds settled into winter camps along the Yellowhouse Canyon in the 1880s. Westward migrations of Anglo-Americans relentlessly skipped over the Great Plains, including the Llano Estacado, most of them pronouncing the place unfit for human habitation. Even the Comanche called the Llano *the place where no one is*. Towns and cities out here were first populated in the last decade of the nineteenth century and began their incorporations in the first decade of the next. Lubbock, for example, marked its centennial celebration only in 2009. This is young country still, yet to shake off its frontier roots and culture.

Buck's notion of the cult of skill that permeates the frontier also helps explain a quality that I've observed, first-hand, amongst each and every one of the ruthlessly poetic songwriters that hail from the Flatlands. You can turn your quibbler back off for a moment, as there's no arguing this point: these folks are *un*selfconsciously and *un*pretentiously and *un*intendedly marked by a perfect balance of perfect humility and perfect self-confidence. They're not braggarts, but they know that of which they are capable, and in that knowing they do not shy away from the practice of their art, from the execution of their work. Their neighbors—and remember, out on the frontier, everyone is your neighbor—regard it as perfectly normal that, if you're able to play the guitar or sing or write the song or paint the picture, you should go on and do it.

Which brings us to the final conundrum, *nothing else to do*. On its face, such a statement is demeaning to music and art. Something that you do when you have nothing else to do is rearrange your sock drawer, or polish your spittoon, or watch bowling on television, or play video games on your smart phone. Not music. Not art. Those things aren't afterthoughts, those things aren't the idler's choice. On the contrary, they demand everything you have to give, and more.

Pardon my rant. I don't mean to be mean. For folks mean something very different when they invoke the there's-nothing-else-to-do line to explain away the tremendous outpouring of art and music that comes from the Llano Estacado. For one thing, it's evidence of that humility that I mentioned a few paragraphs back, a shrugging-off of a compliment, a wordy *aw, shucks*. For another thing it's a sly and mischievous tweaking of the lion's tail, a way of saying that there's nothing *better* to do.

But here's the most important thing. On the frontier there's always plenty else to do, because it's an exacting place, requiring both energy and attention just to stay alive. To make a crop. To put back what gets blown away. A place where the big horizons and the big skies are constant reminders of how small a person really is out here. A place where the constant wind and the rough weather are constant reminders of how a frail a person really is out here. So when there's plenty else to do, to choose to write songs over all the other things that can and, maybe, should be done *just to stay alive* is to say that poetry is the most important thing, a thing worthy of an everyday ruthlessness in its pursuit.

Ruthlessly poetic. I'm beginning to understand it now.

ROOTS OF STEEL

The Poetic Grace of Women Texas Singer-Songwriters

Kathryn Jones

The evening of music at Austin's Continental Club in December 2012 was billed as a benefit show featuring Patty Griffin and her "driver." Fans of Griffin's soulful lyrics listened to her solo material for the first half hour. Then she made a brief introduction. "Three years ago a guy with big hair and a British accent called me and said he needed help singing on their record," Griffin told the audience with a smile. She was referring to the group Band of Joy. "I followed him on the road for eighteen months and after it all he said he'd be my driver." Laughter followed as the "guy" she referred to, with his mane tucked beneath a black chauffeur cap, emerged from the shadows and took the stage. He was Robert Plant, the legendary lead singer of Led Zeppelin. Plant tossed off the cap and stepped into the spotlight next to Griffin, his one-time on- and off-stage partner.

Notice the words "next to." In the past, Plant might have been the main attraction and Griffin the opening act. Not so anymore. *Rolling Stone* magazine's headline on its account of the performance noted, "Robert Plant Joins Patty Griffin Onstage for Austin Benefit Show," with the subhead "Griffin introduces Led Zeppelin frontman as her 'driver.'" A quibble: it would have been nice to see a headline that read, "Patty Griffin Joined by Robert Plant," but headline writers typically like to use active voice.

Regardless of who came first in the article's title, the night was Griffin's, not Plant's. Her solo acts so absorb audiences that *Texas Monthly* magazine dubbed it the "Patty Griffin Effect": "When she sings, people listen. Really listen." Much of her material came from her 2013 album, *American Kid*, which drew on themes of death and tragedy—intimate and yet universal. She wrote the tribute "Go Wherever You Wanna Go" when her father, a World War II veteran embittered about the nation's direction, was dying (he passed away in 2009). "It was just one of those moments you think about when you think you have some time from it and you don't know exactly how the hell you're gonna get through that," Griffin explained about why she wrote the song. "So I just wrote about it, while I was going through it, while he was getting ready to go, so I was getting ready to let him go."

A TV news story Griffin saw about a soldier who signed up for military service after the September 11 terrorist attacks, then returned home with post-traumatic stress disorder and committed suicide, inspired another song on the album, "Not a Bad Man":

> I bet you see a stranger
> When you look at me
> When I look in the mirror
> I know that's what I see
>
> Got some pills to get my head right
> And they don't work so well

> So I drink a little more tonight
> And here's where I fell

Throughout her career, Griffin's songs have been called "spare and folky," "hushed," "volatile," "pensive," "mourning," "confessional," and "haunted," and her voice described as "full of sorrow and steel." As *The New York Times'* music critic Jon Pareles put it in a review of one of Griffin's performances, "she doesn't write many happy songs. Hardly any, in fact. Her folk-rock strummers and countryish waltzes are full of lonely travels and painful separations, of forebodings and sad memories." She and Plant split in 2013 and he returned to England; Griffin went on to make *Servant of Love*, her tenth album and her first release on her new self-owned label imprint with Nashville company Thirty Tigers. Regret makes a recurring appearance in her lyrics, as it does in most human lives. So does struggling against life's currents, as in "Rowing Song" (*Impossible Dream*, 2004) when Griffin sings about making a long emotional journey, "all of the way, alone and alive."

Other women singer-songwriters whose lives or music took root in Texas have made a long journey, too. When surveying the panorama of this musical landscape, the men who are well known as singer-songwriters clearly out-number the women and—Townes Van Zandt and Guy Clark being prime examples—often overshadow them. Kathleen Hudson, founding director of the Texas Heritage Music Foundation at Schreiner University in Kerrville, recalled she was "shocked" to learn that more than eight hundred women were listed in the Texas Industry Music Guide, but most music festivals around the state featured the "boys club," as she called it. "Even Willie's picnic lacks female performers," she wrote in *Women in Texas Music: Stories and Songs*. As of this writing, the Texas Heritage Songwriters' Hall of Fame had inducted only one woman—Cindy Walker. And in this book, most of the essays are about men.

Why the glaring disparity? Is it because women singer-songwriters haven't been "known" in influential musical circles that often resembled a good ol' boys' club and in a music industry dominated by men at the decision-making level? Were they considered more vocalists and musicians than songwriters? Was it because radio stations would not play their songs or record labels would not record them? Or because of sexism—or sex, which led some female singer-songwriters to cohabitation, marriage, and babies, which placed other priorities on them? Is it because their songs didn't make an emotional connection—or because they did, but not with the "right" audience in marketing terms? Did they get typecasted as writing "chick lyr-ics" because many of their songs dealt with themes of love, relationships, and heartbreak? Or were they, like their male counterparts, bending music genres into an eclectic style that record executives couldn't categorize? Too country for Los Angeles and too rock 'n' roll for Nashville, as music industry execs told multiple Grammy-winner Lucinda Williams early in her career?

The answer is bits and pieces of the above, but the last reason carries the most weight. Creating music that defies classification in an industry that wants to slap on labels is not the ticket to the top. Many of the women included in this essay emphasized the conscious choice they made between commercial stardom and artistic freedom. "I knew right away I didn't want to be a star," Terri Hendrix told me in an April 2014 interview in Stephenville, where she and Lloyd Maines performed at the annual Larry Joe Taylor Music Festival. "I just don't like it. When we played the Cotton Bowl, I felt like I needed a GPS to find everybody. I will do anything to avoid being backstage. I don't like to schmooze. It's about the music." Singer-songwriter Susan Gibson told Hudson she didn't feel like she'd ever been discriminated against, but added that she didn't think a man should view a feminine trait as a "negative thing," either. She has the perspective of a woman singer-songwriter who's opened for Guy Clark and written a monster hit recorded by the Dixie Chicks, "Wide Open Spaces," which she penned after moving from Amarillo to Montana. "We are preservers, recorders, communicators, storytellers," Gibson said. "Being a woman makes you do all these things. It's our nature, our clay. Texas music seemed like cowboys around a campfire for a while. That makes sense too. But now I'm really seeing the contribution of women. . . . I'm trying to incorporate this idea of a Greek goddess in a cowboy hat. There are so many archetypal roles that women play . . ."

San Antonio native and San Marcos resident Hendrix wrote the song "Invisible Girl" (*Places in Between*, 2000) after she played at music festivals years ago with mostly men. She recalled she had felt invisible. "It irritated me," she added. "And now, I don't care. My job is to keep practicing that harmonica and then get to be around fifty-five or sixty . . . and if you're going to ignore me, I'll throw it at you." She laughed. "My job needs to be about the song and try to write as good as I can and continue to grow. . . . Look at Wendy Davis running for (Texas) governor. Look at Hillary Clinton when she ran for president. There's still a long way for women to go as far as looking at the person and not the gender." Women making music are held to a high—not to mention double—standard, she added. "Name me one woman artist that's not a great musician. It makes you a better singer and a better player if you can't get away with it—if you can't do less than stellar music. And looks will only get you so far. Eventually, you have to play."

I write this as a female journalist who contemplated similar questions in my own field a few decades ago when starting my career. Why weren't there more women at the top? Why were there so many more men than women in newsrooms? Why were more women covering "soft" news and features than writing hard-hitting stories and doing investigative reporting? Certainly, some of that had to do with chauvinistic attitudes, but some of it also had to do with the fact that many women I knew had other priorities than living for their work. Female journalists don't have to ask as many questions as much anymore. Men may still outnumber women in many newsrooms and editors' offices, but more women are there, as reporters and editors and managers, and the news business is different—and better—for it.

So is Texas music and the singer-songwriter tradition. More women are better known now, but it's not like they were strangers to the scene. Women have been there all along, tucked into niches and coffeehouse corners, writing songs for others and for themselves, breaking out and breaking in, choosing the indie route and taking center stage, remaining unknown (in some cases, even preferring to) and carving a big name for themselves. There's no one factor to blame for their relative (double underline that word) lack of recognition and numbers compared with their male counterparts. Like male Texas singer-songwriters, women write songs that are meaningful to them and that they hope will connect with listeners. As Hendrix noted, it is the art, not fame and fortune that drives them. "Sometimes I suspect that if I had been wildly successful, I would have stopped growing as a human being and that would have affected the music in an unfortunate way," Austin-based singer-songwriter Eliza Gilkyson told an interviewer in 2008. "So, it may be better to struggle and be a little hungry." Some of the women in this essay had to leave Texas—or even the United States—to find a label and an audience. Others, such as Hendrix (see Brian T. Atkinson's essay, "Roll On: Terri Hendrix") went the indie route—"own your own universe" is her motto—and started her own label. Still others have focused less on recording and more on hitting the road and performing in live venues such as clubs and music festivals.

It also would be unfair to stereotype the diverse group of women who have been part of the Texas singer-songwriting tradition for decades, or their music that ranges from blues to rockabilly, country to gospel, soul to folk, and genre-bending blends. When I think of women singer-songwriters who are from or are strongly influenced by Texas, I think of early trailblazers such as Nanci Griffith, Tish Hinojosa, and Sara Hickman, who played at a church coffeehouse down the street from my east Fort Worth apartment in the 1980s. Their music is as varied as their voices. They don't fit into musical pigeonholes. Other than their gender, what they share is a love of writing musical stories and a rootedness in Texas, either by birth or adoption of the state as their muse. Listen and you hear Texas—and a sense of place and perspective—in their lyrics. And it's not the macho, cowboy stereotype. It's the Texas of small towns and gravel roads, of loneliness in a big city, of neighborhoods and families, of friends and lovers, of unsung heroes and blue-collar workers, of intersecting—and interwoven—cultures.

The title of pioneer singer-songwriter Griffith's twentieth album is, in fact, *Intersection*. "It's emotional for me, and it's personal, and it makes my heart pound, thinking I'm going to be totally exposed here," Griffith posted on her website after releasing the album in 2012. She could be speaking about her entire career, starting with her 1978 debut album, *There's a Light Beyond These Woods*. Raised in Austin, Griffith landed on the music scene as an early rebel who crossed lines between folk, country, and pop before it became common or cool—some critics, struggling with a category for her sound, called it "newgrass." Emerging from the acoustic coffeehouse tradition, Griffith in the 1980s released a string of critically successful, self-revelatory records—*Poet in My Window, Once in a Very Blue Moon, Last of the True Believers, Lone Star State of Mind*, and *Little Love Affairs*. The cover of *Last of the True Believers* featured Griffith holding a volume of poetry and standing outside a Woolworth's store. One of the most commercially successful songs on the album, "Love at the Five and Dime," which Kathy Mattea covered, tells the romantic story of a couple, Rita and Eddie, who waltzed the aisles of the local Woolworth, got married, endured hardships, and years later still dance to the radio: "Now Eddie played the steel guitar and his mama cried / 'Cause he played in the bands and kept young Rita out late at night / So they married up in Abilene, lost a child in Tennessee / Oh, still that love survived 'cause they'd sing."

Griffith's songwriting often reveals inner personal struggles. But like the folkies of her era, she also infuses her lyrics with politics and activism in America and abroad. As one of the few musicians to perform in Northern Ireland despite threats of terrorism, she wrote about the country's political battles in "It's a Hard Life Wherever You Go": "If we poison our children with hatred / Then, the hard life is all that they'll know / And there ain't no place in Belfast for that kid to go." One of her best albums, *Other Voices, Other Rooms* (1993)—the title is taken from Truman Capote's first novel, a copy of which Griffith embraces on the cover—celebrates songwriting by others. Her interpretations of songs such as Van Zandt's soulful "Tecumseh Valley" and Dylan's "Boots of Spanish Leather," on which he played harmonica, won Griffith a Grammy for Best Contemporary Folk Album.

Politics, personal pain (she's had two bouts with cancer and a disorder affecting her fingers), and up-from-the bootstraps persistence permeate the lyrics on *Intersection*. Some of the songs sound peaceful and reflective, but others are downright angry. In 2012 Griffith left Texas, moving from Austin to Nashville after clashing with music critics. She even penned a letter to some and has vowed never to perform in Austin again. "I've had a hard life, and I write it down," Griffith sings in the title track on *Intersection*. She vents about economic hardship in another song, "Hell No (I'm Not Alright)," which often brings audiences to their feet in a show of camaraderie, and laments the demise of blue-collar jobs in "Bethlehem Steel." Another song, "Bad Seed," is based on the difficult relationship between Griffith and her father: "Now that I've gone crazy, with no love of my father / Am I the bad seed he always said I would be?" Hopefully, Griffith won't permanently hold her grudge against Texas. She may be able to take herself out of the state, but she can't take Texas out of her music.

Neither can Tish Hinojosa, a Texas singer-songwriter whose work cannot be contained in one word, one language, or one country. Born in San Antonio, she melds folk, country, blues, rockabilly, bluegrass, *and* Tex-Mex. Hinojosa's career took her to Taos, New Mexico, where she worked with Michael Martin Murphey, then to Nashville, then back to Austin, and then Europe. She sings in English, Spanish, and sometimes both in the same tune. Her songs often paint portraits of people and places—slices of life that transform the mundane into the poetic.

As the youngest of thirteen children born to Mexican immigrants, the bilingual Hinojosa knew their struggles from stories and from traditional Mexican folk songs she listened to growing up in the city of the Alamo. Then she made up her own version of the *corridos*—traditional Mexican narrative ballads about oppression, social issues, or people in communities—as in "West Side of Town" (*Homeland*, 1989):

> Felipe was a young man when he crossed the Rio Grande
> Headin' north to Texas where he grew into a man
> He fixed cars and worked the wars and raised a family
> San Antonio was home on the West Side of Town
>
> Young Maria dreamed of singin' in a concert hall
> Past the plaza and the village church adobe wall
> Hard times stole her innocence but drove the woman's heart
> San Antonio bound to the West Side of Town

When Hinojosa's lyrics don't tell stories about people, they often turn everyday objects or images into metaphors, as in "Fence Post" from 2000's *Sign of Truth*:

I'm feeling like a fence post
Looking at a rail yard
Everthing's grey
My heart's pinned away
My feet are nailed to the ground
I'm wired standing up
I'm broken and cut
But I can't seem to just fall down
And something about the sound out here just kills me

Not exactly the kind of song that's going to get a lot of air play on the top FM stations. But although her work may not be regarded as "mainstream" in the United States, Hinojosa's music went multi-platinum in Asia—where, strangely enough, her Spanish ballad "Donde Voy (Where I Go)" was the theme song for a hit Korean TV show. Like many Texas singer-songwriters, she also cultivated a following in Europe. After living in Hamburg, Germany, Hinojosa moved back to Texas and released her sixteenth album, *After the Fair*, in 2013. It's an eclectic mix of Austin, Germany, and Tex-Mex—one reviewer called it "Tex-Deutsch folk pop." Hinojosa even recorded Paul McCartney's song "A Certain Softness" in Spanish for the album. In a 2011 interview for "Writers Talk," a program of Ohio State University's Center for the Study and Teaching of Music, Hinojosa recalled that she wanted to embed Spanish into her music from her beginnings as a songwriter. The first thing she did in that regard was to translate Irving Berlin's "Always" into Spanish for her breakthrough album *Taos to Tennessee* (1987, re-released in 1992). Some of the early songs she wrote were bilingual pieces, such as "Who Showed You the Way to Your Heart." Feeling "very isolated" from her culture when she was living in Nashville during her twenties, "that's when I think it was important to hang onto my mother tongue by playing with songwriting," she explained. Hinojosa finds Spanish to be "wavy and soft and round . . . you can find something a lot more simple and it just sounds really beautiful in Spanish." Writing in two languages also challenges her to find rhymes. "I'll think of the idea or something will come to me in English or in Spanish and I have to try to mirror-reflect that and try to find words that work and also that rhyme," she said. "It's kind of like a puzzle for me."

Finding the right pieces of the puzzle and exploring "unknown territory" also led Hickman into songwriting. The 2010 State Musician of Texas began writing songs when she was seven years old. Since then, she's produced a prolific variety of music—songs from poems and visions, music for newborns, toddlers, and families, love songs, Christmas songs, and songs that strike a balance between introspection, reflection, and whimsy. Her 1989 debut album, *Equal Scary People*, followed by *Shortstop*, received positive critical reviews, but didn't score commercial hits. When the Elektra label dropped her, fans chipped in to help finance the buyback of her master tapes. Hickman dedicated her next album, *Necessary Angels* (1994), to them. One of the numbers, "Shadowboxing," covered by Willie Nelson and Brave Combo, speaks of longing for more and then realizing what a futile fight that can be:

> Shadowboxing with the moon
> It's a tiny pearl in God's eye
> And every step I take
> And every swing I make
> Brings me closer than I was before
> Shadowboxing with the moon
> The night's silver cup pouring down on me
> Ebb and tide, day and night
> Keeps me wanting so much more

A testament to the craft of songwriting is, of course, how many other singer-songwriters cover someone else's tunes. In 2001 the album *The Best of Times* featured Texas artists such as Marcia Ball, Shawn Colvin, Ruthie Foster, Jimmy LaFave, Edie Brickell & New Bohemians, and Robert Earl Keen performing Hickman's songs.

Hinojosa and Hickman, among other women Texas singer-songwriters, were also mothers who found that after having children they couldn't, or didn't want to, stay up all night playing around the campfires at music festivals or live on the road. Many of the women who write songs and perform speak of trying to find a balance—and not always succeeding—between their relationships and children and the lure of work and traveling to the next gig. They also didn't buy into the notion that they needed to be unhappy to find an artistic voice. Even the queen of heartbreak songs, Lucinda Williams, rejected the accusation that getting married had watered down her songwriting ability. "The thing that's so inane to me is the idea that you can't be quote unquote happy and create. That's just a myth," she said in an interview with Rick Mason for Citypages.com in February of 2011, the year she released the album *Blessed* after her marriage.

Other singer-songwriters haven't been quite so blessed. The music industry is strewn with the bodies of performers who fell into depression or in love with a bottle, a needle, or pills, burned up and burned out, died too young, and landed in music mythology. Port Arthur's Janis Joplin, the first female rock superstar who fused rock and Texas delta blues into her powerhouse pipes, may be the most famous example of that among women. Known more as a vocalist than a songwriter, she wrote or cowrote several of her songs, such as "Move Over" and "Mercedes Benz," from her second solo album, *Pearl.* Her wild ways caught up with her and Joplin died at age twenty-seven in 1970 after a drug overdose. *Pearl* was released after her death and Joplin ascended into music history as a legend. Other women singer-songwriters determined not to go that route. "I had already decided I wanted to have a long life and have a long career," pianist and songwriter Marcia Ball said in *Women in Texas Music: Stories and Songs.* "I just didn't want to burn out. The flip side of that is that a lot of the people who have struggled the hardest are also the most creative artists that we know. Townes Van Zandt is the perfect example of someone who created a masterwork out of a mess. In spite of his habits." Hendrix noted that if a woman singer-songwriter passed out in the middle of a set, as Van Zandt was known to do, it could end her career. "What woman do you know who can sound real hoarse, out of tune and grope through a song and maintain a career in music?" Hendrix asked. "A lot of men sure do and they just make a living in Texas. But you name me one woman who can get away with that—one woman who can fall off a stool and continue to get booked."

It seems unfair that the often-out-of-control Joplin, who had a relatively short career, would be so well known—and not the brilliant Cindy Walker, who arguably was the ultimate shatterer of stereotypes and a barrier-breaker among women Texas singer-songwriters. "I like so much her diversity and the fact she didn't write as a woman," Hendrix said. "If you didn't know it was a woman, you'd think it was a man who had written the songs." Born in the tiny Texas town of Mart in 1918, Walker carved a long career as a prolific songwriter who figuratively spilled her guts into her old-fashioned floral patterned typewriter. Stars past and present recorded her songs—Bing Crosby, Elvis Presley, Willie Nelson, Ray Charles, Eddie Arnold, Mickey Gilley, Van Morrison, Patti Page, Roy Orbison, Bette Midler, the Byrds, Cher, Michael Bolton, Kenny Rogers, and Emmylou Harris, to name a few. Walker's songs made the Top 40 or pop charts more than four hundred times over four decades from the 1940s to 1980s. Texas "King of Swing" Bob Wills recorded more than fifty of her songs and helped write some of them. Walker also wrote thirty-nine tunes for Wills's Western movies. Her Western songs sometimes dipped into sentimentality, but Walker also wrote fearless lyrics about love and heartache. Take the opening brutal lines of "You Don't Know Me," about a shy man who can't express his true feelings to a woman:

> You give your hand to me
> And then you say hello
> And I can hardly speak

My heart is beating so
And anyone can tell
You think you know me well
But you don't know me

Nelson recorded the tune when he released an entire album of Walker's songs in 2006, *You Don't Know Me: The Songs of Cindy Walker*. After hearing it, music critics asked what took Willie so long—Walker's songs fit his old soul so well. Fort Worth's Katy Moffatt, who has performed at the Kerrville Folk Festival and all over Europe, called "You Don't Know Me" her "very favorite song in the world." "To my knowledge, I've never heard a woman do that song," Moffatt told Hudson in *Telling Stories, Writing Songs*. "I heard it and I had to do it." One of the most successful singer-songwriters from Texas ever, Norah Jones, also recorded it for one of the discs by her country cover band, the Little Willies.

When Walker was inducted into the Country Music Hall of Fame in 1997, country songwriter Harlan Howard called her "the greatest living songwriter of county music." Added Fred Foster, Roy Orbison's producer, in an interview with the *Austin American-Statesman* in 2004: "Cindy Walker has never written a bad song in her life." With her track record, you'd think Walker's name would be well known alongside other Texas singer-songwriters. But she chose to take a low profile and did not like being in the limelight, rarely granting interviews. Walker mainly cared about living simply with her mother, Oree, in a modest three-bedroom house in Mexia and writing songs. Eventually, she gave up singing to focus on songwriting. Walker and her mother would go to Nashville every year for several months, lease an apartment, and market the new tunes. Oree sometimes even wrote the melodies to her daughter's lyrics. "Worldly things were of little meaning," her niece told the Associated Press after Walker died in Mexia in 2006. "She lived for hamburgers, ice cream, pencil and paper." Walker broke ground for women singer-songwriters in Texas, and new generations of women who came after her were ready to build on that foundation and lay some steel into the structure of their songs.

In the 1960s singer-poets like Joni Mitchell and Carole King inspired more women to sit down at the piano or pick up the guitar and write songs. One of them was Waco's Carolyn Hester, who grew up in the era of Dylan and Peter, Paul, and Mary and immersed herself in New York's Greenwich Village folk music scene. Hester had known and worked with Buddy Holly and Dylan. In his autobiography, *Chronicles Volume One*, Dylan said Hester "was going places and it didn't surprise me. Carolyn was eye-catching, down-home and double barrel beautiful. That she had known and worked with Buddy Holly left no small impression on me and I liked being around her." While meeting with Hester and playing harmonica and guitar on some songs she was thinking about recording, Dylan met a Columbia Records exec who signed the young musician and launched him into a superstar. Initially labeled a folksinger and dubbed the "Texas songbird," Hester returned to her home state and in the 1970s met Kerrville Folk Festival co-founder Rod Kennedy, who became a long-term professional colleague and friend. At first Hester and Bonnie Hearne were the only women performing at the festival, but Kennedy was an early supporter of women singer-songwriters and brought in others, such as Nanci Griffith. Hester met Griffith at the festival and mentored her; they performed a duet on "Boots of Spanish Leather" at a 1992 tribute to Dylan at Madison Square Garden—an example of women singer-songwriters taking center stage and helping each other.

Other Texas women writing songs and performing also got their breaks in the 1970s. Born and raised in San Antonio, Holly Dunn started writing songs by the time she was in high school and as a teenager sang with the Freedom Folk at the White House bicentennial celebration in 1976. She moved to Nashville and became part of the songwriters' pool, writing hit songs for Louise Mandrell and Marie Osmond, among others. A single from her first album, "Daddy's Hands," written as a Father's Day present to her dad, soared to No. 1 on country charts: "I remember Daddy's hands, / folded silently in prayer / And reaching out to hold me / when I had a nightmare / You could read quite a story / In the calouses and lines / Years of work and worry / had left their mark behind." The song launched Dunn into an overnight success. By 1989 she was named to the regular cast of the Grand Ole Opry and continues to write songs. Dunn has been nominated for a Grammy three times, been named BMI Songwriter of the Year, and has retired from recording but continues touring.

Some women—and men—writing songs in Texas, though, not only had to leave the state to find audiences and venues, but also had to cross oceans. Lubbock's Kimmie Rhodes has written so many songs for others that her name, too, often gets overshadowed by the big-name stars who record them, such as Willie Nelson, Trisha Yearwood, Joe Ely, Waylon Jennings, and Emmylou Harris. "With a voice like fine dry wine and imagery as sharp as steel, this singer-songwriter is compelling," music writer David Zimmerman observed in *USA Today*. "Will America ever discover her?" European audiences did. "Up until recently there hasn't really been a market in America that could accommodate my artistry the way it is," Rhodes said in *Telling Stories, Writing Songs*. "Fortunately, in Europe there is a market that can accommodate the singer-songwriter the way they are." Her 1996 first American release, *West Texas Heaven*, included 12 original songs and duets with Nelson, Jennings, and Van Zandt. The title song speaks of the emptiness of the wind-blown plains:

> I left West Texas heaven (it was the only one I've ever known)
> I've been on the road down here driving with my blinders on
> All life was to me was like a truck stop where you want to stay
> I never even saw it when you built your dream right in my way
> No, I just passed on through it like a lonely town

"I am really fortunate to be able to write," Rhodes said in a 1997 interview. "It's a quicker way to be able to express what's going on inside me. And as a performer, if you don't write those songs, you have to go out and find songs that express the way you feel. If you can write those songs and perform them, you have it all because you're not trapped inside yourself with no way out."

While singer-songwriters like Rhodes found Europeans more receptive to their work, some from out-of-state moved to Austin to find their musical home. Betty Elders, who was born in 1949 in Raleigh, North Carolina, grew up writing poetry, counting Robert Frost, Robert Louis Stevenson, and Dylan as inspirations. She released her first cassette of her songs, *After the Curtain*, in 1981 before moving to Austin three years later. Elders's husband, Gene, played fiddle with George Strait's Ace in the Hole Band, and she began performing at venues such as the Austin Outhouse and meeting fellow songwriters such as Barb Donovan and David Rodriguez. In 1988 Elders entered the Kerrville Folk Festival's New Folk Songwriting Competition. She was a finalist and didn't win, but she went on to appear regularly at Kerrville.

Over the next six years Elders released three albums—*Daddy's Coal* in 1989, *Peaceful Existence* in 1993, and *Crayons* in 1995. Joan Baez covered two Elders songs, "Crack in the Mirror" and "Long Bed from Kenya," and the two performed together at the Newport Folk Festival. The lyrics to "Crack in the Mirror" tell a chilling story of incest and robbed innocence:

> Now you say you don't remember
> This thing she can't forget
> You say that life must go on
> Time to bury the hatchet
> And if she was so damned afraid
> You're sure you would remember
> Children will exaggerate

Other singer-songwriters discovered Elders, including Steven Fromholz, who tapped her to sing harmony on *A Guest in Your Heart,* and Lucinda Williams, who collaborated with Elders on "He Never Got Enough Love." When Icehouse Music in Austin released *Ten in Texas* (2005), a compilation of ten up-and-coming singers performing work by Texas songwriters, Terri Hendrix chose to perform Elders's tune "Cowboy":

> There's a cowboy in Texas loves loud, loud music
> There's a cowboy in Texas likes to kick a little dirt
> There's a cowboy in Texas loves to ride the wild ponies
> Likes that "Home on the Range," can't remember the words

Eliza Gilkyson also migrated to Austin and dove into its musical melting pot. Born in Hollywood, California, Eliza had music in her blood as the daughter of folksinger Terry Gilkyson and songwriter Jane Gilkyson. After living in New Mexico and Los Angeles, she broke out of the "New Age" mold—she once was married to Andreas Vollenweider—and, beginning with *Redemption Road* in 1997, found an independent voice. At fifty-five and a grandmother, Gilkyson was nominated for the first time for a Grammy for Best Contemporary Folk Album for *The Land of Milk and Honey* (2004). Joan Baez, Bob Geldof, Tom Rush, and Rosanne Cash covered some of her songs, and Gilkyson toured solo around the world. She also performed with Patty Griffin, Mary Chapin Carpenter, Dan Fogelberg, the Woody Guthrie Review, Jackson Browne, Pete Seeger, and Kris Kristofferson. Like Griffith, Gilkyson's activism and political causes soaked into her lyrics. After the 2004 earthquake and tsunami in the Indian Ocean, Gilkyson wrote the reflective song "Requiem" (*Paradise Hotel*), which found a new audience after Hurricane Katrina devastated New Orleans a year later and was among the songs Baez covered:

> Mother Mary, full of grace, awaken
> All our homes are gone, our loved ones taken
> Taken by the sea
> Mother Mary, calm our fears, have mercy
> Drowning in a sea of tears, have mercy
> Hear our mournful plea
> Our world has been shaken
> We wander our homelands, forsaken

The album's anti-war song "Man of God," about the George W. Bush administration, contains some of Gilkyson's most political lyrics:

The cowboy came from out of the West
With his snakeskin boots and his bulletproof vest
Gang of goons and his big war chest
Fortunate son he was doubly blessed
Corporate cronies and the chiefs of staff
Bowin' to the image of the golden calf
Startin' up wars in the name of God's son
Gonna blow us all the way to Kingdom Come.

Man of God, man of God,
That ain't the teachings of a man of God
Man of God, Man of God
That ain't the preachings of a man of God.

After *Paradise Hotel*, Gilkyson released a live album recorded at Austin's Cactus Café, and a string of albums—*Beautiful World* (2008), *Roses at the End of Time* (2011), and, in 2014, the darkly themed *Nocturne Diaries*, in addition to a collaborative album with John Gorka and Lucy Kaplansky, *Red Horse* (2010). Many of the songs deal with troubled times and issues that recur with deadly consequences, as in "An American Boy" about a troubled teenager contemplating a rampage:

Posted pictures on my Facebook site
A shooting star in a long, dark night
Only kid that needs a basement light
Thunder in his hands
My parents wonder if I'm doing all right
They keep the gun case locked up tight
With the key hanging there in plain sight
While I made my plans
Won't be long before I come undone
No tomorrow for a wayward son
What will they say about their pride and joy
Their American boy

Another Austin transplant, Carolyn Wonderland, was born in Webster and raised in Houston. She can belt out the blues and rock tunes, drawing comparisons with Joplin. But her songs meander into folk and country, too. On her album *Peace Meal* (2011), the first song is a cover of Joplin's "What Good Can Drinkin' Do" (Wonderland used to drink, but says she doesn't anymore). Toward the end is a cover of Dylan's "Meet Me in the Morning."

But most of the songs on her five albums to date are her own poetic compositions with a strong narrative thread, as in "Feed Me to the Lions," from 2001's *Alcohol & Salvation*:

> One night on the town is just tease enough
> The open road it's calling
> She buys one more drink with the change in her purse
> Gets the rest from a man who calls her Darling
> Thinking about him, it ain't hard to do
> The hard part is keeping from crying
> With friends all around she retreats to the car
> To sleep off intentions of flying

Nine-time Grammy winner Ray Benson, of Asleep at the Wheel fame, produced her 2008 breakthrough album *Miss Understood*, after Dylan, who was in Austin for a show, asked Benson about Wonderland and what she was doing. "Playing shitty clubs in Texas," Benson told him, as related in Margaret Moser's 2008 profile of Wonderland in *The Austin Chronicle*. Wonderland couldn't believe Dylan even knew who she was—*Alcohol & Salvation* and *Bloodless Revolution* (2003) had been critically well received, but she was sleeping in her van or staying with friends when she wasn't performing. *Miss Understood* brought Wonderland national attention, and she remains a popular performer on the Austin music scene.

So does Marcia Ball. The Texas singer-songwriter tradition often involves playing an acoustic guitar, but Ball created her own niche with a piano and a sound that fuses Gulf Coast blues with Cajun flavor. Born in Orange and raised ten miles across the border in Vinton, Louisiana, Ball writes songs that range from soulful ballads to boogie-woogie to rousing roadhouse tunes. She recalled in a profile in *Women in Texas Music* that she hung on to country music until 1980, when she returned musically to her Louisiana roots and began writing and playing rhythm-and-blues. As an English major, Ball also found inspiration in poetry and short stories. Ball said Edna St. Vincent Millay's poems inspired the song "She's So Innocent" from the 2001 album *Presumed Innocent*: "She holds the world in the palm of her hand; she's just a girl in the arms of a man / And when she's hurt she folds like a fan."

Over the next decade, Ball wrote her own songs and recorded others' work as well. But her 2011 album, *Roadside Attractions*, marked the first time in her forty-year career that she wrote or cowrote every song. They tell rich stories studded with images and metaphors. Take the opening of the title cut:

Concrete dinosaur, Jesus in a screen door
They don't hold a candle to you
I get no satisfaction from roadside attractions
And honey I have seen me a few
They got the blue ox, chimney rocks
Two-headed livestock, alligator jumparoo
I can turn my back on all manner of distraction
'Cause I'm just passing through

Many of her songs are condensed short stories set to music. The song "This Used To Be Paradise" tells of an old man who was a fisherman until "the oil man came / He gave us jobs and everything changed / We still run our boats and we drag our nets / But every day we get less and less and less."

Ball's energetic and polished vocals sound like the opposite end of the musical universe from another singer-songwriter with one foot in Texas and the other in Louisiana, Grammy-winner Lucinda Williams. Born in Lake Charles, Williams grew up in a dovetailed world of words and music. Her father was a literature professor and poet who introduced her to literary figures such as Flannery O'Connor and became her mentor. "Instead of going to college and taking creative writing, I learned by writing, by trial and error, and by showing (my father) what I was working on and listening to his criticism" she told the *Journal of Country Music* in 1996. Both of her parents played piano and Williams started writing songs at age six, took up the guitar, and was performing live at seventeen. She moved a lot around the South, lived in Mexico, and landed in Austin in 1974 before hopscotching to Los Angeles and then Nashville. Williams collected musical influences along the way—country, rock, folk, blues—and developed a writing style that captures a sense of place. Some of her songs mention cities and towns by name—Jackson, Greenville, Lake Charles, Ventura, Minneapolis—so that you feel you've been there, traveling on the melody. She also picked up some famous fans of her work, such as Tom Petty, Emmylou Harris, and Mary Chapin Carpenter, who scored a big hit recording Williams's song "Passionate Kisses" (*Sweet Old World*, 1992).

Williams's work drew critical praise, and her ragged, languid drawl made her songs feel rough-hewn and raw. The unadulterated quality was by design—Williams was a perfectionist and spent six years on her next album, recording and re-recording until she was satisfied with a song—sometimes to make it sound less produced and rehearsed. Steve Earle, who appeared as a guest artist, described the experience as less-than-pleasant. But the diligence paid off for Williams. *Car Wheels on a Gravel Road*, released in 1998, won a

Grammy Award for best contemporary folk album and went gold. The lead song described a restless rural mother who finds solace on the back roads: "Cotton fields stretching miles and miles / Hank's voice on the radio." The ballad "Drunken Angel" drove home that Williams wasn't just the daughter of a poet, but a poet herself:

> Sun came up it was another day
> And the sun went down you were blown away
> Why'd you let go of your guitar
> Why'd you ever let it go that far
> Drunken Angel
> Could've held on to that long smooth neck
> Let your hand remember every fret
> Fingers touching each shiny string
> But you let go of everything
> Drunken Angel

After the album's release Williams toured with Dylan, played on a tribute album to Gram Parsons, and veered away from a country sound and more into alternative music. *TIME* magazine even crowned Williams "America's best songwriter," male or female.

By the time her seventh album, *World Without Tears*, came out in 2003, Williams's music sounded unlike any other woman singer-songwriter—often melancholy, frankly sexual at times, and twangy—some have called her voice "gorgeously flawed." Her spare lyrics, as on the song "Real Live Bleeding Fingers and Broken Guitar Strings," can slice to the bone:

> You've got a sense of humor
> You're a mystery
> I heard a rumor
> You're making history
> Photographic dialogues
> Beneath your skin
> Pornographic episodes
> Screaming sin
> 'Til it's real live bleeding fingers
> broken guitar strings

Although her eleventh album, 2011's *Blessed*, contained more songs about finding love and less about heartbreak, a notable exception is the heaviest rock song she performed on the album with Elvis Costello, "Seeing Black," about the emotional aftermath of suicide: "Did you feel your act was a final truth / The dramatic ending of a misspent youth / Did you really feel you had all the proof." The album cemented Williams's place as the quintessential songwriter of any gender in the minds of many fans.

Out to challenge Williams is a new generation of women drawing richly from the singer-songwriter tradition but adding their own twists. Carrie Rodriguez, the daughter of Texan singer-songwriter David Rodriguez, also had music, words, and art in her blood—her mother, Katy Nall, is a painter and her grandmother, Frances Nall, a Texas essayist. She toured with her father in Europe as a teenager, then studied classical violin at Oberlin Conservatory and plays not only the guitar, but also the Mandobird and the fiddle. Rodriguez launched her career after performing with other Hispanic artists at the South by Southwest festival in Austin in 2001 and toured with singer-songwriter Chip Taylor ("Wild Thing," "Angel of the Morning") in Europe, recorded four duet records with him, and then broke out on her own with a 2006 critically acclaimed debut album, *Seven Angels on a Bicycle*. In 2013 she released her fifth album, *Give Me All You Got*, which took her country-folk roots into new territory with some darker lyrics and plaintive love songs, as in "I Cry for Love": "If I fall I get up / Am I tough, tough enough? / For I bend, I don't break / If I want, I just take / If I cut I bleed / If I bleed, I don't cry." Rodriguez has toured with Williams, recording one of her songs on a 2010 album of covers, *Love and Circumstance*.

It would be remiss not to mention Norah Jones, who not only bends genres, but also bonds generations, even though many of her best songs were written with collaborators. The key to her success has been her crossover appeal, jumping from jazz to folk, country, and pop in soft—only in volume—music that has won her an armful of Grammys. Jones was born in 1979 in New York, the daughter of Indian sitar musician Ravi Shankar and Sue Jones, a former concert promoter. Her parents divorced, and Norah moved with her mother to the Dallas-Fort Worth suburb Grapevine and attended the Booker T. Washington High School for the Performing and Visual Arts. She sang in church choirs, played guitar and piano, and enrolled in the University of North Texas' respected music program, majoring in jazz piano. While studying jazz, Jones met two songwriters, Jesse Harris and Richard Julian, who were visiting from New York. They influenced her to move to Manhattan, and Jones became a regular at the Living Room, a Lower East Side club favored by singer-songwriters. She played gigs with other artists and bands before being signed by a record company, Blue Note, and recording her 2002 debut album, *Come Away With Me*.

Low-key, with deceptively simple melodies and lyrics that captured a range of emotions, the album sold more than twenty million copies worldwide and won five Grammy awards. Jones wrote or cowrote only a few numbers on the first album—Harris wrote her biggest single hit to date, "Don't Know Why." Identified with the piano, Jones switched to writing songs on her guitar. Three more albums followed—*Feels Like Home* (2004), *Not Too Late* (2007), and *The Fall* (2009), each of which sold more than a million copies. Failed relationships figure into many of the songs, but Jones doesn't fall into sentimentality. The song "Don't Miss You at All" from *Feels Like Home* (and set to a Duke Ellington melody) recalls Cindy Walker's matter-of-fact "You Don't Know Me":

> As I sit and watch the snow
> Fallin' down
> I don't miss you at all
> I hear children playin', laughin' so loud
> I don't think of your smile
>
> So if you never come to me
> You'll stay a distant memory
> Out my window I see lights going dark
> Your dark eyes don't haunt me

Jones teamed with Brian Burton of Danger Mouse to cowrite the songs on the edgy, experimental album *Little Broken Hearts* (2012). But she returns to country roots music with her side country band, the Little Willies, and worked with Dylan on his project *The Lost Notebooks of Hank Williams* (2011), with a dozen unrecorded Williams songs set to music and performed by Merle Haggard, Sheryl Crow, Alan Jackson, Lucinda Williams, and Jones.

Other young women from or in Texas who are writing and performing songs have found an audience and recording industry that's more open-minded about music that blends styles and stresses poetic lyrics—to a point. One of them, Kacey Musgraves, grew up in East Texas and counts Alison Krauss and Lee Ann Womack as influences. Her sound is country with a modern twist, but some fans in that conservative genre found her too edgy and slapped her with the "rebel" label, which Musgraves rejects. "Follow Your Arrow," one of the songs from her 2013 breakout album *Same Trailer Different Park*, was a call for staying true to oneself despite society's pressures. But some critics blasted Musgraves, saying the song condoned drug use and homosexuality:

> So make lots of noise
> Kiss lots of boys

Or kiss lots of girls
If that's something you're into
When the straight and narrow
Gets a little too straight
Roll up a joint or don't
Just follow your arrow
Wherever it points

Musgraves found the controversy much ado about nothing. "If you listen to Willie Nelson, Loretta Lynn, Glenn Campbell, they were all ahead of their time," Musgraves told *The Wall Street Journal*. "And I don't know for sure, but it doesn't feel like they based their careers on templates or models of how country stars should be. So I try to stay open-minded and let an array of things influence me rather than picking from a small box of what is usually popular here." Some of her lyrics speak directly to women and challenge stereotypical roles. The song "Merry Go 'Round" is one of the most personal on the album, about being in the middle of nowhere and wanting to break away and experience the world rather than settle:

Mama's hooked on Mary Kay
Brother's hooked on Mary Jane
Daddy's hooked on Mary two doors down
Mary, Mary quite contrary
We get bored, so we get married
Just like dust, we settle in this town
On this broken merry go 'round and 'round and 'round we go
Where it stops nobody knows and it ain't slowin' down.

The singer-songwriter tradition as it relates to Texas women isn't slowing down, either, and women aren't settling for the back seat. Like Patty Griffin, they are taking the wheel from the chauffeur and driving themselves to write the lyrics of their souls. That means staying true to their roots when it comes to their best songwriting and penning a personal poetry of place and time. "Your old connections turn out to be your true connection," as Ball put it. "Sometimes, you just go home."

FROM DEBAUCHED YIN TO MELLOW YANG

A CIRCULAR TRIP THROUGH THE TEXAS MUSIC FESTIVAL SCENE

Jeff Prince

"Me and Billy the Kid" is foot-stomping revisionist history in which the protagonist out-badasses the famous Western gunslinger at every turn, even stealing his girlfriend. It's an outlaw song in meaning, genre, and attitude, the kind that makes revelers at Texas music festivals pump their beer-filled fists. Joe Ely's no fool; he encored with "Billy" a few years ago at the Larry Joe Taylor Texas Music Festival & Chili Cookoff.

Festivals don't come much wilder than this one, and the crowd roared its approval. Ely waved, bowed, and disappeared into a dimly lit, roped-off area behind the outdoor stage. A crewman took Ely's battered Gibson J-45 guitar and handed him a bottle of red wine and a glass. The Lubbock legend slid into a golf cart seat, kicked up his boots on the dash, and gazed skyward. The stars, lacking competition from city lights, blazed brightly above this Erath County ranch in Central Texas.

Taylor's festival debuted in 1989 at a small pasture in Mingus, whose population barely tops two hundred residents. Less than half that amount showed up. Taylor tried again the next year and drew several hundred people, although some of the younger ones slipped through a flimsy fence to avoid paying. That youthful exuberance was a good sign. A quarter-century later, Taylor's festival stretches six days and attracts more than twenty-five thousand fans. Most are twenty-somethings who, as it turns out, will fork over admission if they can't figure a way to sneak inside.

Money was tight in the beginning, but Taylor was happy to break even. He'd created a festival because clubs wouldn't hire him to play. Taylor's fan base was mostly limited to campfire friends he'd see each year at the Terlingua International Chili Cookoff. So he made his own gig. Musician buddies agreed to play whether they got paid or not, and Taylor used what little budget he had to hire a "name." Ray Wylie Hubbard topped the bill even though the "Up Against the Wall, Redneck Mother" author was just sobering up after a decades-long bender and wasn't landing many gigs back then either.

Taylor's lineup still mixes veterans such as Hubbard and Ely with new artists scrambling for a fan base. "Larry Joe has done a lot to redefine the whole Texas vibe," Ely said. "His festival helps spread the word about up-and-coming songwriters."

Texas music festivals put songwriters at the top of the heap for a change. Visitors don't care whether you're a golden-throated pretty boy on stage or a gravel-throated nobody sitting on a dusty ice chest beside a campfire at 4:00 a.m.—move them with a well-written song and they'll embrace you. Pat Green went from a face in the crowd one year to a stage act the next because Taylor kept hearing people talk about a college kid from Lubbock killing it at the campfires.

I witnessed the evolution of LJT's festival, although some details are admittedly lost in the fog. After missing the two Mingus shows, my buddies and I attended every festival for the next twenty years, watching it stagger from a sparsely attended one-night party to an iconic cultural happening. The event outgrew several locations before finding permanent footing at Melody Mountain's four hundred-plus acres.

Ely poured another glass of *vino* and mentioned he'd just returned from Australia, where constellations look altogether different. "Orion is upside down," he said.

The festival scene seemed upside down as well, at least for me. This would be my last year to attend LJT. Elements that once attracted me were becoming repellant. My friends felt the same. We'd grown older, less tolerant. But that's the beauty of Texas music festivals—hundreds are spread out across the state, big, small, rowdy, tame, an atmosphere for everyone. These days I'm back to the basics, hitting smaller festivals such as Pickin' in the Pines in East Texas, places that draw fewer people and offer little in the way of amenities, but harken back to simpler times.

The vaunted Kerrville Folk Festival introduced me to the wild and wonderful world of camping out for days on end while being steeped in lyric-driven music. Something divine comes from immersing oneself in music too unique and obscure to get radio exposure, particularly in those prehistoric days before websites and YouTube. Producer Rod Kennedy debuted the festival in 1972 with thirteen acts over three concerts. The event drew almost three thousand fans to see pioneers of the "Austin sound" that combined folk, country, and a touch of rock 'n' roll, a style of music that eventually evolved into "progressive country," "outlaw," or just plain "Texas Music." Ely, Michael Murphey, Allen Damron, Bill and Bonnie Hearne, and Kenneth

Threadgill played that first year. Willie Nelson, Jerry Jeff Walker, Townes Van Zandt, and B.W. Stevenson followed the next. But it was Peter Yarrow who most shaped the Kerrville festival, and, by extension, every Texas music festival since.

The co-founder of Peter, Paul and Mary urged Kennedy to showcase unheralded songwriters who couldn't catch a break in the music business. Yarrow had done the same at the Newport Folk Festival in the 1960s by establishing the New Folk concerts. Kerrville's New Folk shows became the heart of the festival, infusing a sense of discovery and surprise, one reason the event has lasted four decades. Nobodies who became somebodies after winning the New Folk competition include Lyle Lovett, Steve Earle, Nanci Griffith, James McMurtry, and Robert Earl Keen.

Kerrville moved outdoors and out of town to the Quiet Valley Ranch in 1973. The grounds blossomed with a professional stage, rented outhouses (if outhouses can "blossom"), and a mantra of "spiritual optimism" that soaked visitors of all shapes, creeds, and cultures. The three-day event stretched to four, then eight days. By its tenth anniversary, the event lasted eleven days and drew ten thousand people.

My first taste of Kerrville came in the mid-1980s after it expanded to eighteen days and attracted many thousands of visitors from across the country and overseas. My buddies and I were a hard-partying bunch of college kids and aspiring singer-songwriters attracted by stories of the late-night campfire guitar pulls. What we discovered was better than we'd imagined. Kerrville was like a huge outdoor listening room. People hung on words, responded with enthusiasm, wanted more. The musical poetry set against a backdrop of stars, crickets, and firelight was cathartic and damn near holy. It's no surprise that a European fan secretly recorded some of those campfire songs and released an infamous bootleg album called *The Texas Campfire Tapes*.

Spring rains could be problematic. They'd sometimes settle in for days, driving people inside tents, cars, and campers for relief from the slog. The first year we attended, my little gang set up a large tent that slept five. Almost immediately a storm settled over the ranch. We sat cross-legged on our sleeping bags for hours, drinking beer and playing guitars over the din of rain slapping against our tent. We marveled at how well the canvas repelled rain.

"I heard that if you touch the inside of your tent it will leak; I wonder if it's true," my friend Raul said as he reached up and touched the tent ceiling.

It's true.

But soggy bedding didn't kill our high. After the skies cleared we walked around the festival grounds for the first time, meeting people and feeling the love. The crowd was huge but friendly. I saw more tie-dyed T-shirts that first hour than I'd seen in ten years. We camped near a large group of American Indians who kept a simple drumbeat going 24–7. The frog-strangling rain followed by sunshine and warmth produced a Woodstock feel, complete with mud between your toes (and, for some, an accompanying acid trip as well). Over the next few days I met rednecks, longhairs, gypsies, yuppies, and punk rockers enjoying peaceful co-existence. The mellow security guards blended with the crowd.

"Everybody has the opportunity here to be an individual with dignity," Kennedy told me.

Music at the Ballad Tree, where singer-songwriters shared their "babies" to a rapt audience, could be incredibly moving. A few years earlier, an amateur Lovett had ruled the Ballad Tree. Now he was a stage headliner. "This is the friendliest place in the world and the first place I got to play my music for people who listen," Lovett said during his set that year.

Lovett and Nanci Griffith were the folk darlings back then, both having been signed by MCA. I asked Kennedy to predict the "next big thing out of Texas," figuring he'd choose one of them. Instead, he said the still unknown Robert Earl Keen would be next to blow up. Keen's lyrics were edgier and tougher than most, and his lone album at the time (*No Kinda Dancer*) included soon-to-be classics "Front Porch Song" and "Swervin' In My Lane." His songs would become even edgier over time and influence a generation of outlaw singers and hell-raising fans that would soon lead to an explosion of Texas music festivals.

Producers such as Kennedy are discriminating when it comes to stage talent. Campfire jams, on the other hand, are typically open to anybody with gumption and a guitar. Over the course of an evening the performances can range from astounding to woeful, although magic lives in even the sourest notes when the mood is right, which is most of the time at Kerrville. Musicians swapping songs can wait thirty minutes or more for their turn to come back around. After several days and nights you begin to feel like a priest in a New Orleans confessional, listening to everybody bare their soul in three-quarter time. Maybe that's why so many people relate to festivals on a spiritual level.

Strangely, one of my favorite moments at Kerrville involved no original music at all. A buddy and I swapped original songs for two nights at campfires and eventually grew weary of so much brutal self-revelation. The next night we decided to stay at our own camp beside our own little fire and play nothing but cover songs. The more obvious the better—Elvis, Hank, George. Sometimes visitors approached our camp, sniffed in disapproval, and sauntered off. But others would settle down by the fire, pop a top, and

sing along to the familiar lyrics. They requested other old songs. Simon &
Garfunkel, Elton John, whatever. More musicians joined in. My buddy and I
didn't command other musicians to play covers, but everyone intuitively followed suit. Hours later with the sun flashing pink on the horizon, more than
fifty people were still there listening to half a dozen pickers pulling out every
three-chord Johnny they'd ever learned, allowing everyone to sing along, just
like in church. And it was church.

We returned to Kerrville for several years but eventually started feeling . . .
contained. The stage shows and campfire jams were wonderful. But Kennedy's
campground policies seemed overzealous. My gang was young, rowdy, thirsty,
and, like many Texans, intuitively resistant to rules.

One afternoon I was napping beside my tent while listening to George
Jones on a cassette player. A stranger woke me up to tell me that canned
music was forbidden. Another time I was gently chastised for playing a cover
song at a campfire. I'd done it because one of the other pickers was playing
long, droning songs about saving whales and rain forests, and I could see
people's eyes glazing. I figured (wrongly) they'd appreciate hearing something familiar.

It all became a bit much. The hippie-dippy package and self-policing
atmosphere rubbed the whiskey crowd the wrong way. Not that Kerrville
needed us. The festival remains one of the biggest and best celebrations of
singer-songwriters in the world. The aging Kennedy sold the festival to
investors in 1999. Ten years later, the Texas Folk Music Foundation raised
money, bought the festival, and established it as a nonprofit event. Kerrville
was always family friendly and has grown more so.

About the time my gang backed away from Kerrville, we discovered Taylor's
bash—the debauched yin to Kerrville's mellow yang. We dubbed it our honky-
tonk festival. Music on stage and around the campfires remained poetic and
honest, but campground rules were nonexistent. Freedom reigned. Babylon
brewed. In 1991, the festival moved to a parking lot next to a large smokestack
along Interstate 20 in Thurber. Public-radio host Roy "The Commander"
Ashley spent a week gabbing about the upcoming event on his "KNON Super
Roper Redneck Review," ensuring the largest crowd yet.

"Roy was an incredible cheerleader for the thing," said Obie Obermark,
another KNON deejay. "You listened to Roy's show back then and you
would think the festival was really the Second Coming. He made it sound so
appealing that you were going to be hopelessly un-hip if you weren't there."

Several hundred people attended in 1991. Tarleton State University students from Taylor's hometown of Stephenville came out in force. The stage
was nothing more than a flatbed trailer perched on cinder blocks, a few of
which collapsed during Gary P. Nunn's set and almost tossed musicians onto

the pavement. The heat was brutal, and the parking lot lacked shade. Someone was selling the previous year's T-shirts emblazoned with "*No Chingas Con Mingus* (Don't Fuck With Mingus)," and many in the crowd purchased them and tied them over their heads as sweatbands/turbans, making them resemble hillbilly sultans. Late in the evening, the entire crowd formed a conga line that snaked around the small parking lot and danced in bumper-car fashion to Nunn's "Corona Con Lima" while a camera crew filmed a television commercial. It never aired. The crowd appeared too intoxicated for public viewing.

After the stage show ended, a lone campfire became the gathering spot for the remaining crowd. A song swap was underway when someone discreetly dropped an unopened can of beans into the fire. The explosion splattered everyone with bean goo. Nope, this wasn't Kerrville. But it was a blast. Taylor even made a profit for the first time—$313.

The next day Taylor and a few hung-over pals spent hours cleaning the site and gathering an ocean of empty beer cans into a huge pile. Exhausted, they sat down to rest before loading the pile into a bin. A helicopter appeared out of nowhere and landed in the adjacent field, creating a gale force wind that sent the cans and litter flying. Taylor was crushed. And done. He'd thrown his last festival. Or so he thought.

A buddy volunteered to take over festival planning in 1992. Just show up and play, he told Taylor. Six weeks before the festival, the volunteer disappeared. "I think he went to Mexico," Taylor said. "My name was on the festival and I didn't want it to fall apart that bad, so we were back in the festival business."

Taylor's business-minded wife, Sherry, took control and has been a driving force ever since. Along the way, an older crowd evolved into a much younger bunch. The buzz created by Tarleton students spread to other campuses. Larger crowds prompted a move to a Possum Kingdom Lake campground the following year. The open setting made it easy for people to skirt admission, and ticket sales plummeted. Taylor was poised to lose hundreds of dollars and face difficulty in paying stage performers. Radio disc jockey Mike Crow grabbed a microphone and urged everyone in the crowd to fork over a few bucks or risk losing what was becoming North Texas's best festival. The crowd stuffed spare bills into a bucket. Taylor still ended up losing $67 that year, but the crowd's show of faith convinced him to try again the next.

The quality of stage acts kept growing, with Green and Charlie Robison appearing several times in the mid-1990s in the early part of their careers before both migrated to Nashville. "If everybody played there every year there would be no room for the new guys to come along," Robison said.

"Larry Joe has to kick you out of the nest after a little while and let the new groups come along and show you how it's done."

Green described the festival as iconic. "You just kind of have to go," he said. "What a powerful, wonderful thing it is. I'm proud to be part of the history of it."

A few of the old guard, Taylor's musical heroes, enjoyed open invitations. Hubbard, Steven Fromholz, and Rusty Wier returned almost every year. Playing to a new and younger audience revitalized all their careers. Wier was a forerunner of the 1970s Austin sound and a vital player in the progressive country movement. But by the 1990s, he was reduced to hosting an open-mic night at an Austin bar once a week.

"The festival has helped me tremendously," Wier told me in the late 1990s. "When I first started playing Larry Joe's festivals I was destitute and I wasn't getting any jobs. It was getting to the point where I was going to have do something. I don't know what in the hell I would do if I had to get a job. Larry Joe got my name back out there. He is one of my heroes."

Artists cemented a kinship with fans by cruising around the campground in Taylor's golf cart and surprising people by sitting in on campfire sessions. "That's what I have so much fun doing," Wier said. "I go a day early just for the hell of it. I make all the fires on Friday night and play the stage on Saturday night."

Wier died of cancer in 2009, and Taylor installed a metal sculpture of his likeness backstage. Artists can rub ol' Rusty's guitar on their way to the stage. I attended the unveiling in 2010, and I could hear Wier's voice in my head as I recalled his reaction ten years earlier when I'd used "progressive country" to describe his music.

"They called it progressive country music which is, excuse my expression, bullshit," he said. "Some of it wasn't country at all. Asleep at the Wheel, Jerry Jeff Walker, it was all outlaw."

New waves of artists led by Green, Cory Morrow, Jason Boland, and others were continuously added to the bill. Larger audiences meant longer festivals, more stages, day shows, night shows, midnight rambles, all music all the time. Nowadays the festival draws more than fifty thousand visitors.

Something Wier said in 2001 foreshadowed the future: "People seem to get along here," he said. "Nowadays if you don't break windows or swipe cars it seems like you're not having any fun."

The breaking and swiping eventually took root. Running herd on a few hundred hard-drinking musicians and fans is one thing. Managing tens of thousands is altogether different. The lack of rules meant everyone was free to be themselves or, more accurately, themselves after way too much booze and drugs. One year Taylor allowed a company to rent golf carts to fans. By nightfall that first day, the festival was overrun with drunken drivers careening at twenty-five miles an hour across dark fields thick with campers. And remember my anguish at being told to turn off my George Jones cassette in Kerrville? At Taylor's festival, I was stuck camping one year next to a moron who played a Jerry Clower "comedy" cassette nonstop for twelve hours until I finally cracked, yanked it out of his tape player while he was sleeping, and threw it in the bushes. Another year, somebody set up a karaoke machine and blared Jimi Hendrix and Led Zeppelin songs all night. Another year, a nearby camper blasted Kid Rock through his car stereo and refused to turn it down after we asked politely. So we asked un-politely. The no-rules setting that my friends and I had longed for was biting us in the ass.

The crowds at the stage shows could become disrespectful as well. Artists sometimes admonished fans for throwing beer bottles and cans at them during songs. The Taylors tried to curb the craziness by creating rules. Bottles and public use of golf carts were the first to go. But monsters aren't easily tamed. The crowd grew bigger and wilder. Taylor's festival moved to the Tres Rios campground in 1995, secured sponsors to boost its music budget to $20,000, and rented better staging, sound, and lights. Keen, like Jerry Jeff Walker before him, had turned hell-raising into an art, and the new breed of musicians and fans followed suit. By 1997, the campground manager complained that the crowd was "the largest collection of white trash I've ever seen," an insulted Taylor recalled.

The festival moved to Meridian in 1998, and five years later moved to the much larger Melody Mountain Ranch. More space meant more fans. Fighting increased. Thievery surfaced. Trust is vital at festivals because people leave guitars, food, and alcohol untended at campsites while enjoying the stage shows. That first year at Melody Mountain Ranch marked the first time I'd ever returned to my camp and discovered that someone had stolen food and beer. Nearby campers reported stolen items as well. A couple of days later I noticed a deputy sheriff handcuffing a young man next to a tent not far from my own and went to check it out. The kid had filled up his tent with stolen goods. The police officer asked me to spread the word among the victims to come look inside the tent and grab what was theirs.

The strangest occurrence, however, involved drunken fools mistakenly wandering into camps and crashing out in other people's tents and campers, thinking they were their own. When you'd try to wake them up and kick them out, they'd want to fight. One guy stumbled into our camp and tried to open the door to a camper where my buddy's daughter was sleeping. We tried to tell him he was at the wrong camper, but he wouldn't listen. He started swinging at one of us, and we pinned him against the camper. We tried to talk sense to him, but he continued to struggle. About that time a deputy sheriff pulled up in a golf cart, got out, and, as he approached us, told us to let go of the man. We did as we were told. "These assholes are . . . ," the kid began, but he didn't finish his sentence. The deputy slammed the guy face-first in the dirt, planted his knee in the guy's back, and began slapping his head. "Why (slap!) are you bothering (slap! slap!) these people (slap!) you stupid (slap!) son of a bitch (SLAP!)?"

Taylor began relying more heavily on Erath County deputies to maintain peace.

"We try to keep ourselves apart from a big-time party, big-time drunk-fest," Sherry Taylor said. "That's not what we want to promote in any form or fashion. When you get a big crowd together you want everybody safe and happy, and you don't want people driving. That's why we've always had a place you could camp."

By 2003, some of LJT's older fans had fled. Deputies sought help from local police agencies to manage the crowd. More than seventy arrests were made that year, many for minors in possession of alcohol. The deputies tended to arrest people coming into the event or leaving the event. Those who got inside were pretty much free to do as they pleased. Some spent much of their time cruising around the ranch roads in pickups with stereos blaring. Dust covered the campsites. The stereo music drowned out singer-songwriters at campfires. "It broke my heart at Larry Joe's when the kids were driving around in their trucks yelling instead of listening at the camp-fires," longtime performer and LJT regular Tommy Alverson said. "When you get that big, you get the undesirables."

Taylor banned nighttime cruising.

Drunken fights were inevitable, but that year a guy lost part of his ear after confronting a knife-wielding thief trying to steal an ice chest. Each year Taylor would have to fashion more rules to address the previous year's problems. The list of rules grew longer. In time, the rules and the presence of law enforcement officers helped curb the bedlam. Still, the sheer numbers of fans could be overwhelming. Intimate, up-close performances were harder to come by. The mosh pit mentality in front of the stage pushed the lawn-chair crowd farther and farther back.

Alverson, who played every year at LJT's bash, created his own festi-val. The Family Gathering at Hog Mountain Retreat in Mineral Wells is smaller and tamer by design, drawing about two thousand visitors over three days. "Bigger is not always better," Alverson said. "I can't imagine trying to wrangle as many people as Larry Joe does."

Alverson's festival and others, such as Terry Razor's three-day "Raz On The Braz," appealed more to my aging gang of former hellions. We weren't seeking quiet sanctuary, just a smidgen of control amid the chaos. As one woman in her fifties told me, "Who wants to come if it's just a bunch of old people? It wouldn't be as much fun without the kids. The older people were just like those kids once, and some of us never grew up. That's what Texas music is all about."

All my bellyaching in this chapter doesn't change the fact that Texas music festivals are a blast to attend. You might have to search for one that fits your style. And your style might change in time. I wrote an article some years back about clashes between young and old patrons at music festivals. For research purposes I hooked up with a group of Burleson guys in their early twenties and hung out with them for a night at Alverson's festival. The fellows seemed more interested in raising hell than listening to music. And even though they planned to stay for several days, they'd brought no food, only beer and weed. Late in the evening my new buddies were walking toward their campsite when they passed an older gentleman about my age, asleep in a chair, chin on chest, boots stretched out toward his campfire.

"Dude, this guy's been passed out for hours," one of them said.

"We should fuck with him," another said.

"Yeah, let's put hot coals on his nuts!"

They casually decided against aggravated assault and kept moving. This was their second year to attend the festival, and they vowed to return every year for the rest of their lives. I remember thinking the same thing about Taylor's festival all those years ago, until I matured. Now I'm feeling an old familiar pull. Kerrville's gentle vibe is calling, bringing me full circle, right side up again. Like Orion.

Vignette—Bobby Bridger: "Heal in the Wisdom," Creating a Classic

Craig D. Hillis (interview with Bobby Bridger)

More than any other songwriter featured in this book, Bobby Bridger incorporates the time-tested tenants of epic poetry into his work, most notably in *A Ballad of the West*. And, along with other polymaths we analyze—the multitalented Terry Allen is probably the best example—Bridger incorporates a cross-section of the literary, musical, and visual arts to bring his creativity to life. In this interview he talks about "Heal in the Wisdom," the official anthem of the Kerrville Folk Festival.

CDH: Bobby, I'd like to know how "Heal in the Wisdom" came to be? What were the circumstances surrounding the song's inception and how did it find its way into the heart and soul of the Kerrville Folk Festival?

BB: The song took shape around 1978. There was a fellow named Michael Eakin who wrote for the *Austin Sun*. Michael was a real "storm the Bastille" kind of investigative reporter, and we happened to be good friends. Michael was murdered in Houston while following some lead, and his murder was never solved. His death had a profound effect on me. Around the time I began to emerge from the grieving process of Michael's murder, I was spending a considerable amount of time with a friend from Kerrville named Antler Dave. He made all these wonderful antler jewelry pieces for the Kerrville crowd and was the quintessential hippie character. Tragically, Dave was in a car wreck and died. The timing of both deaths sent me into a tailspin of grief. Losing two friends in a three- to four-month period kind of freaked me out. It was as if I had a case of "spiritual goose bumps" where there are things going on that you don't know about.

During this period, I went to Louisiana to visit my parents. My dad and I were riding around in his truck, and I was talking to him about the whole thing of grieving, and he said, "Well, Bobby, there are just some things in life that we're not supposed to understand." I had just written this song called "The Hawk." It was a song about man and the earth and their mutual dependence that contained the phrase, "What will they do when the earth needs their wisdom to heal." I started flipping around the phrase "wisdom to heal," and began to blend it with what my dad said about "understanding."

This combination triggered memories of that old Baptist hymn "Farther Along" that featured the line, "Farther along we'll understand why." That hymn had a great feel and a gentle, rolling melody, and I figured that if Woody Guthrie and Pete Seeger could borrow melodies for their lyrics, then so could I! So I began by using "Farther Along" as a musical template. But as I began to set words and ideas into that structure, it seemed to stretch and bend into a distinct melody line that provided a much more comfortable vehicle for the lyrics I was developing for the verses.

As the verses took shape, I knew that I needed a different direction and feel for the chorus—not only because that's how choruses generally work, but because I needed to make a universal statement in contrast to the personal and worldly nature of the verses. I needed to make sure that the *melody*, *intent*, and *effect* of the chorus would stand together in support of the message. And I believe that this is an important point to make about the craft of songwriting. With this song, I wanted to make sure that the chorus injected a positive affirmation into the concerns voiced in the verses. The chorus had to offer a possible solution. I can best describe this by taking a closer look at the lyrics.

"Farther along we'll understand why" flipped into "And one day together we'll heal in the wisdom, and we'll understand." That's what it's all about, and that's what triggered the whole thing. Regarding the verses, "I knew a man who had it all for awhile": Both of those men—Michael Eakin and Antler Dave—had it all going on. Both men were young, in the prime of life, and then suddenly they were gone.

Then I thought, "Well, this really needs a woman's perspective too." The woman depicted in the second verse was a real woman, but there's another story to that that I won't go into here. "I knew a woman with nothing at all. With no one to help her she had a great fall." And I wanted to express the great strength she developed in recovering and how she could then teach her brothers "that they can be free."

Anyhow, the male and female verses had me perplexed for a time because I didn't know where the song was going to go to make the bigger universal statement I wanted to make. I decided to go directly to that point of the lyric that addressed the country, and then in the final verse, I moved to the collective people who form the country.

With that, I had the four verses, but I still considered it a "work-in-progress" because when the chorus came around in between each of the verses, I felt it made the song far too long. I also thought the song made the jump from the man and the woman to the country and the people too quickly. This suggested that it needed a transitional verse, which would make the song even longer. At that point, I was really struggling to either pull all of those various themes into the larger theme to create one long, cohesive piece, or to drastically edit the entire effort.

CDH: But, as I recall, Rod Kennedy had a hand in resolving that issue.

BB: Yes, he did. I was backstage at the 1979 Kerrville Folk Festival, and as usual John Inmon was playing with me. Also, our old friend David Amram was sitting in with us, and I was playing "Heal in the Wisdom" to get their feedback on the length of the song. Just as I was explaining all that and playing the song for John and David, Rod Kennedy, the festival's founder and director, came around from his announcer's perch to tell us to get ready to go on stage.

He heard the song we were playing, and asked, "Did you write that song, Bobby?" I said, "Well, yes, but I don't think it is finished yet. I'm just teaching it to David and John here to see if I should take out a verse." Then Rod said, "I want that to be the anthem of the festival." I said, "Wow, that's very flattering but don't you think we should at least play it for the audience first and see how it goes over? Besides, David and John are just now learning it." Rod agreed that was a good idea, but then proceeded to the stage and promptly announced I was coming out with John and David to perform the new official anthem of the Kerrville Folk Festival! So we played it and everybody immediately jumped right in, locked arms and started humming and singing. It started like that and it has been going on from that very moment.

CDH: It was a home run from night one.

BB: Yes, and I think I touched on something relevant to that period in time. In a documentary film about Kerrville, Rod Kennedy offered an interesting insight about "Heal in the Wisdom." He said that most of the festivals of that period usually closed with one of two songs—either "Will the Circle Be Unbroken" or "This Land Is Your Land"—and he wanted something that was new and different, a unique statement that related to the Kerrville Folk Festival. Evidently, "Heal in the Wisdom" fit the bill.

Now, after nearly four decades as the festival anthem, it has developed quite a colorful history. It made its way around the national folk-music circuit, and soon a number of younger artists were learning and singing my song. It's generated a good deal of support from other sources as well. . . . In this way, the song seems to have become a "hit" that didn't make it to the radio!"

INTERLUDE

What Do We Do with Willie?

I. Willie (An Early Encounter)

Craig D. Hillis

I remember an early encounter with Willie, an encounter that holds a special place in my thinking about Willie's role in the evolution and growth of Texas songwriters during the 1970s and beyond. It was 1972, and I was playing in Michael Murphey's band. Murphey's first album, *Geronimo's Cadillac*, had just been released, and the title cut was enjoying strong radio airplay in various American markets. The single was particularly popular in West Texas, so A&M Records sent us out to the High Plains to chase the airplay. The label, in conjunction with Texas concert promoters, arranged for several dates in college auditoriums in towns like Abilene, Lubbock, and other secondary markets.

When we arrived at the first date, we discovered that there was an opening act on the bill, Willie Nelson. Amazing but true! Murphey was the hottest item in the scene that was unfolding in Austin. Willie was in the process of moving back to Texas from Nashville, he didn't have an album out at the time, and the era of the glorified singer-songwriter was still in its formative stages.

As the lights dimmed on the evening of the first show, I sat in the back of the auditorium to catch Willie's act. I believe the venue was Abilene Christian College, but I'm not sure. I am sure, however, about my impression of Willie's performance that night. It left a mental imprint I'll never forget. As I settled into my seat, an off-stage announcer introduced "Mr. Willie Nelson," and when the stage lights came up, I was truly surprised by the configuration on stage. I had never seen Willie perform live, and I didn't know what to expect, but it certainly wasn't what I beheld on that West Texas stage. It was just Willie and a drummer. That was it! No bass, no piano, no lead guitar, no steel. Had it been simply Willie and a guitar, well, that made sense, but *just* drums? Strange! I moved toward the stage to take a closer look, and as I got closer to this curious combination, things got stranger.

As I closed in on Willie and his band of one, I noticed he was playing a Martin N-20, which is a nylon-string classical model. There's nothing strikingly strange about that—you will occasionally see a country artist with a classical guitar, although most prefer steel-string instruments. What really caught my attention were Willie's playing style and his "guitar rig." He was playing the gut-string Martin with a pick—most classical guitars are played with the fingers—and he had the guitar set up with some sort of pickup that he ran through an amplifier. Keep in mind it was 1972 and the "electrified acoustics," so common today, were rare at that time. I remember wrangling with Murphey's acoustic trying to attach a Barcus-Berry transducer—an ad hoc guitar pickup—to create a direct line into the PA system so his guitar would cut through all the band racket! That was a dicey proposition because a transducer operates by translating the vibrations from the face of the guitar into an electronic signal, a signal that often reflects the unwanted percussive sounds of the player's strumming hand hitting the face of the instrument. Evidently, Willie had a very clever guitar tech situate a pickup in the bridge of the Martin, which alleviated a great deal of the percussive noise associated with "face mounted" transducers. He then ran that signal through a stage amplifier, and the amp was a real doozy! It was a Baldwin amp, made by the piano and organ company. It had solid-state circuitry, a collection of brightly colored controls fashioned like the slide bars of an organ, all encased in a baby-blue Formica frame with buffed aluminum highlights and a shiny black grill cloth. It looked like it had just been "beamed down" from the bridge of Captain Kirk's *Enterprise*. The sound of this guitar and amp combo as Willie bore down on the nylon strings with a flatpick was an audio texture like no other. There were the warm, round tones of the classical guitar, the sharp edge of the flatpick, the hint of a processed signal from the bridge pickup, all powered by the clean wattage of the solid-state amp. A very unique sound. A signature sound.

Then of course there was the band of one, drummer and longtime Willie pal Paul English, who had definitely "beamed over" from an undisclosed location somewhere in Transylvania. His jet-black hair was slicked back, and he wore black jeans, shirt, and boots to match. He had dark sideburns meticulously trimmed to resemble the tail fins of a 1959 Cadillac complemented by the perfect mustache and goatee, and a black cape with red lining from a Bela Lugosi movie set. This striking fashion statement, however, was not an indication of his drumming style. He played with a delicate touch that was hardwired into Willie's sense of time and meter, and Willie's groove moved with the feel and the emotional highlights of the story expressed in the song. Standard meter was a secondary consideration. Contrary to my initial reservations, this unusual combination of drums and gut-string Martin, all dominated by Willie's distinct vocal style, worked very, very well.

Willie moved at a relaxed pace from one song to the next. He rarely stopped to speak, yet he seemed to build an implicit dialogue with the audience. Like so many others in the room, I focused on his voice to keep pace with the story line. Willie didn't let the absence of support instruments compromise his momentum. The comfortable flow of his familiar tunes established a tacit musical foundation that enabled him to step outside of the song and play a lead break. He simply leaned back from the mic and delivered a blend of single notes and double stops with the conviction of a soloist fronting a symphony. Then, with a seamless segue, he slipped back into the song and continued with the story at hand. The ultimate effect was a common current between the songwriter and the listener.

So what does this isolated performance on an obscure West Texas stage forty-three years ago have to do with Willie's place in the pantheon of prestigious picker poets and the enduring music scene that they fostered? The significance is very simple—after more than four decades, the essence of

Willie's show has not changed a lick! Sure, there are more people on stage. The "band of one" has grown into a traveling family ensemble with boundless loyalty to the patriarch. The crowds, the album releases, the hits, the awards, and the international notoriety have all reached unprecedented levels. Yet Willie is still playing the same nylon-string Martin N-20 with the imbedded bridge pickup routed through a stage amp. I'm not sure if the Baldwin "Star Trek" amp still survives, but the same signature tone is front and center. That old guitar reflects the countless road miles with signatures of friends and fellow pickers etched into the Sitka spruce top, and there is a hole between the bridge and the sound hole created by his aggressive picking style. And Paul still has Willie's back, tapping out time focused on the feel of the song rather than the mechanical cadence of a metronome. Same vibe, same spirit, different century!

The twenty-first century Willie Nelson show still moves in a steady song groove. The stage lights come up, Willie kicks off "Whiskey River," a tune written by longtime friend and band mate, Johnny Bush, then continues with his own timeless classics and various interpretations of songs from fellow songwriters. He smoothly shifts from one song to the next, and the stage patter, now as then, is sparse. With the support of the family band, he has a rich musical bed for his guitar solos, but the seminal spirit of the show is unchanged. He communicates through the compositions and continues to create a common current between the songwriter and the listener. The performance is a communion of common song, a litany of message and meaning presented in verse and melody. Decade after decade, it is still about the song, which has always been the critical mass at the core of Willie's creativity.

II. WILLIE (ON EVERYTHING)

Craig Clifford and Craig D. Hillis

Willie Nelson comes up in a number of the essays in this book, and over the four years leading up to its publication, we've gone back and forth on how to deal with the immense subject of Willie Nelson. Nelson didn't emerge as a Texas folksinger like the initial generation of the ruthlessly poetic songwriters that we deal with in Part One, yet he has had a profound impact on their songwriting and their careers. He's hardly a typical country artist, yet he's written an enduring string of country classics and reigns as one of the biggest names in country music. Rather than commission an essay based on the format represented in this book—which of the three parts would we put it in?—we decided on an editors' interlude. We reasoned that this approach might enable us to explore the impact that

Nelson's venerable musical pilgrimage, his experience, and his insights have had on the careers of these ruthlessly poetic songwriters.

Nelson, born in 1933, was already writing country classics before the Texas folksinger phenomenon started to capture the imagination of a new audience in the late sixties and early seventies. While living in Houston in the late fifties, Nelson penned "Funny How Time Slips Away," "Crazy," and other songs that became country classics. These songs are brilliant and poetic in the way that the songs of Hank Williams Sr. are brilliant and poetic. Indeed, titles like "Crazy" and later tunes like "Nightlife" and "I Never Cared for You"—all songs that feature exceptional lyrics—also display sophisticated chord structures and melodic components that further highlight the unique quality of Nelson's early songs.

Patsy Cline's version of "Crazy" was the second hit from her 1961 Decca album, *Patsy Cline Showcase*. It rose to number five on the *Billboard* Country Chart. Billy Walker had a national hit with "Funny How Time Slips Away" in 1961. The song was eventually certified as a "Million-Air" recording by BMI (Broadcast Music Incorporated) for receiving over a million "spins" or radio plays. Capitol Records country artist Faron Young, popularly known as the "Hillbilly Heartthrob," recorded Nelson's "Hello Walls" on his 1961 album release of the same name. The single reached No. 1 on the *Billboard* country chart and crossed over to the *Billboard* pop charts to peak at number twelve. Ray Price recorded "Night Life" on his 1963 Columbia album of the same name. The single reached No. 1 on the *Billboard* Country Chart. Reputedly, "Night Life" was one of the most "covered" country songs of the late twentieth century. Roy Orbison recorded "Pretty Paper" on his 1964 Monument Records album, *More of Roy Orbison's Greatest Hits*. Although "Pretty Paper" was never released as a single and consequently never had a run on the national charts, it became a Christmas classic in the rock and country world.

Had Willie Nelson's career abruptly ended before he came back home to Texas in 1972, he would still hold an honored position in the history of country music. But there was a shift in the country center of gravity in the late sixties and early seventies as a new generation of folksingers began to register their creative presence in the music marketplace. Guy Clark and Bob Dylan were both born in 1941, and they were responding to many of the same influences and facing the same kind of lyric-loving coffeehouse audiences as they came of age as songwriters. Van Zandt was born in 1944, Murphey and Fromholz in 1945. In 1964 Willie Nelson, living in Nashville, became a member of the Grand Ole Opry; in 1965 Townes Van Zandt was playing covers of Bob Dylan and Lightnin 'Hopkins at the Jester Lounge in Houston for ten dollars a night.

But when Nelson left Nashville for Texas in 1972, intending to fashion a new phase in his career, he became immersed in the Austin counterculture, and, not unlike the Great Joe Bob in Terry Allen's song, Willie "grew his hair, then he give up prayer, said football days is done." The rest is of course history—the origins of the so-called "outlaw" movement, with Willie Nelson as the titular gang leader, coincide in time and place with the coming of age of the Texas folksingers who are central to this book. To what extent do these traditions or movements overlap?

The outlaw movement was, at least in part, just that—a movement. It was a movement complete with anthems, anthems that had as their main purpose to rally the faithful to the cause. The outlaw movement was also an enormously successful commercial venture, complete with a brilliant marketing and branding campaign, and Music City made a tidy return on its investment. Still, it was undeniably a revolt against the confining standards and shallow pieties of 1970s Nashville. That revolt took the form of a return to Texas roots, a return to a kind of hell-raising spirit of independence. The primary motive for much of the songwriting of that movement was not to produce poetic lyrics but to stir things up.

And yet that spirit of independence included a call for artistic freedom. In the early seventies, Neil Reshen, a New York attorney, represented both Waylon Jennings and Willie Nelson. He renegotiated Jennings's contract with RCA so that Jennings could produce his own albums, starting with *Lonesome, On'ry and Mean* in 1973. He negotiated Nelson's release from RCA and his move to Atlantic Records. He later negotiated a contract with Columbia Records that guaranteed Nelson complete creative freedom in the production of his albums. It's arguable that Nelson would never have created his masterpiece concept album, *Red Headed Stranger*, without the artistic freedom that the outlaw artists demanded and Neil Reshen negotiated. This recording project was a curious confluence of the old and the new, a loosely connected tale of love, loss, and revenge in the American West. The arrangement of this album was so sparse that Columbia executives thought it was a demo. Nelson released this high-risk concept album over the objections of the record company executives—thanks to the contract Reshen had negotiated for him—and it sold almost three million copies. One of the songs, "Blue Eyes Crying in the Rain," a country-music standard penned by pioneer Nashville songwriter and publisher Fred Rose, became a No. 1 country hit.

Did Nelson insist on releasing this album because he knew that it would sell millions, or did he insist on releasing it because of his artistic integrity? Who cares! *Red Headed Stranger* is a classic example of a "Williefied" cultural product. Ignoring all of the rules again, in 1978 Nelson released *Star-*

dust, featuring his unique arrangements of standard tunes from the American songbook. It sold over eighteen million copies. This successful album connected several generations of songwriters and underscored the staying power and vitality of well-crafted songs, and it demonstrated once again how much Nelson writes his own rules.

The demand for independence and artist freedom that played a role in the outlaw movement overlaps with the classically Romantic embrace of art for art's sake that motivated the Texas folksingers in the coffeehouses of Houston, Austin, and other Texas cities. It was of course an age of revolt against convention and authority, an age that valued freedom and self-expression. That self-expression ranged from silliness to profundity, depending on the talent and background of the person.

What is the legacy of Willie Nelson and the outlaw movement? It's not hard to see a connection between the rowdy I-love-Texas side of the outlaw movement and the dumbed-down let's-party-in-my-truck mainstream Texas country music of today. It didn't take long for the outlaw movement to descend into some crowd-pleasing romps like "Mamas Don't Let Your Babies Grow Up to Be Cowboys," recorded by Nelson and Waylon Jennings in 1978. "On the Road Again" from 1980 is fun, but shallow, a far cry from Hank Williams Sr.'s dark song of the road, "Ramblin' Man." You can draw a line from "I just can't wait to get on the road again" to Josh Abbott's "Koozie's in the console, beer's on the floor, and everybody's gassing up their Fords" in "Road Trippin'." But some of the early anthems had more going on than meets the eye. There was a kind of self-effacing irony to "Good-Hearted Woman" and a bit of self-effacing humor in "Ladies Love Outlaws," and a deeper look into the outlaw soul in "Lonesome, On'ry and Mean" that is lacking from much of the rowdy Texas music of today.

For better or worse, Willie Nelson did play a huge role in the marriage of country music with hippie rock 'n' roll in the early 1970s. On August 12, 1972, Willie Nelson, rejuvenated by his interaction with the counterculture of Austin, played Armadillo World Headquarters. Many commentators see this show as the seminal event in the creation of what came to be known as the "Cosmic Cowboy"—longhaired hippies listening to, and liking, the music of the songwriter who had penned "Crazy," "Hello Walls," and other country music classics. The times they were a-changin'.

This country-rock mix was central to the outlaw movement. Longhaired Willie and Waylon were still as country as you can get, but they infused that country sound with a heavy dose of rock 'n' roll—and we ended up with what Jan Reid called "redneck rock." Meanwhile, the Texas folksingers, influenced by the country music of their youth and rooted in the Texas soil, were feeding off of the same longhaired Age-of-Aquarius culture. Fromholz's *Texas Trilogy* is about small town and rural life in Bosque County, Texas. Guy Clark's songs are filled with old-school country folks. And Townes Van Zandt wearing a beat-up straw hat and shooting a BB gun in one scene of *Be Here to Love Me: A Film About Townes Van Zandt* looks like an episode out of *The Beverly Hillbillies*. But the age of experimentation led, for Fromholz, Clark, Van Zandt, and company, to a marriage of rooted country themes with the storytelling ethos and musical sensibilities of traditional folk music. If Willie Nelson could play at Armadillo World Headquarters, Townes Van Zandt could sing songs that sounded like three-hundred-year-old Irish ballads with a Texas twang. And, if Willie Nelson ushered in the age of the Cosmic Cowboy with his performance at Armadillo World Headquarters in 1972, you might say that Townes Van Zandt ushered it out when he played one of the last shows there on December 6, 1980, opening for Taj Mahal.

Perhaps even more important to the development of Texas music in the 1970s was Willie Nelson's 1975 performance on *Austin City Limits*, the pilot that launched the program onto the national stage. In the fall of 1974, KLRN recorded two pilots: B. W. Stevenson one night and Willie Nelson the next night. The KLRN crew decided to use Nelson's. Bill Arhos, the program director, convinced PBS to use the pilot in its 1975 pledge drive. Thirty-four PBS affiliates picked up the show, and it was a huge success. *Austin City Limits* brought Texas music to the nation, and it started with Willie Nelson. It is, and has always been, an eclectic show, and it has not confined itself to Texas music. But it provided one of the essential venues for the Texas folksingers. Townes Van Zandt played the show in 1976 and 1983. Guy Clark debuted there in 1977, and has played *ACL* numerous times since then. Steven Fromholz played three shows in the seventies. Michael Martin Murphey has played *ACL* eight times, Nanci Griffith ten times. Most of the line-up from what we call the second generation of ruthlessly poetic songwriters have played there multiple times: James McMurtry, Lyle Lovett, Steve Earle, Robert Earl Keen, and Lucinda Williams. And there's been a good showing from the third generation as well: Miranda Lambert in 2006, Ryan Bingham in 2009, Hayes Carll in 2013, and Kacey Musgraves in 2014. Whether the show would have gotten off the ground without Willie Nelson's pilot, no one can say; but it was his pilot that sold the show to PBS, and all of the ruthlessly poetic songwriters of three generations are standing on his shoulders when they play *Austin City Limits*.

Nelson has also been a champion of many of the poetic folksingers this book focuses on by recording their songs and contributing to their recordings in other ways. He recorded Steven Fromholz's "I'd Have to Be Crazy" for his 1976 album *The Sound in Your Mind*. He made Rodney Crowell's "Till I Gain Control Again" a regular in his live performances, and it appears on *Willie and Family Live*, released in 1978. Nelson turned "Last Thing I Needed First Thing This Morning," written by Gary P. Nunn and Donna Farar, into a hit when he released it as a single off of his album *Always on My Mind*. Townes Van Zandt has become a kind of songwriter's songwriter, almost a cult figure in some quarters, but how many people have been led to his esoteric body of work by Willie Nelson and Merle Haggard's No. 1 hit recording of "Pancho and Lefty," the title track of their 1983 album. Nelson has teamed up with Kimmie Rhodes on several albums, starting with Rhodes's 1996 album *West Texas Heaven* and culminating with a collection of duets on *Picture in a Frame* in 2003. Nelson was essential to the so-called outlaw movement, but he has been just as essential to the tradition of ruthlessly poetic songwriting that started in the coffeehouses of the late sixties and early seventies, both as a songwriter and as a performer.

So where do we locate Willie Nelson? Is he part of the tradition of ruthlessly poetic songwriting that this book focuses on? He has certainly written songs that merit inclusion, both before and after the so-called outlaw revolt. But that is probably the wrong question. Truth is, you can neither *locate* nor conveniently *categorize* Willie Nelson. As long as he has been around, as talented as he is, as broadly as his artistic vision roams, and as compelling and unique as his personality is—well, Willie Nelson is everywhere, he's transcendent. It's little wonder that you can't situate him in any one tradition, movement, or genre the way you can, say, quintessential singing poets like Townes Van Zandt and Guy Clark.

In the end, it's highly misguided to try to pigeonhole Willie Nelson as the leader of the outlaw movement. He intersected with it, just as he intersected with everything else that was going on in Texas music at that time, but he was and is much bigger than that. He doesn't monitor the pulse of the industry or tap into the latest trend to move forward. He doesn't go out to find new angles, new adventures, new movements. Nelson is quite at home doing what he does, and movements have a way of attaching to his star. After all the hubbub, Nelson is still on the bus, stepping up to the next microphone, communing with a bunch of old friends, and making some new ones. That spark of artistic independence that came to the fore when he broke away from Nashville is a feature of Nelson's psyche that's been there from day one. It didn't take a movement to create that. His independent spirit intersected with the great tradition of country music, the great tradition of American popular music standards, the jazz of Stéphane Grappelli and Django Reinhardt, the outlaw movement, hippie rock and the counterculture of the sixties, and the ruthlessly poetic singer-songwriter tradition of Texas. Much of what this book is about wouldn't have happened without him. Willie Nelson isn't the leader of a movement—he's a force of nature.

PART TWO

THE SECOND GENERATION

Garage Bands, Large Bands, and Other Permutations

"Gettin' Tough"

Steve Earle's America

Jason Mellard

Steve Earle's debut album *Guitar Town* exploded onto the scene in 1986. In contrast to the decade's gospel of wealth, such songs as "Good Ol' Boy (Gettin' Tough)" took a harder look at just where America stood. The song's protagonist reads off the ledger of his life. He has a job and works hard, but it does not seem to be enough to pay off debts owed on his truck, his home, and to the IRS. You can hear the frustration behind his laments, that despite the omnipresent up-by-the-bootstrap rhetoric, things just do not add up. "I was born in the land of plenty now there ain't enough," Earle sings, but "Nowadays it just don't pay to be a good ol' boy." Such lyrics invited apt comparisons to Bruce Springsteen both then and since, with observers claiming Earle as a workingman's poet. It goes further than that, as it is easy enough to trace both Earle's and Springsteen's themes to such forebears as Woody Guthrie. Earle's "Good Ol' Boy" lyric even echoes Guthrie's "Pastures of Plenty." There is a great deal of history that stands between Guthrie and Earle, though, and that distance makes a difference. Where Guthrie's songs entered the streams of protest that helped form the New Deal that arbitrated the conflict between labor and capital, Earle's voice first issued over the airwaves after those grand bargains had largely collapsed. Coincident with the shocks to public trust of Vietnam and Watergate in the 1970s, New Deal and Great Society reformism faded as Rust Belt industry folded to economic malaise and globalization. Popular music has not always done the best job of narrating these shifts, nor is there reason to believe that it should. Mainstream pop aims at escape, a utopia where all desires continue to be fulfilled, collapsing the distance between our wishes and the real world. Where folk, country, and the harder edges of rock meet, though, Steve Earle's home turf, there is a rich history of plumbing the canyon that separates America's promise and its reality.

As songwriter, musician, author, actor, and activist, Steve Earle defies easy categorization. Indeed, the same might be said of most of the Texas artists profiled in this collection. They overflow the easy bounds of genre despite the fact that many found their first success in the country field. The designation is a hat-tip to geography, accent, performance styles, and the commercial networks centered on Nashville (and, to an extent, Austin). That many have migrated into "Americana" or its regional sibling "Texas Music" cuts closer to the content of the songs themselves. The label fits Steve Earle not because he is a rigid traditionalist (far from it), but because a certain vision of America proves to be one of his most enduring subjects. Earle writes of a vibrant nation that has promised much, occasionally triumphed, and often disappointed. Through autobiographical ballads and love songs, protest anthems and roadhouse rockers, he has consistently and evocatively narrated the country's broken social compact of the twentieth century.

Born in 1954, Earle grew up outside of San Antonio. He took to the guitar, as so many young men of his generation did, in imitation of Elvis and the Beatles. His coming-of-age marked the convergence of rockabilly's fifties rebellion, the British Invasion's sixties brashness, and the earnest politics of the lingering folk revival. Earle's prolific recording career generally plays out over two arcs. After moving to Nashville, Earle burst onto the scene in the 1980s wave of neo-traditionalists that included George Strait and Dwight Yoakam. This first commercial wave runs roughly from *Guitar Town* of 1986 through the album *The Hard Way* of 1990. Earle's much-publicized bouts with addiction and the law interrupted this early success. Where many artists have been swallowed whole by such tragedies, Earle has embarked on a remarkable second act inaugurated by the album *Train a Comin'* of 1995 and carrying through to the present. Lauren St. John's *Hardcore Troubadour: The Life & Near Death of Steve Earle* and David McGee's *Steve Earle: Fearless Heart, Outlaw Poet* have both dealt with Earle's biography at length.[1] Here, I am more interested in the broader vision that Earle's songs convey and their connections to the kind of "ruthlessly poetic" voice theorized in Texas songwriters by Craig Clifford and Craig Hillis.

That Earle stands in the genealogy of Texas singer-songwriters born of the 1960s and 1970s progressive country wave is clear. *Guitar Town* did not come out of nowhere. When Earle moved to Nashville in the early 1970s, he entered the fraternity of Texas expatriates in Tennessee who had come up through Houston's 1960s folk scene, including Guy Clark, Townes Van Zandt, and Rodney Crowell. Clark and Van Zandt proved to be powerful mentors. Each of these men has had the sobriquet "poet" attached to his name, but Earle has at times resisted the label. He possesses the facility for beautiful language, surely, but it is less his lyricism than his narrative voice and ability to craft complicated characters in song that define his artistry.

McGee and others have noted that Earle's hard-luck antiheroes often distract from his poignant love songs or the autobiographical and often abstract depictions of pain found in such pieces as "My Old Friend the Blues."

It is true that Earle's body of songs address the breadth of human experience, but my focus will be on his vision of the American nation, the songs that have branded Earle as a political artist. Politically engaged art, and especially song, has long been suspect in American history. In keeping with the nation's individualist ethos, the culture often frames art as a medium of purely individual expression, rather than an avenue for exploring shared experience or social problems. The genres of American "folk" and "country" are both based on the vernacular traditions of Southern music, white and black, casting back to a sense of the collective ownership and value of song. However, country music's commercial evolution has rendered its connections to folk at times barely visible, at others anathema. Woody Guthrie, for example, worked professionally in country radio in Southern California before becoming a "folk" icon in New York City, but he remains little recognized by the country establishment.

Guthrie and Earle bespeak a thematic continuity, but the history that separates them is equally important. Between Guthrie's folk moment and Earle's neo-traditionalist one, an entirely new conception of songcraft arose. Guthrie's "folk" era celebrated the supposedly anonymous, collective body of American vernacular song. This is not to detract from Guthrie's status as a writer—far from it—but critics obscured that status by foregrounding his generation's creativity as that of the "folk" who shared his circumstances. By the 1970s, the "singer-songwriter" had appeared, keeping folk's quiet aesthetics and heartfelt sincerity while inverting much of its original meaning. As opposed to the thirties or fifties folkie channeling the voice of the people, the seventies singer-songwriter became a kind of virtuoso auteur expressing a highly individualized point of view. We tend to treat this evolution as a product of Greenwich Village or Laurel Canyon, but it also carries a Texas accent. When John Lomax Sr. first collected cowboy songs in Texas in the early twentieth century, he was among the first to assert that contemporary Americans could create folk traditions rather than simply serve as the vessels of medieval British ballads back in the hollers and hills. When his son Alan publicized Jelly Roll Morton or Lead Belly, the focus shifted to individual artists as the agents of this American tradition.[2] By the time John Lomax III served as Steve Earle's first manager, the focus had shifted yet again to the songwriter-as-auteur. While country music maintains its purported ties to American tradition, the question of a vernacular folk, its shared history and challenges, has largely faded from view. The Cold War cleaved the connections between folk and country. McCarthyism trounced the left-wing allegiances of the folk revival, and intellectuals savaged the WPA aesthetics and broader popular-front Americanism that gave folk its political edge. The breed of political song that shored up the worker's voice and the labor insurgencies of the 1930s came to be seen as awkward, kitschy, and even un-American in the face of the global threat of Soviet Communism.[3]

What do we make, then, of Earle's arrival as a political voice, a working-man's poet, in the 1980s?[4] If the country establishment distanced itself from folk's left-wing commitments, it retained a proud populism that cannot easily be classed on the political spectrum. *Guitar Town* spoke with this populist voice that echoes throughout Earle's career. Through a series of tightly sung narratives, *Guitar Town* foreshadowed Earle's later political bent, but expressed through the material challenges facing individual protagonists. The title track is in some ways a take on Chuck Berry's "Johnny B. Goode" or Bobby Bare's "All-American Boy," a semi-autobiographical portrait of the artist as a young man gunning for stardom. Songs such as "Good Ol' Boy (Getting' Tough)" shadow this rags-to-riches aspiration, though, giving a sense of the constricted opportunities for the American working class as the New Deal order began to crack. Earle historicizes the shift frequently, having his contemporary protagonists compare their situations to those of their parents or grandparents. He does not engage in simplistic nostalgia when telling the story of the "greatest generation," but rather recognizes the historical circumstances that made for the grand bargain of the mid-twentieth century, and the conditions that led to that bargain's deterioration. In songs such as "Johnny Come Lately," for example, recorded with the Pogues for 1988's *Copperhead Road*, Earle contrasts perceptions of the American experiences in World War II and Vietnam. The song's narrator attaches a jaunty heroism to his grandfather's service in the former, while wondering why no one greets him at the airport as he returns from the latter.

Vietnam looms large in narratives of the broken American promise. It was in the 1970s, as Earle began his career, that the war began to symbolize the United States losing its way. Paired with Watergate, the oil crisis, and the end of the long post-World War II boom, the national malaise brought all kinds of former certainties into question. "In the 1970s Americans did not merely bump into the limits of the ideas that had governed the mid-century world, they crashed," journalist David Frum has observed, and the "distrust and despair that seized them were the wounds from that collision."[5] *Copperhead Road* doubled down on these themes. The album's songs strum the tension between America's promise and the reality of the constraints experienced by so many of its citizens. The title track's John Lee Pettimore is a quintessential Earle character, and the song showcases Earle's ability to distill a novel's worth of narrative into a spare, meaningful verse. Pettimore hails from a family of moonshiners who had long existed outside of and in conflict with the law. He joins the army to fight in Vietnam, returns home without a sense of what to do next, and takes up the standard of his rebel forebears by growing marijuana and fighting the DEA.

Beginning around the 1997 album *El Corazón*, Earle's politics moved from the subtext of his stories into the lyrics themselves. The album opens with "Christmas in Washington," a dirge lamenting the absence of a critical, populist politics in an age when there are "no more FDRs." Earle pleads for the return of such figures as Woody Guthrie, Joe Hill, and Emma Goldman, artists and activists who foregrounded a working-class perspective on the issues of the day. In such songs, the broken social compact, symbolized by busted unions and torn red banners, comes to be seen as a shared social problem rather than an individual tragedy. It is not just that Earle's protagonists have had a fit of hard luck. The greater body of his work demonstrates how they operate in a system that is rigged against them from the start. This focus does not simply concern the economic condition of the working class. With cutting wit and intellectual acumen, Earle extends his critique to all manners of state-sanctioned violence that are the darker side of the government's broken promises. "Ellis Unit One" and "Over Yonder" excoriate the country's death penalty, while the wars in the wake of 9/11 have also proved fertile ground for Earle's dissident voice.

Perhaps no song better displays Earle's tremendous power of empathy and willingness to tweak the mainstream's sensibilities as "John Walker's Blues." From 2002's *Jerusalem*, the song imagines the motivations and life story of John Walker Lindh, a young American who joined the Taliban in Afghanistan and was captured by American forces in 2001. Predictably, the song served as a lightning rod for the sort of knee-jerk critique that permeates the 24–7 media culture, but few of the critics listened to the song. It does not defend John Walker's actions as such, but aims to understand and contextualize them. Earle fleshes Lindh out as an American character, and, as he so often does, is able to distill capital-H History into the lived conditions of individual experience. John Walker thus becomes another Earle protagonist caught up in the all-American theme of ceaseless mobility. In Earle's songs, though, this mobility is not a source of liberation. Rather, it telegraphs a kind of pathological wanderlust amid the constricted opportunities of the postindustrial landscape. Earle's characters light out for the territories, but never seem to find the bountiful frontier. They defend the country they love, but have little to show for it in return. The national-security state trumpets its protection of freedoms even as it shows an increasing callousness not only to civil liberties but to the lives of individual human beings, "enemy combatants" such as John Walker, surely, but also of those Americans who serve abroad. Take, for examples, Earle's song "Home to Houston" that describes a truck driver contracted to haul supplies in Iraq or "The Gringo's Tale" about an intelligence agent exiled from the United States once he is no longer useful. The world of Earle's songs is one where wealth is no longer gained nor authority exercised by the work of one's hands. Trust and certainty would seem to be in short supply.

Taken together, though, Earle's broad body of work, combining his songwriting and musicianship with acting, literary pursuits, and activism, communicate something more. That most of his characters do not surrender nor accept the situations in which they find themselves shows a conviction, a continued belief in the power of political agency. Steve Earle exemplifies this conviction in his own person as well as his art, the American singer-songwriter perhaps best fitted to inherit Woody Guthrie's mantle. And I'll stand on top of Bruce Springsteen's coffee table and say that.

LYLE LOVETT AND ROBERT EARL KEEN

COSMIC AGGIES

Jan Reid

One night in the mid-1980s I went to the Paramount Theater in Austin for a John Prine concert. The years were long gone since I'd been first mesmerized by his songs "Sam Stone" and "Angel from Montgomery." I'm sure my appreciation of a splendid songwriter was rewarded, but what I remember about the evening was the opening act. A young man with a shy manner and a startling hair style was playing an acoustic guitar and singing country songs in a fine tenor voice, backed by a cellist!

His name was Lyle Lovett.

He grew up in Spring when it was an unincorporated farming and ranching community, not yet consumed by the Houston suburbs. While Austin fans packed in the Armadillo World Headquarters, the Texas Opry House, Castle Creek, the Saxon Pub, and other venues, in College Station Lovett volunteered on a student union committee of Texas A&M that booked musicians for a roving campus coffeehouse called the Basement Committee, and he profiled them in the campus newspaper, *The Battalion*. He graduated with a journalism degree at A&M but stayed on two more years and took another degree in German. He explained that it was easier to tell people he was a student than a struggling musician. One summer day in 1978 he was riding his bicycle down a street in College Station and saw some youths playing and singing on the porch of a house they rented. One was Robert Earl Keen Jr. They chatted a while, Lovett got off his bike, and someone handed him a guitar. At 22, Keen was not quite two years the older. They were inseparable that summer, talking and playing through days that stretched far into the nights.

Keen grew up in southwest Houston. He joked that he lasted fifteen seconds in five attempts to ride bulls in junior rodeos, likening the experience to "getting in your car and driving down the freeway seventy miles an hour, and then chunking your steering wheel out the window." His parents had a house in the country, and he liked to hang out at polka dances of the ethnic Czechs and Bohemians who lived in those rolling hills. An older brother introduced him to Willie Nelson's songs and phrasings, and in 1974 he went to Willie Nelson's Fourth of July Picnic, which took place on an auto racetrack outside Bryan-College Station. It was a woeful experience for the teenager. His date abandoned him for another guy, and a fire erupted in a grassy parking lot and consumed Keen's Ford Mustang. Some guys backstage felt the pain of the forlorn teen, and they took him to Willie's bus for some personal consolation. "He told me, 'I'd really like to stay and rap, but I've got to go jam with Leon Russell.'"

A year or so later his sister gave Keen a guitar that she'd lost interest in. He changed his major from animal science to English and, with his housemates, started playing on that porch on Church Street. Lovett and Keen wrote a song together that summer of 1978, later recorded by Lovett as "This Old Porch" and Keen as "The Front Porch Song." The song was a metaphorical string of images—a Hereford bull shifting under the sparse shade of a mesquite tree; a plate of greasy enchiladas; a main street movie theater darkened since *Giant* came to town; a Brazos River flood plain that no longer produced sugar cane or much cotton; a seventy-year-old rancher "doing all he can not to give in to the city."

Keen often injected his brand of talking blues into live performances. Accompanied by a mandolin player, he would drawl, "We used to sit on this old porch on Church Street, right across the Presbyterian church, and play bluegrass and folk music, dream of being big songwriters, and talk about girls and where we were going to move when our parents got our grades. We always looked forward to Sunday mornings there on the porch. We'd crawl out at about eleven thirty in our underwear, among four or five hundred beer cans, strap on a banjo or guitar, and wait for the Presbyterians to come out of church so we could sing 'em a little gospel music. Give 'em something to talk about—on the way to Luby's."

By the time they wrote that song, "the Great Progressive Country Scare," as the late Steven Fromholz phrased it, had just about run its course. Austin would not likely have nominated itself as any kind of music capital if Willie Nelson hadn't left Nashville disgusted by its music industry bosses. Another motive was that his house burned down. Subsequently he appeared with beard and long hair onstage at Armadillo World Headquarters in 1972. But it's useful to recall that Nelson's commercial breakout en route to being an international phenomenon bore little resemblance to his endless series of honky-tonk road shows. *Stardust*, released in 1978, was instead a legendary songwriter's tribute to great songwriters of the past—among them Hoagy Carmichael, Irving Berlin, George and Ira Gershwin. And so it was with the younger singer-songwriters rounded in the herd of the so-called cosmic cowboys. The expression was born as Michael Martin Murphey's metaphor in a song, which he soon regretted, and he put Austin in his rearview mirror. Murphey, Fromholz, Jerry Jeff Walker, Rusty Wier, and other notables graduated from being folksingers perched with a guitar on a bar stool in small folk venues. Songwriters all, they figured out how to afford hiring a band, and what came together was a happy amalgam of country, rock, blues, gospel, bluegrass, and Western swing. But *foosh*, all at once it was gone.

Musicians don't like to be crammed in a box any more than other kinds of artists. Austin music wheeled on its boot heels and went the way of the blues-inflected rock of Stevie Ray Vaughan and the Fabulous Thunderbirds, and bands like the Skunks and Wild Seeds fueled an avid punk scene. Delbert McClinton, Doug Sahm, and Marcia Ball fit in easily with the blues players, but many singer-songwriters and bands of the seventies were left with little to show for it but their cowboy hats.

But then came another crowd and fashion shift. The cosmic Aggies, Lyle Lovett and Robert Earl Keen, charged forth in the company of Steve Earle, Jimmy LaFave, Bruce and Charlie Robison, Nanci Griffith, Kelly Willis, the Dixie Chicks, and Kevin Russell of the Gourds and Shinyribs. Progressive country and its fundament of artful songwriting hadn't died. It was just taking a nap.

Lovett was the beneficiary of uncommon breaks as a young musician. After the A&M days he had carved just enough of a niche to hail a ride to the European circuit that continues to support Texas musicians. "I'd come to realize I didn't know anything about the business of music. I was in Luxembourg that September, playing an American-music tent at a fair, and met some musicians, Billy Williams and his band, from Phoenix. I'd never recorded with a band before and was curious what it would sound like. When I got back, they helped me make a demo tape, and in '84 I went to Nashville."

Gone was the hostility to Nashville and other music capitals that partly defined but also limited careers of the cosmic cowboys. Lovett went straight to the American Society of Composers and Publishers, and soon his rep there was setting up appointments for him with publishers. He left a demo tape with an admiring note at the publisher of one of his heroes, Guy Clark. The Nashville veteran said, "I finally got around to listening to it, and it flipped me smooth out. I was making everybody listen to it. I was just obsessed. Then one day I was walking through a restaurant and saw a friend, an Irish guitar player. He introduced me to this guy he was sitting with. I took one look at him and pegged him for a French blues singer. I went on and sat down and then finally lights and bells went off. That was the guy who left me all those incredible songs."

For Lovett a contract with a label like MCA was a gateway, not a catch corral. He recorded at a studio in Scottsdale, Arizona, with remix and over-dubs in Nashville. Billy Williams was an associate producer and played electric lead guitar. Roseanne Cash and Vince Gill, the onetime soaring voice of Pure Prairie League, contributed background vocals, and thirteen instruments were brought into the mix. But the sound was all restraint—nothing should take away from the sureness of Lovett's writing and the style of his singing.

Subjects of those songs were heartbreak, beer joints, and rodeos "Farther Down the Line."

> Let's have a hand for that young cowboy
> and wish him better luck next time
> Hope we'll see him back in Fargo
> and farther down the line
> But this time he sure drew a bad one
> One that nobody could ride

Smooth and tight, and with ongoing double entendre: Was it about a young man riding a bull, or had he come out of the chute with a lover who pitched him right away?

It wasn't that smooth an ascent for Keen. After six years as a collegian Keen got his degree from A&M in 1980, just in time to find the folk-friendly cosmic cowboy scene had evaporated. He moved to Austin, pushed paper at the Texas Railroad Commission, and scrabbled for what scarce gigs he could find.

He won a New Folk songwriting award at the 1983 Kerrville Folk Festival, but that only made him feel better for a while. A new friend from San Antonio, Steve Earle, advised him to get out of Austin before he wound up like so many of its musicians, drinking too much and not knowing when to quit. With his girlfriend Kathleen, later his wife, he moved to Nashville, where he dug ditches, worked in a print shop, and got a little studio time from a foundation associated with Waylon Jennings, but the critique of the song he submitted came back scathing. "They couldn't even believe somebody would even submit this as a song. 'There's no hook!'"

In addition to that bruising experience, Keen felt himself being lumped by others' perceptions into Lyle's entourage. "There wasn't anybody to blame," Robert told me. "Lyle got some immediate great success, and I was going the other way. I was trying to make my marriage work, make my life work. Every ounce of me wanted to be in this business, but I could feel it slipping farther and farther away. And I just about quit playing. In Nashville you have to stand in line and be auditioned for an open mic three months later, and then you play three frigging songs? For free? I'd say, 'Jesus, this is nuts.'"

The last straw was when the Keens' car broke down when they were on the way back from a gig in Kansas. On a roadside, a bus swept by Robert and Kathleen bearing his friend Steve Earle and his band. When they got back to Nashville, they found their apartment had been burglarized. They fled Music City and moved to Bandera, where Keen's wife's family lived, and fixed up a house beside a golf course. He felt like he had come back to Texas with his tail between his legs. But reliable gigs at Gruene Hall led to Billy Bob's Texas, he won a contract with the respected North Carolina independent Sugar Hill, and a San Antonio radio station pushed his music hard. Those returns on his psychological investment restored his confidence. He developed a cult following that included great numbers of Texas Aggies. But he knew how he would have to make it, if he made it all. His songs and stage presence defined him as a roadhouse rowdy.

Keen told me once, "I've always been a little embarrassed about my voice. I kind of get by. But I wish I could really sing—for one hour—just to know what it feels like. Somebody like Vince Gill. It must just reverberate in your head." He has learned to stay within the range of his baritone, and his career born on the road proved him worthy of the success that came his way. Coming off those dark days of rejection in Nashville, Keen released a string of sparkling albums that include *West Textures*, *A Bigger Piece of Sky*, *Gringo Honeymoon*, *No. 2 Live Dinner*, and *The Party Never Ends*.

On *Gringo Honeymoon* he hit a masterfully droll key with a song about a dysfunctional Sunbelt family's game attempts to celebrate Christmas. "Merry Christmas from the Family" was a sensation that resonated far beyond Texas. It got him a rave notice in *The New York Times* and a book out of the hullabaloo. In 1997 he returned to that day when Willie Nelson's Picnic left him devastated. The album cover featured a photo of a Ford Mustang, his own, fully ablaze beside another car. He named the album *Picnic*.

But George Strait, Joe Ely, Nanci Griffith, and the Dixie Chicks haven't covered Keen's songs because of his banter. The songs work because they are filled with emotion and tell terrific stories. Free verse is hard to find in songwriting. Keen achieves some measure of that with his talking blues, but songwriters have to deal with rhyme. Look at how effectively Keen does that in "Dreadful Selfish Crime," one of his most engaging songs.

> I had a little place just up the block
> Had me a French girlfriend, I loved the way she talked
> We'd spend our afternoons watching the TV
> Finding things that we could do for free
> When we split up she said, "You don't do enough for me."
> I am guilty of a dreadful selfish crime
> I have robbed myself of all my precious time

Lyle Lovett got what he needed out of Nashville at the start of his career, but he has created his own audience and demonstrated that his tastes are restless and that he's unafraid of moving on. And his writing thrives on sly twists of humor. On that first country album was a song called "God Will."

Some poor guy wonders in apparent self-pity who is the one who puts up with his girl cheating and lying and running loose on the town, yet is eager to forgive her when she comes home. Then the answer: "God will but I won't / That's the difference between God and me."

His 1989 album *Lyle Lovett and His Large Band* underscored the Willie Nelson and *Stardust* premise that a confident artist doesn't get boxed in by what he or she's done before. And again Lovett delivered the humor. That album featured "If I Had a Boat," a whimsical piece of writing about a man who took his pony on a boat. They might be Roy Rogers and Trigger, there's a suggestion of Noah's ark, and the Lone Ranger who gets Tonto to do the dirty work without pay. Then one day Tonto has enough: "Kiss My Ass I've bought a boat / and I'm going out to sea."

That long-ago night in Austin when Lovett fronted for John Prine, I thought he sounded a great deal like Willis Allan Ramsey. It was no coincidence. On Ramsey's twenty-first birthday in 1972 he recorded one almost perfect self-titled album with major studio help from his Shelter Records producer Leon Russell and other famed rockers named Greg Allman, J. J. Cale, and Jim Keltner. Hardly cowed, Ramsey wrote all the songs on that album, and they have since been covered by artists that include David Bromberg, Jimmy Buffett, Waylon Jennings, and Shawn Colvin. Clint Black once remarked that if he were deserted on an island with just five records, one would be *Willis Alan Ramsey.* Austin's enigmatic boy wonder of the seventies still charms and moves club audiences across the country with "Painted Ladies" and "Spider John" and new songs that measure up to the old, but his long-awaited second album has never come together. It's the legend of a phantom.

"I've sung 'Spider John' more times than I could count," Lovett told me with a smile. "I'll never forget my first conversation with Willis. He and his manager had gone to the fanciest restaurant in Bryan. While I interviewed him, he was eating a filet mignon—out of his hand." He went on about his admiration of an inspiration who's now his friend. "I learned so much from Willis. Listening to his record showed me that you don't have to play straight-ahead blues to have blues be a part of your music. He's so soulful."

In 1997 Lovett's seventh album was a double-disc tribute to songwriters who had schooled him, even if they weren't aware of that or of him. The title, *Step Inside This House,* was taken from a song that Lyle's hero Guy Clark wrote and never recorded but played it for him once. Lyle liked the song so much that Clark gave it to him. Other masterful covers included Ramsey's "Sleepwalking," Steven Fromholz's *Texas Trilogy,* Michael Martin Murphey's "West Texas Highway," Townes Van Zandt's "Flyin' Shoes," David Rodriguez's "Ballad of the Snow Leopard and the Tanqueray Cowboy," and Robert Earl Keen's "Rollin' By."

In 1988, Keen was in Nashville to work on his third album, *West Textures.* The producer of Townes Van Zandt and Nanci Griffith had agreed to work with him, but on a tight ration of studio time. The producer suggested postponing the record's release by saying, "I don't think we have a song to hang our hat on here."

Keen was frightened because he was just about broke. He recalled saying, "Listen, I've got this song that I wrote a few verses for a few months ago. I think if you just give me until Sunday, I'll figure it out. If you like it then, we'll go on. Is that a deal? Otherwise you can cancel it."

He said, "The Sonny and Sherry characters are based on real characters that just couldn't stay out of trouble. And they just, no matter what happened, no matter what fortune fell on them, they would screw that up. That's where it started from." Still, those characters hadn't delivered him but a few verses. Fear and the absolute deadline forced him to find out where his now-fictional characters would wind up. "The Road Goes On Forever" closed that deal with the producer and it became his anthem, signature song. He would joke, "If I ended up in Branson, Missouri, I'd play it five times a day."

It begins with the small-town waitress named Sherry in a beer joint where a charismatic loser and small-time dope dealer named Sonny is hanging out. Some drunk makes a grab up Sherry's skirt.

> Sonny took his pool cue laid the drunk out on the floor
> Stuffed a dollar in her tip jar and walked on out the door
> She's runnin' right behind him reachin' for his hand
> The road goes on forever and the party never ends

The story line was a latter-day takeoff on Bonnie and Clyde. But in this version she keeps the money and drives a new Mercedes in the same nowhere town. "Sonny's going to the chair."

It's hard to think of this pair of songwriters as graybeards of Texas music. But there it is at this writing—Keen was 59 and Lovett was 57. In 2003 Lovett's album *My Baby Don't Tolerate* was one of his strongest and was a good-natured return to honky-tonk country, with a bit of gospel mixed in. The same year, he also released *Smile: Songs from the Movies*. On "Moritat (Mack the Knife)," he sounded more like Chet Baker than Bobby Darin. Again it was about the words, and people who wrote them, not just the melodies. The covers included "Blue Skies" by Irving Berlin, "Summer Wind" by Heinz Meier, "What'd I Say" by Ray Charles, "Straighten Up and Fly Right" by Nat King Cole and Irving Mills, and "Pass Me Not," by the great gospel songwriters Fanny J. Crosby and W. H. Doane.

Lovett has won four Grammy Awards, including Best Country Album for *The Road to Ensenada* and Best Pop Vocal Collaboration for "Funny How Time Slips Away" with the stylist Al Green. Every year he appears at the Frederik Meijer Garden and Sculpture Park in Grand Rapids, Michigan, recently with a fourteen-piece band that included a cellist and fiddle player and two horn players who are veterans of the Muscle Shoals burst of rhythm-and-blues inspiration. He has been honored as Doctor of Humane Letters from the University of Houston and as a Distinguished Alumnus from Texas A&M University. He was a favorite actor of the late film director Robert Altman and, of course, for a while was married to a prominent movie star. He keeps a somewhat lower profile now, though he helped perform a rousing gospel show at the Obama White House.

Keen has released eighteen full-length albums and in 2012 was inducted with Lovett and the late Townes Van Zandt into the Texas Heritage Songwriters Hall of Fame. His most recent release goes back to that front porch in College Station, and the music that got him started. On opening the package of his 2015 album, *Happy Prisoner: The Bluegrass Sessions*, you're offered a short essay titled "Why Bluegrass?" Keen explains in a short essay, "I've been lucky. My lifelong love of bluegrass taught me how to feel music as well as hear it. I've spent countless hours banging out fiddle tunes and murder ballads with rank strangers. We never missed a beat, because we spoke only bluegrass." Keen not only speaks fluent bluegrass, he knows the bluegrass songbook and knows what he's after: "Hot Corn, Cold Corn" by Lester Flatt and Earl Scruggs, "Long Black Veil" by Danny Dill and Marijohn Wilkin, "White Dove" by Carter Stanley of the Stanley Brothers, and the bluegrass-hillbilly classic "T for Texas" by Jimmie Rodgers. Helping out Robert Earl Keen with the high harmonies on the last tune was his old friend Lyle Lovett.

It's about hearing and knowing good songs—most of the time their own but also with respect for someone else's—and doing their best to sing and arrange them right. They're having fun these days, and they've earned it.

VIGNETTE—WALT WILKINS: SPIRITUALITY AND GENEROSITY

Craig Clifford (interview with Tim Jones)

Somehow it seemed appropriate to see Walt Wilkins through the eyes of someone who has experienced the generosity of his spirit, both in his songs and in his willingness to give of himself to others, especially to young songwriters. When Tim's son Buck headed off to Nashville to try to make it as a songwriter and a performer, Walt took him under his wing and co-produced his debut album, *Lucky Star*, bringing in a number of major musicians to back him. On Saint Patrick's Day in 2007, Buck was killed in a tragic accident on the way from Nashville to play a private party in Dublin, Texas. Walt helped to organize several benefit concerts to provide for Buck's wife and infant child. For Tim Jones the spirituality and generosity that he finds in Walt's music is a reminder of the role that Walt Wilkins played in his son's life.

CC: How did you get into Walt Wilkins's music?

TJ: My son Buck had driven over from Nashville, and he said that Walt had invited him to come play with him at a show he was doing at a little place on Interstate 35 called the Roadrunner, a little *turista* curio shop and diner. It's this outdoor venue, it's April the 24, the wind's blowing, it's a little cool, and other than Walt's parents, me, my wife Linda, and my two friends who'd driven up from Belton, the only audience he had was a pen full of guineas. For years Walt talked about how he was playing somewhere down around Abbott for a pen full of guineas while his friend Pat Green was playing for sixteen thousand people in Fort Worth.

That was my first getting to know Walt as a performer, but I was blown away by his songs. The next day we went to the White Elephant, where he and Sam Baker and Brandon Rhyder were doing a song swap, and he invited my son to come along and be there. And Walt had a habit of doing this, I started learning. If he had a young person, a young musician he had taken an interest in, somebody he had worked with, he made sure they knew where he was going to be playing, and once he got a chance he would get them up on stage and let them perform a song or two. And that's the way Walt is. He's just a very generous human being.

CC: I only know Walt through his music, and that generous spirit certainly comes out in his music, but the first thing you hear from anyone who knows him is how generous he is.

TJ: As I got to know Walt, as I told friends of mine, to know Walt Wilkins is to learn to love Walt Wilkins. He is probably one of the most genuine, warm-hearted people I've known.

CC: How would you characterize his music?

TJ: He's a great storyteller. He's in that school of younger artists who went to Nashville to follow in the footsteps of Guy Clark. The thing that I've learned about Walt, he's a very spiritual person, and it's reflected in a lot of the music that he sings. He refers to higher beings, and he refers to a very spiritual type of belief. I've talked to him about being religious, and he says, "I'm not religious." And I asked him about church, and he said, "I don't go to church." My friend John Hollinger, who used to be a DJ in Stephenville, has often said, once you've heard Walt Wilkins sing you've been to church.

Look at the song "Poetry" that Pat Green made a hit. There's an area in there where he talks about how "the clouds make rain, the ocean makes sand, the earth breathes fire, and lava makes land." And there's this little quiet line, "Of course we were created."

CC: I like the way he embraces a kind of ultimate mystery to things, when he says "Just one thing is clear to me, there's always more than what appears to be."

TJ: And in his song "Trains I've Missed," he talks about how he "searched far and wide trying to crawl out of God's hands." But he still, in his own way, comes back to that. He actually went to a seminary for a while, went up north to a seminary and stayed there for a brief period of time, but that wasn't what he was meant to be.

CC: One of the things that distinguishes all of the songwriters that we're including in this book is that they're reflective. They think about life. They think about the different stages of life. Mainstream country right now is, "I want to be eighteen forever." "Trains I Missed" is certainly looking back on life and trying to make sense of it.

TJ: "Trains I Missed" is a very reflective song. Balsam Range has a great bluegrass version of it, and it was the first song of that style to win Song of the Year at the International Bluegrass Music Awards. It was the first time I ever heard at the beginning of a bluegrass song, "Y'all listen to the words."

CC: Another thread that runs throughout our book is the rootedness of these Texas singer-songwriters.

TJ: Walt writes about Texas and Texans, he writes a lot about the Hill Country, but he doesn't write Texas-Texas-beer-beer-Texas-Texas.

CC: It's interesting—you said when he went to Nashville he pretty much saw himself in the Guy Clark school.

TJ: Yes, as a storyteller. Where the stories have meaning and the lyrics really matter. And it didn't necessarily need to be a two-minute-and-thirty-four-second song.

LUCINDA WILLIAMS

POET OF PLACES IN THE HEART

Kathryn Jones

Lucinda Williams emerged from the margins of the music business the way a lot of once-obscure singer-songwriters do—someone else recorded one of her songs and turned it into a big hit. The year was 1988 when her self-titled album included her catchy tune about wanting more, "Passionate Kisses." It won a Grammy for Best Country Song after the more mainstream country artist Mary Chapin Carpenter covered it in 1993. "Passionate Kisses" had a memorable melody and commercial appeal going for it, but the ninth track, "Crescent City," better captured Williams's musical sensibilities and foretold her body of work to come. An homage to New Orleans, where Williams once lived and launched her professional musical career, the song stirs up a gumbo of Cajun-flavored lyrics and Zydeco instrumentation. It also was covered by another, more famous singer-songwriter at the time, Emmylou Harris, on *Cowgirl's Prayer* (1993).

On almost every album since her breakthrough Rough Trade LP *Lucinda Williams*, place plays a major character or hangs as an oozing atmospheric backdrop in the songwriter's lyrics. No other singer-songwriter alive today portrays the South with such a Faulknerian dip of the pen. Her words and melodies conjure images of sultry bayous and creeping kudzu, of drinkers hunched over their bottles at a dark bar in the middle of the day, of slowly spinning fans and perspiration beading on skin. Place springs forth from deep roots, and the best writers use simple, spare language to evoke a sense of place and the emotions connected to it.

Williams peppers her songs with specific references to cities and hamlets, lakes, streets, and other personal markers as settings for her characters— restless young mothers, ghosts of dead lovers, men who do their women wrong, women who get fed up and keep searching for love, drunks who waste away their lives, artists consumed by their demons. Having a sense of place steeped in her soul came naturally. Born in 1953 in Lake Charles, Louisiana, Williams grew up in a world of storytellers and Southern gothic settings. Her father, literature professor and poet Miller Williams, counted writer Flannery O'Connor as a friend and influence and introduced her to the young Lucinda. One of the giants of Southern literature, O'Connor made a lasting impression on the girl, who loved chasing the peacocks on O'Connor's farm. "I discovered her writing when I was sixteen. I understood her completely and she became a hero of mine, and I yearned to write songs the same way she wrote stories," Williams told interviewer Alanna Nash in 2009. She sat in on poetry readings and workshops and listened to poets such as James Dickey who gathered at the Williams home afterward, bouncing around ideas. "No formal education could have ever compared with the richness of the type of 'homeschooling'" she received from her father, her "creative soul mate," Williams said.

The other most significant influence on the budding songwriter was someone Lucinda Williams never met but who shared her last name— Hank Williams Sr. He and the Drifting Cowboys gave a performance at McNeese State College (now University) where Miller Williams was teaching in the early 1950s. After the concert, Miller introduced himself to the singer, and the two went out for a drink. The country music legend left in a Cadillac and Miller never saw him again—Hank Williams would die a few weeks later, on January 1, 1953, in the backseat. Born a few weeks later on January 26, Lucinda inherited her father's love of Hank's music. "Flannery O'Connor's writing and Hank Williams's music explain everything you need to know about me as an artist," Lucinda told Nash after she and her father appeared together in "concert" in 2009—she sang her songs, and Miller read his poems.

In a house that revered language and where her mother, Lucy, played piano, the teenage Lucinda gravitated to music, picking up the guitar and putting her own poetry to music. She also listened to old folk songs by Woody Guthrie and others that mentioned towns and places. Williams traveled more than many children of her generation, living in Baton Rouge, New Orleans, Jackson, Mexico City, and Santiago, Chile, when her father was a visiting professor, and in Fayetteville, Arkansas. She went to college for a while, but dropped out, knowing she wanted to write and sing songs. After launching her career as a folksinger in New Orleans, she moved to Austin in 1974 and played in the state music capital and in Houston at a time when Lyle Lovett and Nanci Griffith were just getting started. Her first album, *Ramblin'*, released on vinyl by Folkways Records in 1979, contained covers of classic country, folk, and blues tunes by her hero Hank Williams, Robert Johnson, Memphis Minnie, and others, but it didn't make much of a blip on the musical radar screen. For her next effort, 1980's *Happy Woman Blues*, Williams determined to write all her own songs. Thus began her travelogue style of writing with the Cajun-country song "Lafayette": "We danced all night long to a sweet Cajun song / drinkin' and jivin' 'til dawn, I could dance on and on / doin' a two-step in my sweet Lafayette." The emotional poetry that would come to define her as a songwriter also emerged in the album's title number. So did the mention of cars, one of her favorite metaphors:

> Tryin' hard to be a happy woman
> But sometimes life just overcomes me
> Everyday I'm workin' just to pay my dues
> Lay down at night, my mind is so confused
> Goin' down south with the New York City blues
> Gotta hit the road before I blow a fuse
> I might buy me a Cadillac or a Chevrolet
> I don't care what model as long as it takes me away

Women folksingers of the day such as Joan Baez and Judy Collins were blessed with lilting, strong voices and depth of range, tone, and pitch. Williams knew her voice had limitations—one reviewer for the BBC described it as "pitched somewhere between Tom Petty and Courtney Love." Williams admitted it took a while for her to come to terms with her unique voice, which critics described as "ragged," "raw," "gorgeously flawed," "twangy," and "idiosyncratic," a back-handed compliment, to be sure. Williams herself drew a comparison with Dylan. People listened to his songs because they were well written and compelling, even though many didn't care for his voice. She decided she was going to become the female Bob Dylan, and when she wrote songs, she fit the melodies to her voice and range.

The rambling kind herself, Williams in 1984 moved from Austin to Los Angeles, got married, then divorced, took voice lessons, and poured her raw energy into the personal songs on her mostly well-written self-titled album, now recognized as a classic. Tom Petty and the Heartbreakers covered "Changed the Locks" for the 1996 *She's the One* soundtrack album (the title changed to "Change the Locks"), and Patty Loveless covered "The Night's Too Long" in 1990. Many years later, in a 2013 interview with *The Austin Chronicle*'s Margaret Moser, Williams revealed that Loveless's label wouldn't release her cover as a single because of its sexual lyrics that mentioned leather, sweat, and roughness. While her songwriting stood out on the album, music label execs couldn't categorize her music—it crossed too many borders between folk, country, rock, and blues, and the term "Americana" didn't exist yet. "Sony LA said it was too country, and Sony Nashville said it was too rock for country," Williams told Moser, one of the state's most respected music journalists who retired in 2014 after a battle with cancer. "So it literally fell between the cracks. It took a punk label out of England not to care. They got hold of the demos, asking me if I wanted to make a record, and the rest is history."

Williams again showed her strength as a songwriter on her next album, *Sweet Old World*, released in 1992. Emmylou Harris covered a song—the title cut—for her 1995 album, *Wrecking Ball*. Two songs on *Sweet Old World* revolved around place. "Pineola" recounts the story of a young man who shoots himself, leaving behind stunned loved ones: "Born and raised in Pineola / His mama believed in the Pentecost / She got the preacher to say some words / So his soul wouldn't be lost." (Moser, who earned a reputation for recognizing musical talent early, recalled that the first time she heard Williams sing "Pineola," she knew the singer-songwriter had "the magic"). "Memphis Pearl" hijacks the heart with a tale of a young woman who marries a man who "was good to her when he wasn't drunk," and thought she'd be buying "dresses that zip up the side / And wear red lipstick, have a nice car to drive." Instead, she lives on the street, bounces a baby on her knee, and hopes things will be different someday.

Still the nomad, Williams moved back to Austin, decided it had lost its rough-around-the edges charm, then returned to Nashville. Many fans still closely identify her with Texas even though she's not a native; she's a regular at the annual Austin Music Awards during the South by Southwest music festival and counts many Texas musicians and songwriters as inspirations—Townes Van Zandt and Blaze Foley, to name a few. The devoted listening base she cultivated with her early albums looked forward to her next release and had to wait six years. Much ink was devoted to the delay, which was due partly to Williams's perfectionist tendencies—she wanted a consciously unproduced sound, even though it was the most produced and polished album she had done to date. Williams rejected takes, even discarded entire songs, and butted heads with some of her musicians and guest artists on the album. But she later explained that she spent two years in the studio on the songs and the release date kept moving because of record company maneuverings. When *Car Wheels on a Gravel Road* finally rolled out in 1998, Williams cemented her reputation as a gutsy, independent singer-songwriter melding folk, country, and rock. *Car Wheels on a Gravel Road* won a Grammy for Best Contemporary Folk Album and went gold within a year.

As the title implies, *Car Wheels on a Gravel Road* tells stories about journeys, detours, and destinations of the heart. The thirteen songs on the disc contained more than a dozen references to Southern places. Three songs—"Lake Charles," "Greenville," with Emmylou Harris singing harmony, and "Jackson"—were named for cities that served as settings for characters. "Lake Charles," one of the most haunting and autobiographical pieces on the album, was about Williams's former boyfriend, Louisiana musician Clyde J. Woodward, who died years after they split up:

> He had a reason to get back to Lake Charles
> He used to talk about it
> He'd just go on and on
> He always said Louisiana
> Was where he felt at home

Moser had become good friends with Woodward and held his hand when he died of cirrhosis of the liver in an Austin hospital. Williams was on a plane en route to see Woodward and didn't make it in time. She tells his story in her lyrics: Even though he was "born in Nacogdoches / that's in east

Texas not far from the border," he "liked to tell everybody / He was from Lake Charles." She recalls in the song how they would drive through Lafayette and Baton Rouge "in a yellow El Camino / Listening to Howling Wolf." The chorus haunts with its stripped-to-the-bone description of death: "Did an angel whisper in your ear / And hold you close, take away your fear / In those long last moments." After Williams performed the emotional song at Antone's in Austin in 1999, Moser recalled she went backstage, put her arms around Lucinda, and "held her like a child."

On one of the album's best tracks, "Jackson," the singer-narrator travels to Jackson via Lafayette, Baton Rouge, and Vicksburg, and observes in each town, "I don't think I'll miss you much." Williams told Brian T. Atkinson, author of a book about the influence of Townes Van Zandt, that the late songwriter had "closely influenced" the song and that she liked lyrics that were "dark and brave." That certainly describes the words on the track "Joy," when Williams sings about a lover who took her joy and vows to go to all the way to West Memphis and Slidell to get it back. She practically spits out the lines with their undercurrent of anger. Besides the title track, another song, "Metal Firecracker," used a vehicle—in this case, a tour bus—to write about lost love: "Once we rode together in a metal firecracker / You told me I was your queen / You told me I was your biker / You told me I was everything." Later, after thinking nothing could go wrong and it does, comes the pleading chorus: "All I ask / Don't tell anybody the secrets I told you." Williams later said in introducing the song at a concert that the song was inspired by one of her "bass player boyfriends" who wanted to keep the relationship low-profile while touring, then dumped her.

Ever the stickler for detail, Williams asked her father to read her lyrics to songs before the album's release, and he had a suggestion for the ballad "Drunken Angel," based on the life and death of Austin songwriter Blaze Foley. One of the most poetic songs on the album, it's dark and bleak, as was Foley's work. Shot to death in 1989 by the son of a friend, Foley rose to cult figure status: "Followers would cling to you / Hang around just to meet you / Some threw roses at your feet / And watch you pass out on the street." Williams's lyrics nailed the self-destructive nature of an artist undermined by demons:

> Some kind of savior singing the blues
> A derelict in your duct tape shoes
> Your orphan clothes and your long dark hair
> Looking like you didn't care
> Drunken Angel

Williams originally wrote the opening line of the song's last stanza, "Blood spilled out from a hole in your heart." Her father suggested she change it to "Blood spilled out from *the* hole in your heart," she recalled in the Nash interview. Her reaction: "Brilliant!" She made the change, of course.

After toiling for twenty years as a singer-songwriter, Williams finally found commercial and critical success after *Car Wheels*, touring solo and as an opening act for Dylan and Van Morrison. Three years went by before Williams released her next album, *Essence*, in 2001. It touched on similar themes of derailed relationships, unsatisfied desires, and personal angst, with her trademark spare lyrics. The sorrowful, emotion-laden songs showed her voice to its best advantage. Reviewers described it as "honest," "naked," "vulnerable," "wrought with feeling," "rough," "husky," and even "sexy." A sense of place didn't come through as strongly on the meditative *Essence* as it did on *Car Wheels*, with the notable exception of "Bus to Baton Rouge." Williams sings of returning to a house on Belmont Avenue "to see if camellias were in bloom" and the sweet honeysuckle whose vines were "switches when we were bad." Details paint a picture: "Company couch covered in plastic / Books about being saved / The dining room table nobody ate at / The piano nobody played." Ghosts of the past follow "wherever I go / I'll never be free from these chains inside / Hidden deep down in my soul."

In 2002, *TIME* magazine named Williams the best songwriter in America. Now that she was a star, the pressure was on Williams to turn out albums every two years. Her seventh album, *World Without Tears*, continued the Americana, alternative, folk-rock vibe with the upbeat "Righteously," and a particularly brutal piece about being discarded by a lover, "Those Three Days." This time, the places that leant their names to two track titles weren't in the South, but were places that still resonated with Williams and reflected her life. She had grown bored with Nashville and had moved back to Los Angeles. Not a single song on the album mentioned a Southern place; most of the songs once again dovetailed with the title—the universal inability to live in a world without tears. Trying to forget a lost love by driving up the California coast forms the plot of one of the most memorable tunes on the album, "Ventura." The chorus expresses a litany of wants: "I wanna watch the ocean bend / The edges of the sun, then / I wanna get swallowed up / In an ocean of love." But the verses cut to the quick about trying to purge the pain:

Stand in the shower
Clean this dirty mess
Give me back my power
And drown this unholiness
Lean over the toilet bowl

And throw up my confession
Cleanse my soul
Of this hidden obsession

Even though the song was set in California, Williams drawled out the words, slurring consonants and elongating vowels, and wore a Western-style hat when performing it live. She was living in LA, but her sound was still in the other La.—Louisiana. Likewise, "Minneapolis" also sets heartache against the backdrop of a city with images of winter written from a Southerner's perspective:

I've been waiting for you to come back since you left Minneapolis
Snow covers the street lamps and the windowsills
The building and the brittle crooked trees
Dead leaves of December, thin-skinned and splintered
Never gotten used to this bitter winter

After recording an album of songs performed live, *Live @ the Fillmore* (2005), Williams named an entire album after a place, *West*. Released in 2007, it received some of the best—and worst—reviews since *Car Wheels on a Gravel Road*. "Dreary, deeply disappointing" and "'roots' music in only the most general sense," Stephen M. Deunser wrote on Pitchfork.com. But *Vanity Fair* called it "the record of a lifetime," and Chris Jones of the BBC decreed *West* "the 'mature but hip' album that we've all been waiting for." Producer Hal Willner went back to Williams's stripped-down sound with her longtime guitarist, Doug Pettibone, aided by jazz guitarist Bill Frisell and drummer Jim Keltner. The cover featured a pensive Williams looking down and holding her signature hat while a road lined with telephone poles ran off into the distance. Change and hope, which the West has symbolized since the days of the great frontier, took root in Williams's lyrics. Her mother, Lucy Morgan, had died, and Williams had suffered through another turbulent breakup. Once again, Williams lived the life she sang about. The album felt cohesive, organized around the subjects of death, depression, and loneliness, but also redemption. One of the most painful and poetic songs, "Mama You Sweet," presses the exposed nerve of anyone who's lost a beloved relative:

There's that ocean in my spirit
It cries through my lips
It scars my heart
And it's burning on my hips

An ocean becomes heavy
And tries to push its way out of the ancient eye
And the memory is my mouth

Southern places also returned on the album—Tupelo, Birmingham, and Gainesville. Williams, in an interview with *Billboard*, described the album as coming "full circle, like I've come through a metamorphosis." The song "Unsuffer Me" sounded like a plea for the chrysalis-to-a-butterfly transformation of spirit:

Unlock my love
And set me free
Come fill me up
With ecstasy

Surround my heartbeat
With your fingertips
Unbound my feet
Untie my wrists

Love, the source of so much of Williams's pain and personal lyrics, also had come full circle. Williams had met and fallen in love with Tom Overby, a lanky Minnesotan and former music executive. By 2008 they were engaged and in 2009 married on stage in Minneapolis, where Williams was performing and where she once set one of her sad love songs. The heartbreak songs didn't disappear after Williams's marriage, but the lyrics on her next albums, *Little Honey* and *Blessed*, sounded more content. Williams for years had said that writing about unrequited love was easier, so the "happier" songs like "Honey Bee," "Sweet Love," and "Tears of Joy" on the later albums challenged her to write lyrics that didn't sink into sentimentality:

Uprooted and restless
I paid the cost
I've been a mess
Misguided and lost
But I've been so blessed
Since our paths have crossed
That's why I'm crying tears of joy

Some reporters pissed off Williams by asking if she could still write good songs now that she was happy. But Williams told Moser she felt more prolific and inspired than ever because she could focus more of her energy on writing songs. "Look, I love Tom," she said, "but that doesn't mean I don't have my bad days or feel sad or think about my mother's death or my brother's mental illness or my sister's physical and mental illness or the estrangement of them. Come on."

In 2012 and 2013 Williams toured the United States, accompanied only by Pettibone. She returned to Austin in January 2013 to perform at the Paramount Theatre. The barebones sound and intimate setting spotlighted Williams's voice and lyrics. She dedicated "Lake Charles" to Moser that night. The South stays with her wherever she lives. But the place she writes about best turns out to be the one inside—the place in the heart that, despite getting stomped in the dust over and over, keeps searching, yearning, and never surrenders.

RODNEY CROWELL

LOOKING INWARD, LOOKING OUTWARD

John T. Davis

It may be that Rodney Crowell figured he'd already done the hat trick.

Beginning with his move from Houston to Nashville in August of 1972, he'd been a student of, and then a peer to, the most acclaimed ex-pat Texas songwriters of the day: Townes Van Zandt, Guy Clark, and Mickey Newbury.

He'd evolved into a highly sought after songwriter; his chart-topping songs had been cut by Emmylou Harris, future father-in-law Johnny Cash, Willie Nelson, Tim McGraw, Jerry Jeff Walker, Etta James, Bob Seger, Jimmy Buffett, Waylon Jennings, Keith Urban, Andy Williams (!), and a host of others. Harris paid him a supreme compliment by recruiting him into her legendary Hot Band in 1975. Crowell would sing harmony, write songs, and tour with Harris for the next two years as his star ascended and his songwriting chops matured.

He'd reaped kudos for his intuitive, simpatico skills as a producer, principally with Rosanne Cash (whom he would marry in 1979; they later divorced), and also Guy Clark, Johnny Cash, actress Sissy Spacek, Jim Lauderdale, Lari White, Elizabeth Cook, and, of course, his own albums.

Then, in 1988, he stunned the world of mainstream country by releasing his fifth solo album, *Diamonds & Dirt*, that generated a then-unprecedented string of five No. 1 singles. Of the album, Allmusic.com reviewer Thom Jurek said, "For contemporary country fans, this disc is such an important part of the development of modern music that it has virtually influenced everything that's come after it, making it impossible to ignore." It was the high-water mark (so far) of his commercial career and marked a significant signpost at the juncture where the rootsy, songwriter-centric Americana back road took leave of the commercial Nashville autobahn.

He is a multiple Grammy winner and a member of the Nashville Songwriter's Hall of Fame, with enough honoraria, plaques, and scrolls to stock a decent-sized pawnshop. Hell, he even penned one of the best musician's memoirs in recent memory, his 2011 volume *Chinaberry Sidewalks*, an autobiography-with-the-bark-off that details his growing up in hardscrabble, blue-collar Houston with a set of parents that Tennessee Williams might have dreamed up.

So if you didn't know him, you might have forgiven Crowell for choosing to do the Big Chill—pen a hit for one Nashville chart-topper in the morning, produce a track for another star in the afternoon, and then hold down the Songwriters' Emeritus chair at a guitar pull at some Nashville showcase club in the evening.

Rather, he did anything but.

His professional bona fides well assured, Crowell turned aside from the well-trodden commercial path and after taking a multi-year sabbatical, he virtually re-invented himself as a songwriter and storyteller.

Beginning in 2001, six years after his most recent release, he recorded a triptych of albums—*The Houston Kid, Fate's Right Hand*, and *The Outsider*—that were not only breathtakingly revealing in their intimacy and candor, but also a riveting examination of how a questing soul comes to grips with, variously, his past, his intimates, his community, and his place in the world.

That sounds like a ponderous set of baggage, but it's not. Crowell's musical touch is, as it ever has been, unfailing. His deft use of country, rock, blues, bluegrass, folk, and even jazz and spoken word all combine to keep the songs light on their feet melodically. Once heard, songs like "Earthbound," "Why Don't We Talk About It," and "Say You Love Me" take up permanent residence in the listener's ear. These and others are radio hits that just don't know it.

These albums and songs are the sound of Crowell getting his head on straight. "Once I had a little taste of radio success, I started making music for 'them,'" he told *Harp* magazine around the time of the release of *The Outsider* in 2005. "And that's (putting) the cart way before the horse. Now I make records for me. If I get it right for me, it's usually right for an audience of some kind."

That being said, he admitted in the same interview, "Talking about song-writing is like doing card tricks on the radio. . . . If you can explain it, it ain't it."

Or, as a wise man once said, everything that's not a mystery is just guesswork.

The three albums, released over a span from 2001 to 2005, are rooted in scrupulous self-examination. One might almost call it auto-dissection. Briefly stated, *The Houston Kid* is a look at Crowell's roots and origins, what molded and scarred him; *Fate's Right Hand* is a meditation on mortality, on self, on fear, and on letting go (one standout tune is titled "Time To Go Inward"); *The Outsider*, several of its songs written from an expatriate's point of view, takes a look at the challenge of keeping a moral center in a world grown increasingly amoral and ethically fungible. What is a person's responsibility to a larger community, and how does one find his place in it? Time to go outward, you might say.

It wasn't as though he had not touched on darkness, anger, or mature, complex emotions before. He'd done both, as far back as "Til I Gain Control Again," "I Ain't Living Long Like This," and "Leaving Louisiana in the Broad Daylight." But the three albums under examination here represent a sustained, almost novelistic examination of one life and how it fits into physical, emotional, and spiritual planes.

Crowell, who took several years off from the professional treadmill to concentrate on fatherhood, may have on some level created this body of work for his children—here's your dad, warts and all.

The passing of his own parents (his father J. W. died in 1989, his mother Cauzette in 1998) seems to have been the spark that ignited both the songs on *The Houston Kid* and his memoir of growing up in Houston, *Chinaberry Sidewalks*.

"I grieved over the loss of my mother much longer than I had for my father," he wrote. "I began to make peace with the possibility that this sorrow would never go away. Out of that reconciliation came the notion that the most fitting tribute to my mother, and indeed my father, would be to put the sadness to better use."

God knows he had enough to work with. His father was a blue-collar worker who moonlighted as a honky-tonk bandleader (Rodney played drums in his daddy's band, the Rhythmaires, when he was eleven). "He was an enigma, and money was an enigma to him," Crowell told a radio interviewer. "He could never keep it in his pocket."

As he recounts in the book and in songs like "The Rock of My Soul" and "Topsy Turvy," whatever inner furies and frustrations were liberated by the hours his father spent marinating in some local icehouse were apt to be vented on his wife—a fervent Pentecostal Holy Roller who also suffered from epilepsy—and son. "Bustin' out the windows with a baseball bat," he sings in "Topsy Turvy," "Daddy's gone as crazy as an outhouse rat / Momma's on the sofa with a big black eye / I cross my heart and tell myself I hope they die."

Both on record and on the page, it's raw and compelling storytelling, unflinching and stark. Even the album's package is steeped in somber tones. For once, the CD cover doesn't play on Crowell's silver-tongued-devil good looks. He is photographed in shadow, pensive and almost unrecognizable. Imprinted on the disc itself is the ominous silhouette of a hurricane, much like the one that did a number on the Crowell family in 1961.

Crowell idolized his father despite his violence and resented his mother for not standing up to him. Yet Rodney's parents lived together and loved one another all their lives, and their offspring—a father himself by now—found a genuine nobility at the heart of their struggling, often-contentious relationship. "I was able to emerge from the dark forest of an angry heart into the light of love that will forever exist between my parents and me," he wrote.

Fate's Right Hand, released a couple of years after *The Houston Kid*, finds Crowell looking in the mirror and wrestling with his parents' legacy—the man that he's become—and the inbred angers and self-imposed cages that accompany that man. It's not necessarily a pretty picture, as the self-loathing "The Man in Me" makes clear: "There's a man in me / He's cold and he's hard / He's got an eye for deception / He's always on guard / He's swimming in concrete / Drowning in fear / And he keeps it all locked in his heart."

"Time to go inward," he sings in the song of the same title. "Would you believe that I'm afraid / To stare down the barrels of the choices I've made?"

And in "Preachin' to the Choir": "My self-importance is a god-forsaken bore / I aim for heaven but I wind up on the floor."

And yet there is an enormous, liberating sense of grace and forgiveness that permeates the album. In confronting and forgiving his own fears, cutting himself loose from old resentments, tearing open the cages he's locked himself inside—in short, by letting go—Crowell makes his way towards a vision of peace and self-acceptance that is buoyant.

It's a journey, as he makes clear in the album's opening track, "Still Learning How to Fly": "My ragged old heart's been blessed / With so much more than meets the eye / I've got a past I won't soon forget / You ain't seen nothing yet / I'm still learning how to fly."

In the bouncing, bluegrass-flavored "Earthbound," he recalls, "Last night's conversation with a real good friend of mine drinkin' wine, wine, wine / Fifty years of livin' and your worst mistakes forgiven takes time, time, time."

Even a chance encounter can offer a glimpse of a bigger truth. Encountering a homeless man on a freezing New York street corner, Crowell offers him his coat (a genuine incident, as he recounts in an interview). No, the man replies, in "Ridin' Out the Storm," "I don't need pity for these choices are my own."

"A lot of times," Crowell told a reporter for the *Chicago Sun-Times*, "I write really for the purpose of understanding who I am."

Disappointment and loss, as recounted in "Adam's Song" and "This Too Will Pass," are inevitable, but can lead to acceptance and, way down the line, a hard-won peace.

Fate's Right Hand, said Crowell, "is an attempt to articulate the day-to-day task of dealing with the uncertainty of a clouded future and the sorrow of a botched past. . . . In the end, adulthood is the complex matter of figuring out who and what to put our your faith in."

According to Crowell, the songs for *The Outsider* were penned during the presidential election year of 2004. Crowell spent a good deal of the time touring overseas where President George W. Bush and the Iraq War were manifestly unpopular.

Touring with "the basic Beatles line-up" of bass, drums, and two guitars, many of the songs on the album were conceived as gritty, stripped-down snapshots of a world teetering on its axis, as the singer struggles to fashion the proper response to shifting political and emotional ties.

That's a tall order for the narrator of the opening tune, the ballsy rocker "Say You Love Me," who confesses, "There was a good time had by all accounts / We were drinking to you in tall amounts," before going on to demand fealty from his lover; "Say you love me . . . Say it!" (Contrary to the other songs on the album, Crowell recorded "Say You Love Me" a decade earlier on his album, *Jewel of the South*).

What follows is one of the album's standouts, the bile-drenched sing-along "The Obscenity Prayer," in which Crowell dons the mask of the ugliest of "ugly Americans," the smug entitled asshole who would toss his mother to the wolves for a hedge fund tip or another line of cocaine.

"I could learn to love the life I lead / Just don't take away the things I need," Crowell sings before adding piously, "Give to me my Aspen winter

/ Sorry 'bout the World Trade Center." God help yourself, before the track is over, you're joining in on the "Gimme, gimme, gimme" chorus. It's a car wreck of a song—there's blood everywhere, but you can't look away.

"Don't Get Me Started" brims with aggression too, with two drunks arguing politics in some smoky pub with, doubtless, a rugby game blaring on the telly. "We ran into trouble scamming for oil / The whole Middle East is coming to a boil. . . . Don't get me started / I came into this bar to unwind / Don't get me started / I'll like as not speak my mind." Crowell—the outsider—looks in vain for nuance when everyone is talking in bumper stickers.

"I was kind of processing some anger, too," said Crowell in the press kit that accompanied review copies of the album. "I was in Europe. I was pissed off. Most of these songs were written in the election year, and I was not happy with what I was seeing. My rule of thumb is always show-don't-tell. I don't think it will ever be my style to take a big mallet and just slam it, bust the window out with it. I have to get there in a more subtle way."

Then there's the other side of the expatriate—the romantic, timeless, out-of-place feeling that Crowell evokes on the luminously beautiful "Glasgow Girl," where the vocalist finds himself out on the Ring Road past midnight, bound for the girl with "skin like milk, hair like silk, and eyes of cobalt pearl." Proof, if any were needed, that Crowell still has many a classic love song up his sleeve.

Unusual for Crowell, he pulls out a cover song, a duet rendition with Emmylou Harris of Bob Dylan's "Shelter From the Storm," an apt inclusion, given the turbulent nature of much of the album.

There's another tip of the hat to the master in the wry and sorrowful "Beautiful Despair (for James)": "Beautiful despair is hearing Dylan when you're drunk at 3 a.m. / Knowing that the chances are no matter what you'll never write like him."

In the end, Crowell reacts to the displacement and turbulence of the world he explores in *The Outsider* with a certain stoic acceptance and a sort of rigorous inner discipline. "In silence lie the keys to how we grow," he sings in one of the album's centerpieces, "Dancin' Circles 'Round the Sun (Epictetus Speaks)."

Bristling with internal rhymes and bouncing along on a twining guitar line and rubbery bass, Crowell paraphrases the first-century Greek philosopher who taught that suffering occurs from trying to control what is uncontrollable: "Disregard what don't concern you don't let disappointment turn you. . . . Know what you can and can't control don't let envy take a toll / It's nothing more than weather passing through. . . . And when the right thing has been done, you'll be dancin' circles round the sun."

Like so much of the music on these three albums, "Dancin' Circles 'Round the Sun" is the sound of an artist's journey of discovery.

Crowell has said he does his best to stay out of a song's way. "Songs are better when they tell me what they want to be," he told a CMT interviewer. "I just listen. I'm like a court reporter when I just listen to what they want to be, and I write them down."

Far from being a hand's off approach, Crowell's methodology demands a fierce, even ruthless self-discipline. In the same interview, Crowell was asked what he would tell an aspiring songwriter. He answered with the precise strokes of a surgeon wielding a scalpel: "I think the first thing you have to do is remove your own mental blocks," he told the imaginary wannabe, who decried the closed nature of the music business.

> Even believing it's hard to get in is a prison of the mind. I think the first thing you have to do is figure out how to dismantle the thought behind that. The next thing you have to do is evaluate your work for what it really is. Is your work really up to a par that is deserving? . . . Does it have a relevance that would work in the music entertainment field?
>
> And then after that, if you can really be honest with yourself about your own mental blocks and the quality of your work, I guarantee that people who are running publishing houses and record companies are wide open to making money. So get rid of your own mental blocks and really make sure your work is relevant in the world—and then go do it.

Crowell did not, of course, rest on his laurels after the sustained critical hosannas that greeted *The Houston Kid*, *Fate's Right Hand*, and *The Outsider*.

He went on to take a tough look at the sexes and the role of women in society in 2008's *Sex and Gasoline*. Four years later, he created an all-star suite of songs, *Kin*, cowritten with Texas poet and writer Mary Karr. In 2013, he reunited with his lifelong friend Emmylou Harris to record an album of duets, *Old Yellow Moon*, which won a Grammy for Best Americana Album. In the spring of 2014 he released his latest solo effort, *Tarpaper Sky*. Last year, he and Harris released a second duet album, *The Traveling Kind*.

In short, Crowell's creative wellspring seems to be flowing undiminished. His body of work continues to grow, and glow, with undimmed luster and nuance.

But in one extraordinary five-year span, Rodney Crowell reached into unforeseen places and took listeners on an extraordinary journey. As he sang in one of the most yearning and revelatory songs on *The Houston Kid*: "Yes, I've had my trouble trying to start all over / No, I didn't give it all I could / Now I get a chance to know what love can heal / And if you want to know the feeling—Why don't we talk about it now?"

VIGNETTE—SAM BAKER

SHORT STORIES IN SONG

Robert Earl Hardy

Sam Baker stands center stage with acoustic guitar, ruggedly hand-some, quietly charismatic. His voice like fine-grain sandpaper, he sings speech-like, with flat West Texas inflection. He finger-picks sparsely but decisively. He writes sparsely but decisively. After a verse of "Iron," I know the main character. After two, I know his wife, their situation. I'm drawn in by nuances, details. With epigrammatic economy, Baker spins an emotionally deep, organically complex story. Songs rarely operate like this. The analogy is not poetry, but literature—the short story.

Baker cites Faulkner and Hemingway as influences—and Dylan, Clark, and Van Zandt. I think of Cormac McCarthy.

The music's simplicity contributes to the literary effect, especially Baker's use of traditional melodies and refrains. Familiar pieces are integrated into new contexts as if they were always there, vessels filled and refilled with the drama of different characters and situations. The dramatic element is strong—the decisive moment that changes everything.

When Sam's finished, I go over and buy *Mercy*, *Cotton*, and *Pretty World* (he's since released *Say Grace*). Sam signs the CDs—slowly, painstakingly, for several extended, quiet moments—moments I later equate with the econ-omy, precision, and grace of his songwriting. When I listen to the albums I learn about the decisive moment that changed everything for Baker, which he writes about in "Steel" and "Broken Fingers": he was almost killed in a bomb blast on a train in Peru. People around him were killed, including a child. Baker was left mangled, almost deaf, and spent months recovering, relearning how to use his hands, how to speak . . . slowly, painstakingly.

Sparsely and decisively, with rare literary skill and precision, Baker con-veys his experience of humanity, adults confronting adult problems, adult joys and sorrows. Decisive moments change everything—they haunt for life, or they liberate. Actions have consequences.

JAMES MCMURTRY

TOO LONG IN THE WASTELAND

Diana Finlay Hendricks

It's the middle of a November Sunday afternoon, and we're at the Whip In in Austin, Texas. Walking distance from the Travis Heights home of award-winning songwriter and musician James McMurtry. We have a plan. Five questions and an overview of the albums. I have a yellow legal pad, a recorder, and all of his albums. He has a bottle of a California Dolcetto and an order of nachos. Those five questions turn into more than three hours of tangents and rabbit trails leading toward fathers and sons, politics, beer joints, and the American landscape. On the record.

"The simple fact is that James McMurtry may be the truest, fiercest songwriter of his generation."

—STEPHEN KING, *Entertainment Weekly*

Songwriter, guitar player, and sometimes actor James McMurtry has released eleven albums—running the budgetary spectrum from $250,000 major label projects (the three Columbia projects) to $10,000–$15,000 independent projects. His songwriting has remained consistent, clean, clear, fierce, and, yes, ruthless.

If ever a description were to fit a writer, this defines James. He has been called a "Texas-tentialist" by the *Village Voice*. Katherine Cole at *Voice of America* says his songs are "filled with characters so real that you're sure they're going to climb out of the speakers and look you in the eyes." And the critical acclaim grows with each project he releases.

An attempt to focus on all of the material in this Grammy-nominated, multiple award-winning, prolific songwriter's catalog would be impossible to cover in this space. This is instead a quick snapshot of James McMurtry's political songs; a discussion of some of his early influences; and, for those aspiring songwriters who read this book seeking insider secrets, a few tricks of the trade.

James recorded his first album, *Too Long in the Wasteland*, at the age of twenty-seven. A songwriter has a lifetime to write that first album and then has to follow up with more and consistently better material. Through the years, James has managed to do just that. After three albums on Columbia, four on Sugar Hill, two on Compadre, and two on Lightning Rod, he has just signed with a new LA-based label, Complicated Game. He will be fifty-two when his next album hits the streets—almost twice the age he was when *Too Long In The Wasteland* debuted.

Too Long in the Wasteland (Columbia, 1998), produced by John Cougar Mellencamp, introduces James's ambivalent, though sharp-tongued, observations with "Painting By Numbers." The song opens with art teachers preaching the virtues of pastels to inattentive school children, ". . . but it won't hurt your grades / cause you're painting by numbers / connecting the dots / they don't have to tell you / you don't call the shots." From the school children to the grad students to the soldier down in the Canal Zone, he returns to the chorus reminding us that "You're painting by numbers, connecting the dots."

In a nod to his Pulitzer Prize-winning father, novelist Larry McMurtry, the final verse of "Painting By Numbers" comfortably lifts a great line from Larry's first book of essays, *In A Narrow Grave*. The senior McMurtry is describing the filming of the movie *Hud*, based on his first novel, *Horseman, Pass By*. As the cowhands set up the ranching equipment and livestock for the scenes, they regarded the directors and screenwriters and stars with what Larry described as "tolerant incredulity." He quoted one of the cowboys wrangling for the scenes as shrugging and summing up the job, "I'm just working from the shoulders down." James uses that as a hook line in the chorus, "You're painting by numbers / connecting the dots / You work from the neck down / as often as not."

Political songs have come to define McMurtry. He writes about the working class, the middle-American who struggles for every break and is fearful of every change.

His "We Can't Make It Here," from *Childish Things* (Compadre, 2005), spent six weeks at No. 1 on the Americana Music Charts and won the Americana Music Awards for Song of the Year and Album of the Year, respectively. How did it happen?

"Steve Earle's the only one I know who can consistently write a good political song," James says. "The problem with political songs is that you run the risk of writing a sermon instead of a song and nobody's going want to hear it. I got lucky with 'We Can't Make It Here.' It turned out that people did want to hear it. The character was identifiable and a lot of people identified with it."

He added, "I live in Texas and I tend to vote Democratic which means that most of my votes don't count. The only power I had was a record deal and access to the Internet through my label. I finished the song and went in and did an acoustic version and bleeped out the radio-sensitive parts. Then I went to the label (Compadre) and said, 'Can you get this on the Internet as a free download so every station can have it?' And they did. And they got more response than anything I've ever put on a record. So by the time I got around to making the rest of the record it already had some momentum."

No one understood the song better than working-class people in union states. "Like Bangor, Maine," James said. "Stephen King owns a huge classic rock station there, WKIT-FM. He was already a supporter. First, he heard the live version of 'Levelland' [*Live In Aught-Three*, Compadre, 2004] and was playing that. Then he heard 'Choctaw Bingo' and he went and talked to his program director and said 'Can we play this?' The guy said, 'Well, we're in Maine, but I guess we can do it.' You know—it's nine minutes, it's about Oklahoma. Nobody in classic rock anywhere else is going to play that song, but they've got some nerve up there in Bangor. They spun it and everybody liked it."

Then, he recalls, WKIT picked up "We Can't Make It Here." At that time, James explains, Maine had lost more than thirty thousand jobs to outsourcing, which is the main thing the narrator complains about in the song. Maine used to be a major manufacturing state and suddenly all the jobs left. So that song really hit home and lit the phones up.

James offers a rare smile as he recalls, "The closest to a Beatles moment we ever had was when we were playing the Grand Auditorium in Ellsworth, Maine. The promoter was not really quite prepared. He didn't have an adequate PA for the size of the crowd or the size of the room. So it's the closest we ever got to being the Beatles at Shea Stadium. Stephen King comes out and introduces us at that show. We are playing through this PA on sticks and the crowd is yelling louder than we can play—way louder than we can possibly play."

But writing political songs is risky, even for successful, veteran songwriters. James admits, "I got lucky with 'We Can't Make It Here.' It turned out that people *did* want to hear it. I was not so lucky with 'Cheney's Toy' [*Just Us Kids*, Lightning Rod, 2008]. It's not as much a *song* as it is a *rant*—but it's pretty good as rants go. But we never should have tried to go with that as a single because it didn't have a chance of being as popular as 'We Can't Make It Here.' There's no character for the listener to identify with. It's a second-person narrative."

Rolling Stone deemed the song "one of the sharpest musical indictments yet of George Bush." "Cheney's Toy" begins with "Another unknown soldier / Another lesson learned . . ." and continues with lines about smiling for the camera and waving to the crowd, leading to the chorus: "You're the man / Show 'em what you're made of / You're no longer daddy's boy / You're the man / that they're all afraid of / But you're only Cheney's toy."

"Cheney's Toy" draws to a close with the poignant lyrics, "One more pin on one more shoulder is all the future brings for another unknown soldier. . . . And he won't get any older and he can't see for the shrapnel in his brain."

James admits, "With 'Cheney's Toy' it was just McMurtry ranting about something. And a lot of that was misinterpreted because people thought I was saying the *soldier* was Cheney's Toy—which was not at all what I was saying. The nature of a popular song is that the listener hears himself or herself in it. They couldn't find themselves in that song. You gotta read *The New York Times* to understand a lot of that stuff and a lot of people don't read *The New York Times*. As a writer, you've got to realize that not everybody's on the same page as you."

So back to the list of questions. What about influences? How did he get here? What caught his attention and who made James McMurtry want to be a songwriter? While it's not in chronological order, this is the list that grew to answer those questions:

> First on my list would be Kris Kristofferson. He was the first "songwriter" I ever heard—and heard of. I had not ever paid attention to where songs came from before Kristofferson. A singer-songwriter. It was about 1971. My stepfather had the *Jesus Was A Capricorn* album, and introduced me to Kristofferson's music.
>
> Johnny Cash would be right up there, too. I was about seven, and got to see him in a big package show with June Carter and Carl Perkins. I think that package show had a lot to do with me wanting to be a songwriter. This was before the big video screens, but Cash had this big voice that was so clear you could hear every word. It came through that bad sound system. The Statler Brothers were also on that show. I was only seven, but realized that "Flowers on the Wall" was a hell of a song. Great songwriters, all of them.
>
> My dad belongs on this list. Larry. He had a random collection of great albums. His influence was subtle but strong. I grew up with him. The thing is, Larry was kind of a splinter. He splintered off from the family trade. His family is all rural, and he never was rural. He always traveled pretty easily and didn't mind leaving the village. Larry loves cities.

His family is scared to death of cities. He was the weird one. In fact, my grandfather once told his brother, "Larry's a good boy, but I don't know if he's gonna make it. All he wants to do is *read*. But if he wants to read, I guess that's okay."

Though he may have loved cities, Larry needed regular treks to the country—or as close to the country as he could get, and he carried James along. James recalls their Houston days, before they moved to Virginia:

I always lived with Larry. We didn't have a washing machine, so we'd go to the laundromat every Sunday. It was in a strip mall, and we'd wait for our clothes and go over and play the jukebox. Three songs for a quarter. We'd listen to Hank Williams sing "Cold Cold Heart," and then "Gates of Eden," and "Like a Rolling Stone" by Dylan. A great mix of music. We also spent a lot of time at this little beer joint-diner-drive in over in Richmond, just outside of Houston. They had a great jukebox too. With those tableside jukebox machines. We'd play Merle's "Working Man Blues" and "Radiator Man from Wasco," and Cal Smith's "The Lord Knows I'm Drinking," and soak up the country.

James continues to explain those early influences:

When Larry was teaching creative writing at Rice, my mother, Jo McMurtry, lived about six blocks away in Houston. She was a graduate student teaching assistant. While I never lived with my mother, we all moved to Virginia at about the same time around 1969. She married a former creative writing student, Mike Evans, who introduced me to lot of songwriters, and took me to see some great shows. My mother taught me a few chords and showed me how to play a little. Mike took me to see John Prine and Steve Goodman. Prine's "Angel from Montgomery" and Goodman's "Ballad of Penny Evans" taught me that I could write from a female point of view. "Rachel's Song" and "Lights of Cheyenne" were greatly influenced by Prine and Goodman.

"And Curtis. My son. He's a fearless songwriter. He has a degree in music comp. He can read. He can score. He can do all kinds of things I can't do. And he's got a work ethic," James says.

James has grown weary of interviewers across the country who have opened countless interviews through the years with the "Larry's Son" line of questioning and has openly disagreed with the notion of genetics playing a part in his talent, but he cannot disagree with the three generations of success behind the pen. It could be argued that someone who grows up in a house filled with professional athletes will most likely have some ability in sports.

By the same reasoning, a child who grows up in a world of good books and quality music and great writing is going to have a literary bent. Twenty-six-year-old Curtis McMurtry, living in Austin, pursuing a career in the music business, is sure to carry that banner forward in McMurtry tradition as a name to follow.

The more we talked, the more influences James wanted to add to this list. I take time to include them in this essay as a primer for would-be songwriters and songwriting aficionados. He mentioned Rogers and Hammerstein, and Gilbert and Sullivan. He went through a Waylon phase and discovered Billy Joe Shaver when Waylon recorded all of Shaver's songs on the *Honky Tonk Heroes* album.

> Let's add Chuck Berry and Bo Diddley. Chuck Berry is one of the best songwriters in the world—"C'est la Vie," "Memphis." . . . And Bo Diddley had that rhythmic sense. I do more Bo in my acoustic shows. That's kind of how I get through those shows—I set open tuning and go. And you need to add the Stones and the Beatles. I learned my first strum patterns by practicing "Here Comes The Sun," and the Stones influenced everything in the sixties and seventies.

Pretty heavy-hitting influences, all writers. Ruthlessly. Poetic. Songwriters.

Speaking of writing, let's get technical. How do you write songs—literally—I ask. He takes out his cell phone and shows me:

> I get a couple of lines and a melody and put them down, and when they start keeping me up at night, I write them into a song. I used to only write on yellow legal pads—they looked like white tablets under a seventy-five-watt bulb. And it had to be a *legal* length because I could fit a whole verse or a thought on a page. Now I write just about everything on my iPhone. With an app called Notes.

What's next? Audiences at James's live shows are getting sneak previews of the new material. His epic "Long Island Sound" is sure to attract critical attention. At first listen, it appears to be a tribute to what Mike Seely describes in *No Depression* as "the everyday resilience of Hurricane Sandy survivors that Springsteen could have penned." But James shrugs and says, "No. I wrote that when Kellie, my girlfriend, and I were up there last spring for Curtis's graduation (from Sarah Lawrence University). We were stuck on the Whitestone Bridge trying to get back to the airport. It was just there. And I wrote it all down."

On the latest album, James leaves the Long Island-Bronx landmark bridge and comes back home for an occasional spin across the floor of the "Copper Canteen" and the "Things I've Come To Know," a love song that is, as Kris Kristofferson would describe, "partly truth and partly fiction."

Overall, James defines his new work for this album as "mostly relationship songs." He adds, in unvetted McMurtry fashion, "Everybody hates politics. Everybody loves pussy."

John F. Kennedy biographer Thurston Clarke said in a *Washington Post* interview, "What makes journalism so fascinating and biography so interesting is the struggle to answer that single question: 'What's he like?'"

James McMurtry takes pride in his misanthropic reputation at times. Longtime followers have seen him stop a crowded show because the audience was singing along. "They paid to hear *me* sing these songs, not to hear *you* sing these songs," he has said, with an eye on the rowdy table at the front of the room.

McMurtry keeps the masses at arm's length, and, yes that is part of the mystique. But describing him can be a challenge for those closest to him as well. What's he like? A combination of the inability to do justice to the bullwhip crack of his humor, and being protective of the vulnerability of this "Ruthlessly Poetic Songwriter" keeps McMurtry's essence just out of reach—at least for now—for another chapter, another book, another time.

PART THREE

EPILOGUE

Passing of the Torch?

DRUNKEN POET'S DREAM

HAYES CARLL

I. GOOD ENOUGH FOR OLD GUYS

Craig Clifford

In one of the essays in *Untimely Meditations*, "On the Advantage and Disadvantage of History for Life," Friedrich Nietzsche outlines three approaches to history: the monumental, the antiquarian, and the critical. The common thread that he finds in these three approaches, properly understood, is the abiding meaning of the past for the present. Monumental history discovers examples to be emulated. Monuments, in this sense, are models for what is possible. Antiquarian history is guided by reverence for the past, but the past as the origin of the present. Revering something just because it's old would mean that we could never replace something old with something new. And, finally, critical history drags the past to the bar of judgment, which frees us to act.

Several years ago, when Craig Hillis and I first discussed this book, we knew that we wanted it to be a book about a vibrant tradition, not just two grouchy old men lamenting the loss of the golden musical age of their younger years. So we decided the final part of the book would deal with some of the young folks who are continuing this Texas tradition of ruthlessly poetic songwriting, even though, as grouchy old men, we were both skeptical about this undertaking, considering the state of mainstream country music these days.

Being the (slightly) younger of the two grouchy old men, I volunteered to do the research, to come up with a few names. I had a few in mind already. I started asking friends for suggestions. I asked my brightest students who they listened to. One name that came up repeatedly was Hayes Carll. I knew his recording of "Bad Liver and a Broken Heart," but of course he didn't write that song. I started delving into his music, and I was impressed.

So impressed I learned a couple of his songs for my band to play. All three members of the band are over sixty, and we pride ourselves on only playing songs by dead or almost dead people, myself included in that group. So if all three of us agree that a song by a young person is good enough for us to play alongside songs by Townes Van Zandt, Guy Clark, Jerry Jeff Walker, David Rodriguez, and Hank Williams Sr., then that's got to be a good song. "It's a Shame" quickly became a part of our regular repertoire. We only played "She Left Me for Jesus" once because a waitress threatened us with eternal damnation if we ever played it again.

In short, Hayes Carll is a fine songwriter, and a quick search on YouTube revealed his connection to the tradition of ruthlessly poetic Texas singer-songwriters. The "monuments" of this tradition have clearly functioned for Carll in the way that Nietzsche says monuments should function. Carll plays Van Zandt's "Loretta" and "Greensboro Woman." He recorded Guy Clark's "Worry Be Gone" for *This One's for Him: A Tribute to Guy Clark*. He cowrote "Drunken Poet's Dream" with Ray Wylie Hubbard. He wrote "Rivertown" with Guy Clark. Carll comes out of this tradition of poetic songwriting, and, apparently, it has embraced him.

Right after I started looking into Hayes Carll, he released another album, *KMAG YOYO* (a military acronym that stands for "Kiss my ass goodbye, you're on your own"). I preordered a copy, and when it arrived I drove around for a couple of weeks listening to it in my car. It's not a concept album in the normal sense, but there is a concept behind it. Carll seems to be making a conscious attempt to pay tribute to or, in some cases, parody the various genres that he's working out of. In fact, he manages to do both at the same time in a number of the songs.

The title song is unashamedly Bob Dylan's "Subterranean Homesick Blues" with new words. In Carll's story a young man enlists in the army and ends up in Afghanistan "stealing from the Taliban . . . / turnin' poppies into heroin." The song evolves into a drug-induced paranoid fantasy, in which the narrator is blasted off into outer space in a rocket ship, a guinea pig in a CIA experiment. But the song crashes back down into grim reality at the end:

> I think I see a bright light
> Something 'bout it ain't right
> Laid down in a spaceship
> Woke up in a fire fight
>
> Tripping from the morphine
> Came down in a bad scene

> God, don't let me die here
> I ain't even nineteen

The lyrics of "KMAG YOYO" actually remind me more of Dylan's "Talkin' World War III Blues": "Some time ago a crazy dream came to me / I dreamt I was walkin' into World War III." Both stories are paranoid fantasies turned into sardonic humor. Writing a song that pays homage to a particular song by a great songwriter like Bob Dylan is gutsy, to say the least. But Carll pulls it off.

Of course, Carll had already paid tribute to Dylan with the cover photo of *Trouble in Mind*, which is based on the cover of Dylan's *Freewheelin'* album, which contains "Talkin' World War III Blues." And Carll often mentions Dylan when he talks of influences. It's not a stretch to say that he aspires to be the Bob Dylan of the Texas singer-songwriters of the twenty-first century.

"Chances Are," by contrast, is a classic country crying-in-your-beer sad song that Merle Haggard would be proud of, but of course with a Hayes Carll twist. Carll's talent for creating self-effacing narrators who see their own frailty comes through in this song: "Chances are I took the wrong turn every time I had a turn to take / And I guess I broke my own heart every chance I had a heart to break."

"Hard Out Here" is a honky-tonk romp, but, again, with Carll's peculiar self-mocking irony: "Everybody's talking 'bout the shape I'm in / They say, boy you ain't a poet, you're just a drunk with a pen."

"Hide Me," with gospel choir, is a traditional spiritual, a combination of dead-serious reflections on life's suffering and the Carll wink: "I took the pain and called it fair." And then, "I'm gonna leave these blues behind / for some other fool to find."

"Bottle in My Hand" and "Bye Bye Baby," both featuring banjo prominently, have a traditional bluegrass feel.

"Another Like You" takes the genre of the dueling duet (can't help but think of Johnny Cash and June Carter's "Jackson") to new outrageous lows. Carll claims that he came up with the idea by imagining what it would be like to try to pick up Ann Coulter in a bar. As we know from "She Left Me for Jesus," Carll is a master of irreverence. *American Songwriter* named "Another Like You" No. 1 on its list of the top fifty songs of 2011. It's almost embarrassing to listen to, but you can't help but listen.

"Grateful for Christmas," like the album's title song, alludes to a particular song, in this case Robert Earl Keen's "Merry Christmas from the Family." Move over, Robert Earl. It comes off initially as a satire without a lot of sympathy, not unlike Keen's song. But there's an underlying sadness as we move from one Christmas to the next, with the loss of yet another family member who used to say the blessing. There's a darkness, but in the end there's a kind of affirmation of family, a real family flawed and fragile as are all things human, as the narrator realizes that the responsibility to say the blessing now falls on his shoulders:

> So let's all gather 'round, I guess I'll say the blessing
> Aunt Jane, she fell asleep, and I never cared for dressing
> But we got all of our friends and family here
> And I'm grateful for Christmas this year

In a critical review of *KMAG YOYO* in *Saving Country Music*, an online magazine, someone writing under the name "Trigger" proclaims: "Not everybody can be Guy Clark or Townes Van Zandt, and that's OK. But if you can't, maybe you shouldn't try."

It's true, if you aspire to write songs like Bob Dylan or Townes Van Zandt or Guy Clark, then you invite comparison to those great songwriters. Van Zandt and Clark compared their lyrics to Dylan Thomas's poetry and viewed themselves as coming up short. But without that high aspiration we wouldn't have Townes Van Zandt and Guy Clark. Without Carll's aspirations to follow in the footsteps of the Texas songwriting greats, we wouldn't have Hayes Carll. Trigger says of Carll:

> Everybody seems to want to crown him as the next great Texas songwriting god. How about just calling him a good songwriter, with above average Texas country music with some soul that's fun to listen to and doesn't make you feel stupid like the stuff on the radio.

When the final tally is in, how Carll will compare to the greats of the earlier generations of Texas songwriting remains to be seen. Time will be the judge of that. But he's a far cry better than "above average" for Texas country music. Even among the minority of Texas songwriters who have eschewed the inanity of mainstream country and aimed their sights higher, he is one of the best. If Guy Clark thinks he's good enough to cowrite a song with, that's a pretty good endorsement.

Audiences pay the bills and exert a huge influence on artists who want to eat, and shallow audiences tend to produce shallow artists. But artists shape the audience as well, and Carll has done his part to bring a new audience to this great tradition of poetic songwriting. He may have a tendency to overdo the drunken part of the drunken poet's dream, the better to attract the drunken revelers with, but, once attracted, they are left to ponder the poetry of phrases like "She laughs for a minute about the shape I'm in / Says you be the sinner, honey, I'll be the sin." For my money, Hayes Carll deserves credit for having the courage to try to write the kind of songs that his heroes have written, and daring to ask for comparisons to them.

II. GOOD ENOUGH FOR YOUNG GUYS

Brian T. Atkinson

The lanky young man pulling drafts stepped out from behind the bar later that evening. He quietly took the stage. Cracked a corny joke. After all, we were in Galveston, Texas, raising glasses at the Old Quarter's sixth annual Townes Van Zandt Wake on New Year's Day 2003. The too-weary troubadour cleared his throat. Strapped on his guitar. He struggled not one single ounce for purchase on perfection. Instead, Hayes Carll effortlessly coaxed Van Zandt's "Greensboro Woman" as breathlessly as the songwriter himself and delved even deeper into the heart of "Loretta." Carll's poised and poignant delivery simply rolled away the stone.

As the youthful songwriter resumed serving drinks, his own songwriting craft emerged. Carll mindfully stuffed bills in the till, but his peripheral glances froze snapshots real and imagined: strangers laughing too loudly, salty sea hands squaring off outside, locals swapping bring-your-own bottles. His eyes owned a gleam and glimmer rarely found. He thought deeply. Broadly. "You know the famous songwriter Hayes Carll," Old Quarter owner Rex Bell had said dryly as he introduced us earlier. "Of course," I said, lying. As I left the Old Quarter that night with the creaky front door closing behind us and Carll's debut *Flowers and Liquor* in my hand, I had no idea I was about to discover my new favorite lyricist.

Carll effectively shot his career from a cannon with *Trouble in Mind's* elegant wordplay five years later. The Woodlands, Texas, native's third album—a vibrant vortex backing machetes ("Faulkner Street") with memories ("Knockin' Over Whiskeys")—immediately catapulted him from rising talent into established tunesmith. High watermarks measured a young poet's wanderlust ("Beaumont") against a seasoned brawler's will ("I Got a Gig"). The golden key: boundless ambition. Carll deepened Tin Pan Alley's dimensions (a re-recorded "It's a Shame") and stretched country music's walls thin (the excellent Scott Nolan cover "Bad Liver and a Broken Heart"). The title track alone effectively redefined roadhouse blues. Beneath everything: lyrics razor sharp.

Trouble in Mind's Technicolor narratives established the droll young man as a poetic songwriter worldwide. His most wistful recall of Van Zandt's finest ("Willing to Love Again") and his wittiest echo Robert Earl Keen at his best ("Wild as a Turkey"). None defines Carll's artistic mission statement more than the album's peak moment, "Drunken Poet's Dream," a bold and dangerous love-struck ballad as limitless as anything drawn from Texas soil this century. He seamlessly frames his beauty's desire: "I've got a woman, she's wild as Rome / She likes to lay naked and be gazed upon / Well, she crosses a bridge and then sets it on fire / Lands like a bird on a telephone wire."

The song offers a most uncommon pleasure: romantic poetry cresting rapid-fire rock 'n' roll. Picture John Keats wearing faded jeans and a six-string. "I always like writing with Hayes because he's fearless," the song's cowriter Ray Wylie Hubbard says. "Hayes takes chances with his writing." Witness the lines following: "Wine bottles scattered like last night's clothes / Cigarettes, papers and dominoes," he sings. "She laughs for a minute about the shape I'm in / She says, 'You be the sinner, honey, and I'll be the sin,'" Four phrases rarely draw more direct lines between sensuality and spirituality. The songwriting pairing, first realized when the duo cowrote "Chickens" on *Flowers and Liquor*, exponentially boosted Carll's craft.

"For 'Drunken Poet's Dream,' I just had this line, 'I've got a woman, she's wild as Rome,' and a groove," Carll says. "He came over to the house and we started writing. We did about half the song and went our separate ways. We each finished the song on our own and ended up with pretty different versions. They're probably sixty percent the same."

"Hayes has his own voice," celebrated Texas songwriter Bruce Robison says. "Those are the ones I tend to like. I'm jealous that he has a real sense of humor. I can hear a lot of influences from Townes to Ray Wylie to Todd Snider. He brings that stuff together and it comes out something special on the other side."

ROLL ON

TERRI HENDRIX

Brian T. Atkinson

Terri Hendrix crafts personal narratives with perpetual motion. "I had a breakdown in a small town, but no one knew a thing / I went about each day with my thoughts in the way," she sings early into her landmark album *The Art of Removing Wallpaper* (2004, 2012). "When I wanted to stop, I kept on moving." "Breakdown" charts her emotional fall and rise and eventual compromise ("Look at me putting makeup on my face / What am I trying to add or erase?"). Hendrix ultimately unifies human spirits, her greatest asset as a songwriter. "If you put yourself in my place / You'd be able to see," the song continues. "We're just skin and bone / We're not made of stone / We're all just skin and bone."

The San Antonio native's a vibrant and vital songwriter, both challenging and compassionate and ceaselessly cornered by her own imagination. She's fiercely independent, a visionary do-it-yourself artist and unwavering creative life force. Hendrix simply handles curveballs gracefully. Her lyrics deliver lessons learned beneath thunderclouds. Her lines shine with endless empathy. She fills pages with unassumingly elegant lines like, "Kiss the evening sky and say, 'Bye, bye, bye' / Tomorrow knows no sorrow like today."

Hendrix disarms with intimacy. "I think songwriting is therapeutic," she says. "Most people write when they are in a funk, but I have to have a clear head and have a good, solid place. I don't think that I purposely set out to write [hopeful] songs, but I do know that I don't like to be the victim in my songs. I don't like to come out on the bottom. I like to come out on the other side and if it's about other people, I want them to come out on the other side. Being positive is something I have to work at every single day. I get up and have to remind myself. Happiness takes work."

She knows challenges. The longtime San Marcos resident has lived with epilepsy for more than two decades. "It's been something that I've always lived and performed with," Hendrix says. "There's stigma and mystery around epilepsy but there doesn't have to be. It's more common than we think. My job is to stand up despite that and live a happy, healthy life."

Such gratitude emboldens *The Art of Removing Wallpaper*. Hendrix fortifies her earthy ("One Way") and ethereal vignettes ("One Night Stand") with an everywoman's elegance. The seamless collection, equal measures of recovery ("Breakdown") and redemption ("Hey Now"), consistently captures everyday snapshots as clearly as celebrated tunesmiths like Guy Clark, Kris Kristofferson, or Billy Joe Shaver. Hendrix deftly doubles down on the deeply personal ("Enjoy the Ride") with acutely political ("Monopoly"). High watermarks transcend temperament ("It's About Time") and time ("Judgment Day").

Hendrix and legendary instrumentalist and producer Lloyd Maines, her musical partner for more than a decade and a half, frame portraits with broad diversity, a boundless stretch between blues and country and folk and jazz. "Lloyd and I are hungry for music," she says. "We're ruthless about digging for music. I'm into techno, drum loops, far-out, weird ethereal music. Lloyd isn't scared of that. He keeps me reaching artistically. He's really hard to work with because he demands a lot more than I can do, but it keeps me on my toes and reaching forward. I feel like I keep him on his toes, because it's always, 'What's next for us to learn?'"

Hendrix's compelling catalog—a dozen self-released albums from her debut *Two Dollar Shoes* (1996) through *Cry Till You Laugh* (2010)—showcases a songwriter constantly evolving. "I'm a big fan of Terri," says Dixie Chicks fiddler and singer Martie McGuire, who cowrote the band's Grammy-winning instrumental "Lil' Jack Slade" with Hendrix. "I think she's a great lyricist and very talented songwriter." *Lone Star Music* magazine editor Richard Skanse goes farther. "Terri is the bar by which I personally measure all other singer-songwriters in the Texas and Americana and folk worlds, and all independent artists of any genre," he says. "Terri's songs can be deeply personal, moving and insightful, or humorous and playful—and sometimes even all of those things at once—but they never sound forced or insincere. Her lyrics almost always sing and read like conversation, but there's the soul of a true poet displayed in those words, too."

Hendrix writes those words organically. "'It's About Time' came when I was riding around in my car," she says. "As time moves faster and faster, I don't feel like I have the time to do what I really want to do. Wow, I'm getting a little older and I have to compromise what I hope to do with my life. 'Dreams vary in size / When I'm down to the wire, I compromise / I can do this or that instead / But first I have to get out of my bed.' Then one day I was making coffee and 'It's carpe diem on a caffeine buzz.' Then five minutes later: 'I'm chemically awake but my brain's in a fuzz.' Next thing, I know I've got something. I just try to get out of the way and let it roll and not think too much about it."

"Terri writes songs that are totally her own style and are not similar to any other writer I know," said late songwriter and Cheatham Street Warehouse owner Kent Finlay, who encouraged Hendrix early on and helped record the album *Terri Hendrix: Live in San Marcos* (2001) at his club. "They are just a fit for her voice and personality—pleasant, positive, and upbeat."

The Art of Removing Wallpaper's cover songs—particularly Jeff Barbra and Sarah Pirkle's meditation "Quiet Me" and K. S. Taylor's equally contemplative "The Long Ride Home"—prove Hendrix understands the poetry in interpretation as well. "Terri is foremost a fan of music," Skanse says. "I've interviewed and come to know a lot of artists in the twenty years I've been writing about music, and Terri is the only one I've ever met who I know for a fact buys and listens to as much music as I do. And she listens to everything: songwriters, classic rock, pop, classical, world music, hip-hop, rap, blues, jazz, techno, even metal. She absorbs and finds inspiration from everything." She effortlessly claims other songs as her own when she sings them.

Accordingly, Hendrix inhabited Guy Clark's "The Dark" like the lyrics were stamped on her heart when she cut the track for *This One's For Him: A Tribute to Guy Clark* (2011). The earthy, warm-eyed songwriter quietly entered Austin's Cedar Creek studio that mild January day. She adjusted her overalls. Sang the truth. "In the dark, you can sometimes hear your own heartbeat or the one next to you," Hendrix whispered over three circular chords. "And the house settles down after holding itself up all day / Shoulders slumped, gives a big sigh / And you hear no one's footfall in the hall." Then she snuck in her spirit: "That drip in the kitchen sink keeps marking time / June bug on the window screen can't get in, but it keeps on trying / One way or another, we're all in the dark."

As she sang the Clark song, her passion and persistence illuminated fireflies and sparks, lightning and stars, campfires and the moon, headlights on cars, the Northern Lights and Milky Way, everything we see—everything that make us feel less lonesome, less vulnerable, more hopeful—when dim fades to black. "When the earth turns its back on the sun and the stars come out," the song goes, "And the planets start to run around / Now, they call that day is done, but, really, it's just getting started / Some folks take comfort in that."

"It's probably one of the best songs that I've clung to," Hendrix says. "That song's a painting, pure poetry. He's talking about his surroundings, but it could be about the dark as a whole, the dark inside of us. My take on a great song would be 'The Dark.' Great lyrics read well and stand the test of time. Guy Clark's a master storyteller because he's able to really nail it emotionally and go to those places with vulnerability, but he's never staring at his shoes and feeling sorry for himself. He's doing it with a whisky glass in one hand and one fist toward the future."

FROM RIDING BULLS TO DEAD HORSES

RYAN BINGHAM

Craig Clifford (interview with Shaina Post)

After seeing the movie *Crazy Heart*, I learned the song "The Weary Kind," and my band recorded it. Who is this Ryan Bingham? I wanted to know. (Rest assured, he isn't asking the same question about me because his royalties from our CD might, at best, buy him a good bottle of wine.) A little research quickly revealed that about a decade before *Crazy Heart*, Bingham had been a student at the university where I direct the Honors College and teach philosophy, Tarleton State University in Stephenville, Texas.

I started asking around. Michael Dooley, one of my colleagues in the English Department, said that Bingham had taken a class from him. According to Dooley, Bingham was already bound and determined to make it as a singer-songwriter. He made his start as a stage performer playing open-mic night at the Agave Bar and Grill and a regular Wednesday night gig at the Water Hole. According to Dooley, Bingham would often come by his office in the afternoon to tell him about his latest gig. One afternoon he dropped off a homemade CD, which, thanks to my colleague, I've had the opportunity to listen to. Raw talent in the making, I thought. Solo acoustic—just Bingham, his guitar, and a harmonica, like the early Bob Dylan.

Originally from Hobbs, New Mexico, Bingham landed in Stephenville, Texas, for part of high school and attended Tarleton in 2000, riding bulls for the Tarleton rodeo team.

At some point, according to his slightly tongue-in-cheek account, he realized that "playing guitar is a lot easier on the teeth and bones" (Newsobserver.com, October 16, 2009).

When he won the Academy Award for "The Weary Kind" (cowritten with T Bone Burnett), I read in the Stephenville paper that Bingham e-mailed one of his classmates about the effect Jennifer Muncey, his high school English teacher, had on his songwriting. "Please tell Mrs. Muncey that she is the reason that I write songs the way I do, and I honestly think of her every time I write a song. She was the only teacher I ever had that actually got through to me. I can tell you that I wouldn't be where I am today if it wasn't for Mrs. Muncey" (*Stephenville Empire-Tribune*, March 9, 2010).

I mentioned Ryan Bingham in my classes at Tarleton, trying to find out how many of my students knew about him. Most had never heard of him, but one of my best students, Shaina Post, knew his music backwards and forwards. I talked to her after class quite frequently about what attracted her to his music. And her answers intrigued and impressed me.

I now know Bingham's music fairly well, and I've done enough research to know that he is coming out of the tradition this book is about—consciously coming out of it. That early homemade CD was strong evidence, but it doesn't take long on YouTube to see how many Townes Van Zandt and Guy Clark songs he knows. Bingham clearly aspires to enter the pantheon of great Texas songwriters. I considered writing an essay about him myself, focusing on his influences. But then it occurred to me—why not have a smart young person talk about his music?

Shaina grew up in numerous small towns in Oklahoma and Texas. She graduated from Tarleton State University in 2012, with a major in history and a minor in philosophy. She spent her final semester in college studying in Tuscania, Italy. Just after we finished this interview, Shaina headed off to the Defense Language Institute in Monterey, California, to train to become a Chinese linguist for the US Air Force.

This dialogue was done by e-mail, but it's not unlike the many conversations we had after class.

CC: What is it about Ryan Bingham's music that you find so appealing?
SP: A few years ago I was half-heartedly listening to country music television when this song suddenly caught my attention. That song, "The Weary Kind," was my official introduction to Ryan Bingham, and I have been a whole-hearted fan ever since. I am a music fanatic. I listen to an eclectic range of artists and genres. My music library includes everything from folk to hip-hop to rock 'n' roll. So when I say I am a fan of Ryan Bingham, what I really mean is that he is near the top of a very long and

varied list of favorite artists. Like all of my most-loved artists, what I like most about Bingham is that every song has soul. I love the grungy, rolling poetry of his songs. Every song tells a story, and every song transports the listener to an almost physical place. When I listen to songs like "Ghost of Travelin' Jones," "Southside of Heaven," and "Dylan's Hard Rain" I can hear the metallic clanking of train cars, I can feel the rolling gait of the horse under my saddle, and I smell the smoky mesquite campfire.

CC: You said you were "half-heartedly" listening to country music television. Do you listen to much mainstream country music? Were you surprised to find a country songwriter who was this poetic?

SP: I do listen to mainstream country music. For the most part, though, it serves as background noise when I'm driving. I find most of the newest stuff too "pop" for my taste. That being said, I am a huge country music fan. I love the artists from the eighties and nineties, and I love the "red dirt" country music coming out of Texas and Oklahoma lately. To put it simply, I am a hillbilly girl at heart, and I like anything with that quintessential twang to it. I honestly wasn't surprised to hear "The Weary Kind" on a country music video station. It is a beautiful song that I think easily appeals to a mainstream audience. I was more surprised to find out that Ryan Bingham was a Texas singer-songwriter from my area. Once I listened to more of his music I was even more surprised. There aren't many "red dirt" artists who can make the leap into mainstream country music. I think the mainstream audience prefers the more upbeat, repetitive, catchy tunes that Nashville is producing lately. Fewer people have the patience for poetry any more.

CC: You've use the term "poetry" a couple of times, and you referred earlier to the "grungy, rolling poetry of his songs," but you also talked about how the stories he tells transport you to another place. This is a probably a false dilemma, but when you talk about the poetic character of Ryan Bingham's songs are you thinking of the way the sounds, the rhythms, and the rhymes are more sophisticated than your run-of-the-mill mainstream country, which they definitely are, or are you talking about a kind of poetic truth, the way his words let us see things in a way we wouldn't otherwise see them?

SP: To be completely honest I am more concerned with the whole package when it comes to a good song. I can appreciate a good song that exhibits a kind of poetic truth that focuses on the poetry and deeper meaning of the lyrics. But for me, it has to have more than that. There is definitely a large part of Bingham's work that "lets us see things in a way we wouldn't otherwise see them." "Hard Times" and "Ever Wonder Why" might be a couple of good examples. I like this part of his music but what most attracts me is the raw musical talent coupled with poetic storytelling. I can appreciate the poetry of artists such as Townes Van Zandt or Bob Dylan. However, I think

I am more drawn to Bingham because his music has more energy, an energy that really brings emotion into the song.

CC: I have a copy of a CD that Bingham made when he was a student at Tarleton. It's just him with an acoustic guitar and a harmonica, and it really sounds like he'd been listening to a lot of early Bob Dylan. And in his live performances, especially when he's playing solo, he has covered Townes Van Zandt's "To Live Is to Fly" and Guy Clark's "Dublin Blues." He definitely seems to locate himself in that "folksinger" tradition, which is why we wanted to include him in this book. But he's also got enough of a rock 'n' roll edge to get mainstream attention. Bingham seems to balance his quieter acoustic songs with a good dose of hard-driving country rock.

SP: I had the pleasure of attending a Ryan Bingham concert at the House of Blues in Dallas when I was a student at Tarleton. I noticed that even the more mellow songs from his playlist were amped up a little for that particular crowd. The whole show was actually very rock 'n' roll, which I enjoyed but it did surprise me a little. Later, when I considered the audience, it made more sense. You can find much of the red dirt audience in honky-tonk bars. So in order to appeal to an energetic, probably inebriated, crowd who just want to dance and have a good time, it is a good idea to keep up the energy. I attended a Sean McConnell event at a honky-tonk bar in Stephenville, and at another occasion on the Tarleton campus. If you haven't heard of Sean McConnell, he is a primarily a songwriter, but he also made a few albums of his own work that are pretty mellow. At the bar event I could barely hear or see the musicians through the smoke and chatter and people standing around. No one paid much attention to the stage at all really, same goes for the campus event. I think part of what makes Ryan Bingham stand out from other red dirt artists is his balance of the slower poetic songs and the more energetic live shows that appeal to a wider audience. Of course, it probably all depends on the venue as well. I think Bingham does do smaller, quieter venues as well, which is a great opportunity to bring out the poetry.

CC: I noticed that you put quotation marks around "red dirt." That term is used to describe some really great music, like Ryan Bingham and the Turnpike Troubadours from Oklahoma, but it's often used to describe the I-love-my-truck mainstream music that is anything but poetic. What does "red dirt" music mean to you?

SP: Well, when I lived in Texas I used the term "Texas Country Music," but I didn't realize that Texas fans had kind of put their label on the whole movement until I moved to Oklahoma. The radio stations here call it "red dirt" music, which I think is more inclusive. Music trends obviously don't adhere to state boundaries, though I know many Texans who would like to think all good things end at the Texas border.

To me "red dirt" means singer-songwriter bands that come out of Oklahoma, Louisiana, Texas, or New Mexico and exhibit similar characteristics. Most are exceptional musicians. If you take a look at any of Bingham's album covers you will notice he plays many of the instruments heard in his songs, and plays them well. Music has always seemed like a kind of magic to me. Artists like Bingham wave their fingers over a box with strings and "voila!" something enchanting happens. Add a good story, a little poetry, and some heartfelt vocals, and you find yourself transported to another place, another state of mind. The so-called "red dirt" artists excel at this kind of magic. They write their own songs, play their own instruments, and sing with a laid back, unaffected sincerity. You will see them in honky-tonk bars and smaller, intimate venues, rather than giant arenas. And even when they "make it big" they always make a point to go back to the small towns, to the audiences that loved them first. When I lived in Texas, I noticed the more popular artists like Cross Canadian Ragweed, Robert Earl Keen, and Pat Green still played the small-town bars (Stephenville, Gruene) whenever they could. I think that is why red dirt fans are so possessive when it comes to this genre. We love them and are proud of them because they are ours. They may not be from our hometown, but they come from a town just like ours. You can hear it in their songs.

When I think of "red dirt" music I hear Hispanic, Irish, and Creole influences. I hear bluegrass, rock, and blues. I hear Texas and Oklahoma good ol' boys, Hank Williams Sr., Woody Guthrie, and a kid and his guitar singing around a campfire.

CC: I'll probably get in trouble for saying this, but I think that two of the most ruthlessly poetic contemporary songwriters in country music—OK, let's call it red dirt music—are not from Texas: Turnpike Troubadour Evan Felker from Oklahoma and Jason Isbell from Alabama. But let's get back to this term "red dirt." Do you think you identify with Bingham's music because your own background is "red dirt"? On one level, his songs are about contemporary people struggling with the realities of life. On another level, they're almost mythical, or at least a harkening back to the landscape of Woody Guthrie: "The man come to shake my hand, and rob me of my farm / I shot 'em dead and I hung my head, and drove off in his car." Shades of Woody Guthrie's "Pretty Boy Floyd."

SP: I would definitely consider my background "red dirt," in the most literal sense of the word. I grew up in a microscopic Oklahoma town for most of my childhood so my siblings and I spent most of our time outdoors in the red Oklahoma dirt. Our town didn't have paved streets or even street signs. There was at least one church that still had an outhouse. We were related in some way to most of our neighbors; everyone had an Oklahoma drawl, and most everyone could play music. At least, that is how I remember it. I grew up hearing my great-uncles play bluegrass, my grandparents listening to gospel, and my parents listening to country. This is how music was introduced into my life. My appreciation and love-obsession with music is rooted in bluegrass, gospel, and country, so it is no surprise that I identify with artists like Bingham, the Turnpike Troubadours, and John Fullbright. If you don't know who Fullbright is, drop what you are doing right now and listen to "Satan and St. Paul."

CC: Fullbright—another Okie! He's very much in this same tradition. OK, one final question about Bingham: I had a hard time getting into his voice. I'm guessing he cultivates that roughness—I can't imagine anyone that young having a voice that rough, no matter how much he's abused himself. And it reminds me of young Bob Dylan. The roughness of his voice—half singing and half talking—fits the kind of songs he writes. How do you relate to his voice?

SP: I was actually able to listen to Bingham's CD from his Tarleton days because you lent it to me. I immediately noticed a huge difference in his singing voice compared to his other albums. Those earlier recordings aren't nearly as husky as his current work. That being said, it did bother me a little when I realized that wasn't a natural singing voice. His voice was one of the things that drew me to him in the first place. I guess it didn't even occur to me that it couldn't be 100 percent natural. I got over it though. I like the grungy, dirty tone it brings to his songs, and I think it works well with the kind of stories he likes to tell. Hard luck, "Dollar A Day" stories. Artists like Ray LaMontagne, Ray Wylie Hubbard, and Lincoln Durham have that same husky quality in their singing voice, and they are also on my favorites list as well.

BAD GIRL POET

MIRANDA LAMBERT

Craig Clifford

In the July/August 2010 issue of *The Atlantic*, Hanna Rosin tells us that "for every two men who get a college degree this year, three women will do the same." In 2009, according to the Census Bureau, 25 percent more women graduated from college than men, 685,000 men and 916,000 women. At many universities the general student population runs from 55 to 65 percent women, while the Honors College or Honors Program is 75 percent women.

Something seems to be going on in country music that reflects the same ascendency of smart women. Grady Smith, writing about the top ten country albums of 2013 in *Entertainment Weekly*, singles out Kacey Musgraves as a welcome challenge to the monotony and stupidity of much of mainstream "bro country." Collin Raye, a major country music star of the 1990s, mentions Miranda Lambert as an example of someone who is bucking the tide of male I-love-my-truck inanity. Is there—dare I use the F-word—a feminist revolt against mainstream bro country?

It's certainly not a second-wave feminist revolt, as a quick look at Kacey Musgraves and Miranda Lambert will confirm. No Army fatigues and hiking boots in their attire, and they obviously have no problem with makeup and cleavage. Many commentators have referred to the women of their generation as post-feminists, even anti-feminists; and I have no idea whether Musgraves and Lambert would apply the F-word to themselves. But some cultural critics have dubbed the assertive women of this generation "third-wave feminists." They are independent and assertive, but one of the ways they assert themselves is through their sexuality. Schooled on second-wave feminism, I have to take a step back in order to understand what's going on when I look at a video or photograph of Kacey Musgraves or Miranda Lambert. They're too damned sexy—and too made-up and dressed-to-kill sexy—to be smart, thinks this aging child of the sixties. But think again. These young women are the country music world's version of *Legally Blonde*, except they're a lot tougher and a lot more likely to be hanging out in the bar than in the sorority house.

Kacey Musgraves's revolt against bro country consists of intelligent lyrics that raise serious issues. Miranda Lambert does that as well, but her approach is more of the *Thelma and Louise* variety. Her signature seems to be a direct assault on proudly stupid men, most notably in "Kerosene," cowritten with Steve Earle, and "Gunpowder and Lead," cowritten with Heather Little. These could be dubbed standard done-me-wrong songs, but it's almost as if they're putting the entire male sex on notice. Don't mess with this bad girl. Lambert claims that she came up with the title "Gunpowder and Lead" while she was taking a concealed handgun class, and it's hard not to notice the tattoo on her forearm of two crisscrossed revolvers.

Other songs might seem to fall into the kind of raunchy let's-have-sex-in-my-truck genre that the men are putting out in droves—"Fastest Girl in Town," cowritten with Angaleena Presley, and "Hell on Wheels," cowritten with Ashley Monroe and Angaleena Presley and recorded by the Pistol Annies—but those songs are really what the cultural critics call "grrl power." The message is clear—the women are running the show. They can be as raunchy as the men, but smarter. Lambert's teaming up with Monroe and Presley in a three-girl band called the Pistol Annies pretty much says it all.

Of course, if this is a revolt, it's one that's managed to steer right down the middle of commercial mainstream country music. Artistic purity and integrity are admirable if they produce artistic songs, which in the case of someone like Townes Van Zandt they did. But the ability to write artistic songs that are also commercially successful takes a special kind of smarts that Lambert clearly has.

And she's not just the queen of the theatrical bad girls. Her more reflective songs are often a challenge to the unthinking status quo. Just as Kacey Musgraves's reference to drugs, homosexuality, and religious hypocrisy in "Merry Go 'Round" and "Follow Your Arrow" raised a few Nashville eyebrows, Lambert's "Heart Like Mine," cowritten with Ashley Monroe and Travis Howard, is a challenge to thoughtless pieties. Where Hayes Carll's "She Left Me for Jesus" is a hilarious ironic romp, Lambert's religious questioning, although funny in its own way, is a serious reflection on human frailty and a deeper meaning of Christianity. She starts off with this self-characterization:

> I ain't the kind you take home to mama
> I ain't the kind to wear no ring
> Somehow I always get stronger
> When I'm on my second drink

Then she says "God Bless" to the "Christian folks" who tell her to stop smoking:

> 'Cause I heard Jesus He drank wine
> And I bet we'd get along just fine
> He could calm a storm and heal the blind
> And I bet He'd understand a heart like mine

In several cases, Lambert has turned to other songwriters for her more serious side, especially when it comes to looking at life from a broader temporal perspective than the eternal now of raising hell, whether it's the inane version of the party boys or the smart version of the renegade girls. But she deserves credit for sniffing out great songs that provide a counterweight to the bad-girl persona. When Lambert chooses to record a song she didn't write, her eye for intelligent lyrics is keen. Lambert convinced fellow Texan Kacey Musgraves to let her record "Mama's Broken Heart," which Musgraves cowrote with Brandy Clark and Shane McAnally. This thoughtful ballad is on one level another third-wave-feminist, girl-power song, but on another level there's a sense of the tragedy of choice and generational conflict, a sense of the inevitability of moral ambivalence.

Another fine song that shows Lambert's more reflective side, "The House That Built Me," was written by Tom Douglas and Allen Shamblin. The narrator of this song, much more vulnerable than Lambert's bad girl persona, returns to her childhood home, now occupied by strangers, looking for the healing power of a return to origins: "I thought if I could touch this place or feel it / this brokenness inside me might start healing." But the song ends with a sense of loss that can't be overcome: "Won't take nothing but a memory from the house that built me."

Lambert said she wished she had written "Mama's Broken Heart," so I'm hoping to see Lambert's own songwriting turn more in the direction of looking at the broad scope of life. She's the country music queen of badass, and what she's done with that genre is significantly smarter than the male songs about pickup trucks and painted-on jeans. And there's an underlying message she and her female cohorts are sending out to the slacker, two-timing, sometimes physically abusive party boys that is worthy of repetition. But, as smart and as called-for as that message is, the "Earl's Gotta Die" motif can become a bit too formulaic and repetitive in its own right. As her own songwriting in songs like "Heart Like Mine" and her selection of songs by other songwriters show, there's a side to her that has room to grow and mature. Of course, mainstream country music now only gives the gorgeous young a few years in the spotlight—it's a world of the young and for the young. A decades-spanning career like Johnny Cash's is unthinkable now in mainstream country music. But, Miranda, I'm pulling for you.

Is Miranda Lambert the next Townes Van Zandt or Guy Clark? Probably not. But who is? Is she as ruthlessly poetic as Townes Van Zandt was? No, but poetic enough, given the context she has to deal with.

Is she the leader of a third-wave feminist revolt that will save Texas and Nashville music from the mindlessness of the party boys? That would be a nice ending to a story that starts with a generation of Texas songwriters that was almost exclusively a men's club—a nice ending to that story, but perhaps a bit far-fetched. Still, there is something to be said for these smart and savvy young Texas women showing that you can be popular and actually have something to say.

CHALLENGE TO BRO COUNTRY

Kacey Musgraves

Grady Smith

Mainstream country music finds itself at a crossroads in the mid-2010s. On the plus side, the format is as popular as it's ever been, and its appeal continues to skyrocket as it adopts a more pop-centered sound. But rapid growth rarely breeds great art, and although the genre's footprint may be getting larger, there's a pervasive sense among industry insiders and country fans alike that quality is taking a major hit. As labels have attempted to reach the broad cross-section of the United States now giving country a chance, mainstream country music has grown increasingly homogenous, and it now appears stuck in a creative (and discouragingly sexist) rut. The weekly *Billboard* rankings find male performers like Luke Bryan, Blake Shelton, and Florida Georgia Line producing chart-toppers with derivative songs about pickup trucks, parties, panties, and Patrón, a phenomenon that *New York Magazine*'s music critic Jody Rosen famously labeled "bro country" in mid-2013.

Typical "bro country" songs are tailgate tunes sung by male artists wearing backwards trucker caps and wallet chains (fashions that seem to have replaced George Strait-approved cowboy hats and wrangler jeans), and they often employ hip-hop-influenced rhythmic cadences and, increasingly, elements of electronic dance music. Country radio can't get enough of the new trend, and debut singles from young artists like Tyler Farr ("Redneck Crazy"), Thomas Rhett ("It Goes Like This"), and Cole Swindell ("Chillin' It") have achieved massive radio success despite loud critical outcry about their narrow points of view and general lack of lyrical substance.

At the same time, female newcomers aren't enjoying such industry support. Country radio currently plays just three solo women on a regular basis: Carrie Underwood, Miranda Lambert, and Taylor Swift—and Swift has lately framed herself as a glitzy pop diva, not a country chanteuse. Distressingly, Swift was the last female artist to have her first two singles reach the Top 10 on *Billboard's* Hot Country Songs chart—and that happened all the way back in 2007. It can't be denied that country music is simply not producing new female superstars, which is both confusing and frustrating considering the creative revolution currently being led by underrepresented women. Talented upstarts like Ashley Monroe, Holly Williams, and Brandy Clark are penning many of the sharpest, wittiest, and most heart-wrenching songs the genre has to offer today, and yet, the collective powers that be don't seem willing to invest in their success. Fortunately, some talent is impossible to ignore.

The shining star of the up-and-coming new class of female country stars is undeniably Kacey Musgraves, a winsome singer-songwriter from Mineola, Texas, whose ability to marry traditional country melodies with unflinchingly honest lyrics have quickly made her the most compelling mainstream artist to arise from the ashes of "bro country." Musgraves has, in fact, become something of a symbol for country fans longing for a return to classic storytelling.

That's not to say Musgraves is pandering to old souls by penning fawning ditties about the good old days. A born iconoclast, she entered the mainstream consciousness in 2012 with a debut single called "Merry Go 'Round," a gothic lament about the broken, drug-addled culture of small town America, which showcased her natural flair for wordplay: "Mama's hooked on Mary Kay / Brother's hooked on Mary Jane / Daddy's hooked on Mary two doors down." The homespun track wasn't a smash hit, but it garnered enough airplay, buzz, and perhaps even controversy to launch her excellent debut album, *Same Trailer, Different Park*, to the No. 1 spot on the country chart in March 2013.

Same Trailer, produced by Shane McAnally and Luke Laird, forsook blaring drum machines and arena-sized pop flourishes, opting instead for acoustic plucking and pedal steel slides. But the disc's spare musical style isn't what made it feel revolutionary in modern country; its quiet power was its sharp lyrics. An accomplished songwriter, Musgraves had already scored a No. 1 cowrite with "Mama's Broken Heart," cut by Miranda Lambert, before she began releasing her own music, and another of Musgraves's songs, "Undermine," was featured on ABC's hit TV drama *Nashville*. So it was wise of *Same Trailer*'s producers to strip back production and allow the starlet's straight-talking lyrics and sassy delivery to take center stage.

It helps, of course, that Ms. Musgraves has a fresh perspective and bold things to say. On "It Is What It Is," she chronicles a sexual relationship that's turned passionless, and on "Blowing Smoke" she channels a world-weary waitress gossiping with her coworkers. But Musgraves's most provocative track, "Follow Your Arrow," is the one that has earned her most of her media attention. The song, which references smoking marijuana and same-sex kissing, subverts most of the norms typically represented in the conservative-minded country world. "Make lots of noise / Kiss lots of boys / Or kiss lots of girls if that's something you're into," goes the chorus of the you-only-live-once anthem. Admittedly, such feelings about the world aren't exactly revolutionary in 2014, but Musgraves's willingness to express them on a major-label country release most definitely was.

And she's not just an outspoken lyricist. Musgraves has gained fans (and ruffled feathers) as an interview subject as well. When asked by *British GQ* what musical trend should die, Musgraves didn't toe the Nashville party line. She responded, "Anyone singing about trucks, in any form, in any song, anywhere. Literally just stop—nobody cares! It's not fun to listen to." It's that direct attitude that has established Musgraves as a fascinating enigma within modern country music. On the one hand, she's an industry darling, an "it girl" who continually earns critical praise and even scored two Grammy awards for her debut album. But on the other hand, she's a conscious outsider that still seems to be on shaky ground with the country establishment. After all, none of her singles since "Merry Go 'Round" have reached the Top 20 of country radio airplay, though her album has sold admirably thanks to public interest.

Musgraves's determination to buck the conventional rules of country music have made her an exciting, and, many would argue, downright essential ingredient in the fight against "bro country." Her frank honesty is a refreshing addition in an industry currently polluted by shameless, rampant posturing to a tailgatin' redneck crowd. Her politics won't be for everyone, but Musgraves speaks clearly and from the soul, without the tired pop gimmicks employed by her peers. She follows her own arrow, and that is something that any music fan can get behind.

BEYOND THE RIVERS

Craig Clifford

In Part Three we include a few songwriters who are carrying on the Texas tradition of ruthlessly poetic songwriting that began with songwriters like Townes Van Zandt and Guy Clark in the late 1960s and early 1970s, a tall order considering the different context and different audiences that young songwriters face today. Because this is a book about the ruthlessly poetic singer-songwriters of Texas, we confined ourselves to the Lone Star State in our search for the heirs to this tradition.

But one of the reasons the music this book covers is so important is that it resonates well beyond the Red River and the Sabine; in fact, it resonates well beyond the borders of the United States. Faulkner wrote stories about people rooted in a thoroughly local culture, but he is read worldwide because at a deeper level his stories touch something universally human. Eudora Welty puts it this way:

> It seems plain that the art that speaks more clearly, explicitly, directly, and passionately from its place of origin will remain the longest understood. It is through place that we put out roots, wherever birth, chance, fate or our traveling selves set us down; but where those roots reach toward—whether in America, England, or Timbuktu—is the deep and running vein, eternal and consistent and everywhere purely itself, that feeds and is fed by the human understanding.

Texas music is rooted in a particular place, but the way it reaches down to the vein that Welty describes explains why the Irish can make sense of Townes Van Zandt.

It's also important to note the impact of this music on songwriters beyond Texas. And, as much as it hurts my diehard Texas heart to say it, when it comes to young songwriters who are following in the footsteps of Townes Van Zandt and Guy Clark, some of the very best are not from Texas. Luckily it's not a football game, but if it were, the Okies would probably be winning.

Evan Felker of the Turnpike Troubadours, whose sound is mainstream country enough to get played on the radio, writes finely crafted songs that provide a stark contrast to the I-love-my-pickup, get-drunk, painted-on-jeans genre that dominates Texas mainstream country radio. While many of the mainstream Texas boys are hanging on to mindless male adolescence with every verse they write, Felker hits us with courageously self-searching explorations of the loss of innocence:

> Life ain't what it was back then, someone smashed the windshield in
> Well you never see it comin' till it's knockin' out your teeth
> And it's the same Saturday, brand new Fords and Chevrolets
> Lined up like they never saw the likes of you and me
> And I watched them as they drove off in the sun

And, perhaps even more important, Oklahoma is producing radically independent, radio-be-damned music that would make Woody Guthrie proud—John Fullbright's poetic precision and beyond-his-years sense of narrative and John Moreland's soulful visions of life in the heartland played out over a percussive finger-picking guitar reminiscent of Townes in his prime. Fullbright and Moreland are honest-to-God folksingers who could be plopped down at Anderson Fair in Houston in 1970 and they would fit right in—their sound but, more importantly, the intelligence of their lyrics.

In *High on Tulsa Heat*, Moreland turns grief and suffering into shimmering art. On the surface, many of these songs are about the agony of love, but for Moreland love is a mirror on life's tragic challenge, that suffering always exceeds guilt. In "Hang Me in the Tulsa County Stars" the narrator is ostensibly talking to a lover, but in the process he offers up to us a vision of life driven by ominous forces that we don't control:

> No, I don't want to come back down to earth
> No, I don't want to come back down to earth
> My heart is growing heavy from the ever-endless hurt
> So I don't want to come back down to earth
> And, babe, I know
> This life will make you cold and leave you mad
> Make you homesick for a home you never had
> Burnin' out the good with all the bad

And a later version of the refrain:

> And, babe, I know
> This world will have the wolves outside your door

Make you leave all that you love to fight a war
But never tell you what you're dying for

That is not an anti-war verse—it's a beautifully unflinching commentary on life. What makes a world that will have the wolves outside your door worthwhile? Life seen through the eyes of John Moreland's art.

What distinguishes Moreland's brand of independence is not an "outlaw" rebellion but a singular dedication to truth:

So, darlin', let the charmers leave the room,
Let 'em have that Nashville moon,
I want to know exactly who you are,
Then hang me in the Tulsa county stars

In "Cleveland County Blues," a mournful love song of yearning and loss, Moreland's lover is a beautiful and dangerous contradiction that he can't escape:

So we're covered up in fiction chasin' something true
And, darlin', damn the luck and damn the consequences too
I could bury all the memories, I could patch up all the holes
But I'd still feel your fingers on my soul
My baby's a tornado in the endless Oklahoma sky
Spinning devastation and singing me a lullaby

It's worth noting here that Texas used to be the land of the endless sky, but too many Texas songwriters now are so caught up in the pseudo-country tropes of pickups and painted-on jeans that the true spirit of place that once was so powerful in songwriters like Guy Clark, Townes Van Zandt, Terry Allen, Steven Fromholz, and David Rodriguez has moved from Texas to Oklahoma. Oklahoma, because of songwriters like Moreland, has endless skies; Texas has bumper-to-bumper pickups.

But if I had to pick one young songwriter who is the true heir to the Texas tradition of songwriting that this book is about, the ruthlessly poetic song-writing trophy buckle would go to Alabaman Jason Isbell. And I'll stand on Steve Earle's coffee table in my cowboy boots and say it. Since leaving the Drive-By Truckers, Isbell has put out five studio albums: *Sirens of the Ditch* (2007), *Jason Isbell and the 400 Unit* (2009), *Here We Rest* (2011, again with the 400 Unit getting credit), *Southeastern* (2013), and *Something More Than Free* (2015). With *Here We Rest* he really hits his stride, with masterful songs in the folk-country tradition like "Alabama Pines," "Daisy Mae," and "Tour of Duty." But his two recent solo releases, *Southeastern* and *Something More Than Free*, establish him once and for all as a wordsmith worthy of comparison to the great singer-songwriters who began the tradition this book is about—and worthy of the tattoo on his arm from Bob Dylan's "Boots of Spanish Leather." The songs on these two albums are fearlessly intelligent and gorgeously lyrical. The lyrics are a combination of Southern storytelling, Faulknerian struggles of loving it and hating it, inspired turns of phrase, and seductive mystery.

Many of Isbell's songs are about the darker demons that haunt us. Philosophers have argued about this issue for a couple of millennia, but I'll go with Plato, who thought that all humans have the darker demons in their souls, and the question we all face, then, is: how do we deal with these demons?

"Cover Me Up," the lead song on *Southeastern* opens with an angry rebel-without-a-cause passage:

A heart on the run keeps a hand on the gun, you can't trust anyone
I was so sure what I needed was more, tried to shoot out the sun
Days when we raged, we flew off the page, such damage was done

But this song is ultimately about redemption through love: "But I made it through, 'cause somebody knew I was meant for someone." It is a deeply personal song inspired, according to Isbell, by his own escape from the destructive throes of alcoholism with the help of Amanda Shires, now his wife. But when the personal is transformed into art, it touches us all.

By contrast, in "Live Oak," a mysterious narrative that reads like a medieval tale of woe, the narrator tries to escape his darker demons but fails. He seeks redemption through love, but when he realizes that his lover was drawn to him because of his former murderous self, he apparently kills her:

Well I carved a cross from live oak and a box from short-leaf pine
And buried her so deep, she'd touch the water table line
I picked up what I needed and I headed south again
To myself, I wondered, "Would I ever find another friend?"
There's a man who walks beside her, he is who I used to be
And I wonder if she sees him and confuses him with me

There is an air of mystery about the entire story, and you're never completely certain you know what's happening, but you know that his darker demons have never left him. Again, this song seems to draw from Isbell's own darker side and darker, booze-addled experiences, and it's perhaps too easy to over-psychologize it into Isbell's fear that his darker side will return and win out. Again, it's the deeper mining of the personal psyche that makes it speak to all of us.

"New South Wales," a tale of desolation and debauchery laced with flashes of insight, is intensely cryptic. At first, I almost gave up on it. It reminded me of some of the pseudo-profound alternative rock. If you say something that makes no sense, everyone will think you're profound. Early Bob Dylan probably sounds that way to someone who isn't smart enough to struggle through the layers of indirection. But, in the end, early Bob Dylan does makes sense, just not in an obvious or immediate way. Isbell's "New South Wales" creates an enigma that draws you in, and one that yields deeper and deeper layers of meaning the more you live with the song. It is a commentary on finding meaning in the midst of desolation:

> And the sand that they call cocaine cost you twice as much as gold
> You'd be better off to drink your coffee black
> But I swear, the land it listened to the stories that we told
> God bless the busted boat that brings us back

And in another version of the refrain, he says:

> And the piss they call tequila even Waylon wouldn't drink
> Well I'd rather sip this Listerine I packed
> But I swear, we've never seen a better place to sit and think
> God bless the busted ship that brings us back

On one level, this song seems to be about a sailor complaining about landing in God-forsaken Australia; on another level, it's a comment on the human condition—the boats that bring us back are always busted, and we should be thankful for a land that listens to the stories we tell and thankful for a place to sit and think.

The title song of *Something More Than Free* at first glance seems to be another homage to the working man: "You see a hammer finds a nail and a freight train needs the rails / And I'm doin' what I'm on this earth to do." But this is not Merle Haggard's proudly defiant working man. The song deepens and darkens with every line. Isbell's working man says he's "just lucky to have the work," but that line follows an expression of gloomy resignation: "And I don't think on why I'm here where it hurts." The narrator is a simple but honorable man trying to make sense of his lot in life. Like many of Isbell's characters, he reminds me of the characters in Faulkner who suffer well beyond their just deserts but still maintain a kind of tragic dignity that compels our attention, perhaps because, deep down, that is the human condition we all struggle with.

In "Flagship," a masterful combination of youthful yearning and ominous foreboding, Isbell again draws a quick sketch that deepens with every listening:

> Baby, let's not live to see it fade
> I'll cancel all the plans I've ever made
> I'll drive and you can ride in the back seat
> And we'll call ourselves the flagship of the fleet

This song is a beautifully constructed reflection on the collision between love's innocence and life's tragic realities. It ends with a plea for embracing love in spite of all of the odds:

> You gotta try and keep yourself naive
> In spite of all the evidence believed
> And volunteer to lose touch with the world
> And focus on one solitary girl

Against the backdrop of the rest of the song, are we supposed to take this passage to be ironic? Or an honest assessment of the Kierkegaardian leap of faith that romantic love requires? Like all of his songs, this one raises questions that we can only answer by living our lives in light of the questions.

When I saw the title "Speed Trap Town," the first thought that crossed my mind was that this song would be just another leaving-my-hometown, the-highway-is-my-home white boy romp. However, from the first verse, it's clear that this song, like all of Isbell's songs, reaches to the universally human, not by repeating the usual clichés that catch the attention of an MP3-buying audience and the radio station DJs, but by digging deeply into the soul of an all-too-real individual. It's not a positive portrayal of a small town, to be sure, but it's not about the clichéd generic speed-trap towns; it's about a particular young man struggling with his lot in life.

With the *in medias res* opening—"She said, 'It's none of my business but it breaks my heart'"—there is no way to know for sure what is happening. But this young man has probably just lost his mother, possibly from suicide since the unidentified woman of the opening line makes it clear that what she's referring to is not something that is easy to talk about in public. After he signs the papers, presumably to take his philandering father off life support, he moves from asking "if there's anything that can't be left behind" to the realization that "there's nothing here that can't be left behind." Mainstream bro country rejects adulthood with every syllable it produces, but Isbell shines a truthful light on the costs and rewards and fateful mysteries of growing up. One of the finest lines in this song is ostensibly about losing a football game to "these 5A bastards" but in the end it's about becoming a man: "It's a boy's last dream and a man's first loss."

"Children of Children" doesn't go for the obvious lament about the difficulties for the child of children. Instead the narrator takes on the guilt of what his birth did to his mother. He looks at a photograph of his mother at seventeen, and he sees his role in her predicament:

> I was riding on my mother's hip,
> She was shorter than the corn
> All the years I took from her,
> Just by being born

Isbell is a master of getting deep into the psyche of an individual character, but he is also a master of showing the interconnectedness of individuals and communities. When you look deep into your own soul, he tells us, you will see the others you are connected to, often in ways that are chosen by the hands of fate, sometimes in ways that are chosen by you. Human dignity, he seems to say, comes from looking at that situation, suspended between heartless fate and human responsibility, with an unflinching eye.

In "Rex's Blues," Townes Van Zandt says, "There ain't no dark till something shines." Jason Isbell's lyrics shine, and often they shine on darkness. But, like the lyrics of the great Texas singer-songwriters this book is about, like the enduring tragedies of Sophocles, like the disturbing short stories of Flannery O'Connor, like the Southern soul-searching novels of Faulkner, Isbell's lyrics are ennobling.

NOTES

Too Weird for Kerrville: The Darker Side of Texas Music by Craig Clifford

1. Adapted from an essay originally published in *Langdon Review of the Arts in Texas*, Vol. 5 (2008–2009).

Townes Van Zandt: The Anxiety, Artifice, and Audacity of Influence by Robert Earl Hardy

1. Mickey Newberry, unpublished interview with the author on May 4, 2000, for *A Deeper Blue: The Life and Music of Townes Van Zandt* (Denton: University of North Texas Press, 2008).

2. Interview with Townes Van Zandt, Dutch MTV, 1991.

3. Bob Dylan, *Chronicles Volume One* (New York: Simon & Schuster, 2004).

4. John Hollander, review of Harold Bloom's *The Anxiety of Influence*. *The New York Times*, March 4, 1973.

5. Paul Zollo, *Songwriters on Songwriting* (Cambridge: Da Capo Press, 1997).

6. Hardy, *A Deeper Blue*.

7. T. S. Eliot, "Tradition and the Individual Talent" in *The Sacred Wood: Essays on Poetry and Criticism*, 1921.

8. Townes Van Zandt, "High, Low and In Between" on *High, Low and In Between*, Capitol, 1971, Bug Music.

9. Townes Van Zandt, "Pancho and Lefty" on *The Late Great Townes Van Zandt*, 1972, Bug Music.

10. Zollo, *Songwriters on Songwriting*.

11. Leonard Cohen, "Tower of Song" on *I'm Your Man*, 1988, Sony/ATV Songs LLC, Stranger Music Inc.

12. Steve Earle, interview by John Nova Lomax, New West Records press release, 2009.

13. Leonard Cohen, interview by Tim de Lisle, *The Guardian*, September 16, 2004.

14. Interview with Townes Van Zandt, Dutch MTV, 1991

15. Mickey Newberry, unpublished interview with the author, for *A Deeper Blue*.

16. Robert Frost, "Tree At My Window," *The Poetry of Robert Frost* (New York: Owl Books, 1979).

17. Zollo, *Songwriters on Songwriting*.

18. Steve Earle, interview by John Nova Lomax, New West Records press release, 2009.

19. Hardy, *A Deeper Blue*.

20. Jan Wenner, "Lennon Remembers: The Rolling Stone Interviews," *Rolling Stone*, January 21, 1971.

21. Lightnin' Hopkins, "My Starter Won't Start," Prestige Music.

22. Townes Van Zandt, "Brand New Companion" on *Delta Mamma Blues,* 1971, Bug Music.

23. Lightnin' Hopkins, "Katie Mae," Prestige Music.

24. Zollo, *Songwriters on Songwriting.*

25. Hardy, *A Deeper Blue.*

Guy Clark: Old School Poet of the World by Tamara Saviano

1. Excerpted from the biography *Without Getting Killed or Caught: The Life and Music of Guy Clark* (College Station: Texas A&M University Press, 2016).

Steven Fromholz, Michael Martin Murphey, and Jerry Jeff Walker: Poetic in Lyric, Message, and Musical Method by Craig D. Hillis

1. The quotations from Walker in this section are from Jerry Jeff Walker, *Gypsy Songman* (Emeryville, California: Woodford Press, 1999).

Vignette—Ray Wylie Hubbard: Grifter, Ruffian, Messenger by Jenni Finlay

1. Ray Wylie Hubbard, interview by Brian T. Atkinson, November 1, 2013.

2. Ibid.

"Gettin' Tough": Steve Earle's America by Jason Mellard

1. Lauren St. John, *Hardcore Troubadour: The Life & Near Death of Steve Earle* (New York: Fourth Estate, 2003); David McGee, *Steve Earle: Fearless Heart, Outlaw Poet* (San Francisco: Backbeat Books, 2005).

2. A process analyzed well in Benjamin Filene, *Romancing the Folk: Public Memory & American Roots Music* (Chapel Hill: University of North Carolina Press, 2000).

3. The connections between the aesthetics of the Popular Front and the politics of the 1930s have been best traced by Michael Denning, *The Cultural Front: The Laboring of American Culture* (New York: Verso Press, 1994). On the intertwined genre histories of folk and country, see Richard Peterson, *Creating Country Music: Fabricating Authenticity* (Chicago: University of Chicago Press, 1997), 198–199.

4. It should also be noted that Earle objects to the kinds of authenticity claims that see him as an exemplar of the working class. His own upbringing was, admittedly, firmly middle class, and he has chosen to document American struggles across the class spectrum.

5. David Frum, *How We Got Here: The 70s.* (New York: Basic Books, 2000), 7.

Selected Sources

Books and Articles

Allen, Michael. "'I Just Want to Be a Cosmic Cowboy': Hippies, Cowboy Code, and the Culture of a Counterculture." *Western Historical Quarterly* 36:3 (2005): 275-300.

Alyn, Glen. *I Say Me for a Parable: The Oral Autobiography of Mance Lipscomb, Texas Bluesman*. New York: W.W. Norton & Company, 1993.

Antone, Susan. *Antone's: The First Ten Years*. Austin: Antone's Records, 1985.

Atkinson, Brian T. *I'll Be Here in the Morning: The Songwriting Legacy of Townes Van Zandt*. College Station: Texas A&M University Press, 2011.

Bane, Michael. *The Outlaws: Revolution in Country Music*. New York: Doubleday, 1978.

———. *White Boy Singin' the Blues*. Cambridge: Da Capo Press, 1982.

Barkley, Roy, Douglas E. Barnett, Cathy Bringham, Gary Hartman, Casey Monahan, David Oliphant, George B. Ward, eds. *The Handbook of Texas Music*. Austin: Texas State Historical Association, 2003.

Belcher, David. "Politics Sung With a Texas Kick," *The New York Times*, February 29, 2012.

Berliner, Louise. *Texas Guinan: Queen of the Nightclubs*. Austin: University of Texas Press, 1993.

Bell, Vince. *One Man's Music: The Life and Times of Texas Songwriter Vince Bell*. Denton: University of North Texas Press, 2009.

———. *Sixtyeight Twentyeight: The Life and Times of a Texas Writer and a Flat Top Box Guitar*. Sante Fe: Vincebell.com, 2006.

Bennett, Andy. *Popular Music and Youth Culture: Music, Identity, and Place*. London: Macmillan, 2000.

———, and Richard Peterson, eds. *Music Scenes: Local, Translocal, and Virtual*. Nashville: Vanderbilt University Press, 2004.

Boyd, Jean. *The Jazz of the Southwest: An Oral History of Western Swing*. Austin: University of Texas Press, 1998.

Boyd, Jean A. *"We're the Light Crust Doughboys from Burris Mill": An Oral History*. Austin: University of Texas Press, 2003.

Branch, Douglas. *The Cowboy and His Interpreters*. New York: Cooper Square Publishers, Inc., 1961.

Breithaupt, Don, and Jeff Breithaupt. *Precious and Few: Pop Music in the Early '70s*. New York: St. Martin's Griffin, 1996.

Bridger, Bobby. *A Ballad of the West: Seekers of the Fleece Lakota*. South Bend: Augustine Press, 1993.

———. *Bridger*. Austin: University of Texas Press, 2009.

Buerger, Megan. "Kacey Musgraves Follows Her Arrow to the Top," *The Wall Street Journal*, February 13, 2014.

Bukowski, Elizabeth. "Lucinda Williams," *Salon*, January 11, 2000.

Bush, Johnny, and Rick Mitchell. *Whiskey River (Take My Mind): The True Story of Texas Honky-Tonk*. Austin: University of Texas Press, 2007.

Clarke, Donald, ed. *The Penguin Encyclopedia of Popular Music*. London: Viking-Penguin, 1989.

Clayton, Lawrence, and Joe W. Specht, eds. *The Roots of Texas Music*. College Station: Texas A&M University Press, 2003.

Clemons, Leigh. *Branding Texas: Performing Culture in the Lone Star State*. Austin: University of Texas Press, 2008.

Connell, John, and Chris Gibson. *Soundtracks: Popular Music, Identity and Place (Critical Geographies)*. London: Routledge Publishing, 2003.

Corcoran, Michael. *All Over the Map: True Heroes of Texas Music*. Austin: University of Texas Press, 2005.

Crawford, Richard. *America's Musical Life: A History*. New York: W. W. Norton & Company, 2001.

Davis, Francis. *The History of the Blues: The Roots, The Music, The People*. Cambridge: Da Capo Press, 1995.

Davis, John T. *Austin City Limits: 25 Years of American Music*. New York: Billboard Books, 2000.

———. *The Flatlanders: Now It's Now Again*. Austin: University of Texas Press, 2014.

Denisoff, R. Serge. *Waylon: A Biography*. Knoxville: University of Tennessee Press, 1983.

Deusner, Stephen, M. "Lucinda Williams: West," *Pitchfork.com*, February 19, 2007. http://pitchfork.com/reviews/albums/9912-west/.

Dobson, Richard J. *The Gulf Coast Boys*. CreateSpace Independent Publishing Platform, 2013 (reprint of Greater Texas Publishing 1998 edition).

Doggett, Peter. *Are You Ready for the Country: Elvis, Dylan, Parsons, and the Roots of Country Rock*. New York: Penguin Books, 2001.

Drummond, Paul. *Eye Mind: The Saga of Roky Erickson and the 13th Floor Elevators, The Pioneers of Psychedelic Sound*. Los Angeles: Process Media, 2007.

Dutton, Monte. *True to the Roots: Americana Music Revealed*. Lincoln: University of Nebraska Press, 2006.

Dylan, Bob. *Chronicles Volume One*. Reprint. New York: Simon & Schuster, 2005.

Ely, Joe. *Bonfire of Roadmaps*. Austin: University of Texas Press, 2007.

Endres, Clifford. *Austin City Limits: The Story Behind Television's Most Popular Country Music Program*. Austin: University of Texas Press, 1987.

Evans, Nick and Jeff Horne. *Songbuilder: The Life and Music of Guy Clark*. Kent, England: Amber Waves/Heartland Publishing, 1998.

Felps, Paula. *Lone Stars and Legends: The Story of Texas Music*. Plano: Republic of Texas Press, 2001.

Filene, Benjamin. *Romancing the Folk: Public Memory & American Roots Music*. Chapel Hill: University of North Carolina Press, 2000.

Ginell, Gary. *Milton Brown and the Founding of Western Swing*. Urbana: University of Illinois Press, 1994.

Goetzmann, William H., and William N. Goetzmann. *The West of the Imagination*. New York: W. W. Norton & Company, 1986.

Govenar, Alan. *Living Texas Blues*. Dallas: Dallas Museum of Art, 1985.

———. *Meeting the Blues: The Rise of the Texas Sound*. Dallas: Taylor Publishing Company, 1988.

————. *Texas Blues: The Rise of a Contemporary Sound*. College Station: Texas A&M University Press, 2008.

————. *The Early Years of Rhythm & Blues Focus on Houston*. Houston: Rice University Press, 1990.

Graham, Don, ed. *Literary Austin*. Fort Worth: TCU Press, 2007.

Green, Archie. "Austin's Cosmic Cowboys: Words in Collision," *Torching the Fink Books and Other Essays on Vernacular Culture*. Chapel Hill & London: The University of North Carolina Press, 2001.

Gregory, Hugh. *Stevie Ray Vaughan and Texas R&B*. San Francisco: Backbeat Books, 2003.

Hardy, Robert Earl. *A Deeper Blue: The Life and Music of Townes Van Zandt*. Denton: University of North Texas Press, 2008.

Harris, Steve. *Texas Troubadours*. Austin: University of Texas Press, 2007.

Hartman, Gary. *The History of Texas Music*. College Station: Texas A&M Press, 2008.

Hillis, Craig D., and Bruce F. Jordan. *Texas Trilogy ~ Life in a Small Texas Town*. Austin: University of Texas Press, 2002.

Holland, Travis. *Texas Genesis: A Wild Ride Through Texas Progressive Country Music 1963–1978 as Seen Through the Warped Mind of Travis Holland*. Austin: B.F.Deal Publishing, 1978.

Hudson, Kathleen. *Telling Stories Writing Songs: An Album of Texas Songwriters*. Austin: University of Texas Press, 2001.

————. *Women in Texas Music: Stories and Songs*. Austin: University of Texas Press, 2007.

Jones, Chris. "Lucinda Williams West Review," BBC, 2007. http://www.bbc.co.uk/music/reviews/83zf

Keen, Robert Earl. *The Road Goes on Forever and the Music Never Ends*. Austin: University of Texas Press, 2009.

Kennedy, Rod, and Hugh Cullen Sparks. *Rod Kennedy: Music from the Heart: The Fifty-Year Chronicle of His Life in Music (with a Few Sidetrips!)*. Austin: Eakin Press, 1998.

Koster, Rick. *Texas Music*. New York: St. Martin's Griffin, 1998.

Krasilovsky, William M., Sidney Shemel, and John M. Gross. *This Business of Music: The Definitive Guide to the Music Industry*. New York: Billboard Books, 2000.

Kruth, John. *To Live's to Fly: The Ballad of the Late, Great Townes Van Zandt*. Cambridge: Da Capo Press, 2007.

Langer, Andy. "The Patty Griffin Effect," *Texas Monthly*, May 2013.

Leigh, Keri. *Stevie Ray: Soul to Soul*. Dallas: Taylor Publishing Co., 1993.

Lewis, George H., ed. *All that Glitters: Country Music in America*. Bowling Green: Bowling Green State University Popular Press, 1993.

Light, Andy. "Stars Add New Tunes to Country King's Lyrics," *The New York Times*, September 23, 2011.

Lomax, John Avery. *Adventures of a Ballad Hunter*. New York: The Macmillan Company, 1942.

Lomax, John and Alan Lomax, eds. *American Ballads and Folk Songs*. New York: Dover, 1994 (reprint of Macmillan 1934 edition).

Malone, Bill, C. *Country Music U.S.A.* Austin: University of Texas Press, 1968.

————. *Don't Get above Your Raisin': Country Music and the Southern Working Class*. Urbana: University of Illinois Press, 2006.

————, and David Stricklin. *Southern Music/American Music*. Lexington: The University Press of Kentucky, 2003.

Martin, Douglas. "Obituaries: Cindy Walker, songwriter," *The New York Times*, March 29, 2006.

McLean, Duncan. *Lone Star Swing: One Scotsman's Odyssey in Search of the True Meaning of Western Swing*. New York: W. W. Norton & Company, 1997.

Mellard, Jason. *Progressive Country: How the 1970s Transformed the Texan in Popular Culture*. Austin: University of Texas Press, 2014.

Miller, Karl Hagstom. *Segregating Sound: Inventing Folk and Pop Music in the Age of Jim Crow*. Durham: Duke University Press, 2010.

Milner, Jay Dunston. *Confessions of a Maddog: A Romp through the High-Flying Texas Music and Literary Era of the Fifties to the Seventies*. Denton: University of North Texas Press, 1998.

Morthland, John. "Songwriter," *Texas Monthly*, December 1999.

Moser, Margaret. "Double-Barrel Beautiful," *The Austin Chronicle*, December 19, 2008.

———. "Going Back to 'Lake Charles,'" *The Austin Chronicle*, October 23, 1998.

———. "Moon-Shaped Panties & the Saint of White Trash," The Austin Chronicle, October 23, 1998.

———. "Rough Trade Talk with Lucinda Williams," *The Austin Chronicle*, September 13, 2013.

———. "Something Wicked This Way Comes: Lucinda Williams," *The Austin Chronicle*, January 15, 2013.

Nelson, Willie. *The Facts of Life: And Other Dirty Jokes*. New York: Random House, 2001.

———, and Turk Pipkin. *The Tao of Willie: A Guide to the Happiness in Your Heart*. New York: Gotham Books, 2002.

———, and Bud Shrake. *Willie*. New York: Cooper Square Press, 2000.

Nettl, Bruno. *Folk and Traditional Music of the Western Continents*. Englewood Cliffs: Prentice Hall, 1965.

Nicholls, David, ed. *The Cambridge History of American Music*. Cambridge: Cambridge University Press, 1998.

Oakley, Giles. *The Devil's Music: A History of the Blues*. New York: Da Capo Press, 1997.

Oglesby, Christopher J. *Fire in the Water, Earth in the Air: Legends of West Texas Music*. Austin: University of Texas Press, 2006.

Oliver, Paul. *Blues Fell This Morning*. Cambridge: Cambridge University Press, 1960.

———. *The Story of the Blues*. London: Barrie & Rockliff, 1969.

Patoski, Joe Nick. *Willie Nelson: An Epic Life*. New York: Little, Brown & Co., 2008.

Patoski, Joe Nick, and Bill Crawford. *Stevie Ray Vaughn: Caught in the Crossfire*. Boston: Little, Brown & Co., 1993.

Peña, Manuel H. *The Texas-Mexican Conjunto: History of a Working-Class Music*. Austin: University of Texas Press, 1985.

Plato, Greg. "Patty Griffin on First Solo Tour in 12 Years: 'The Idea Is to Go Back to an Old, Beaten Path,'" *Rolling Stone*, July 31, 2012.

Porterfield, Nolan, ed. *Exploring Roots Music: Twenty Years of JEMF Quarterly*. Lanham, Maryland: The Scarecrow Press, 2004.

Reid, Jan. *The Improbable Rise of Redneck Rock*. Austin: Heidelberg Publishers, 1974.

———. *The Improbable Rise of Redneck Rock*. Austin: University of Texas Press, 2004.

Reid, Jan with Shawn Sahm. *Texas Tornado: The Times and Music of Doug Sahm*. Austin: University of Texas Press, 2010.

Richards, Tad, and Melvin B. Shestack. *The New Country Music Encyclopedia*. New York: Fireside, 1993.

Rosen, Sybil. *Living in the Woods in a Tree: Remembering Blaze Foley*. Denton: University of North Texas Press, 2008.

Rossinow, Doug. *The Politics of Authenticity: Liberalism, Christianity, and the New Left in America*. New York: Columbia University Press, 1998.

Sanjek, Russell. *Pennies from Heaven: The American Popular Music Business in the Twentieth Century*. New York: Da Capo Press, 1996.

Santoro, Gene. *Highway 61 Revisited: The Tangled Roots of American Jazz, Blues, Rock & Country Music*. New York, Oxford: Oxford University Press, 2004.

Scully, Michael. *The Never Ending Revival: Rounder Records and the Folk Alliance*. Urbana: University of Illinois Press, 2008.

Shank, Barry. *Dissonant Identities: The Rock 'n' Roll Scene in Austin, Texas*. Hanover and London: Wesleyan University Press, 1994.

Shaver, Billy Joe. *Honky Tonk Hero*. Austin: University of Texas Press, 2005.

Southern, Eileen. *The Music of Black Americans: A History*. New York: W. W. Norton & Company, Inc., 1971.

Stevens, Denis, ed. *A History of Song*. New York, London: W. W. Norton & Company, 1970.

Stimeling, Travis D. *Cosmic Cowboys and New Hicks: The Countercultural Sounds of Austin's Progressive Music Scene*. New York: Oxford University Press, 2011.

St. John, Lauren. *Hardcore Troubadour: The Life and Near Death of Steve Earle*. New York: Fourth Estate, Harper Collins Publishers, Inc., 2003.

Swiatecki, Chad. "Robert Plant Joins Patty Griffin Onstage for Austin Benefit Show," *Rolling Stone*, December 16, 2012.

Tosches, Nick. *Country: The Twisted Roots of Rock 'n' Roll*. New York: Da Capo Press, 1985.

Treviño, Geronimo III. *Dance Halls and Last Calls: A History of Texas Country Music*. Plano: Republic of Texas Press, 2002.

Turley, Alan C. *Music in the City: A History of Austin Music*. Cedar Park: Duckling Publishing, 2000.

Wald, Elijah. *Escaping the Delta: Robert Johnson and the Invention of the Blues*. New York: Amistad (An Imprint of HarperCollins Publishers), 2004.

Walker, Jerry Jeff. *Gypsy Songman*. Emeryville, California: Woodford Press, 1999.

Willoughby, Larry. *Texas Rhythm, Texas Rhyme: A Pictorial History of Texas Music*. Austin: Tonkawa Free Press, 1990.

Wilson, Burton. *Burton's Book of the Blues: A Decade of American Music: 1967–1977*. Austin: Edentata Press, 1977.

———, and Jack Ortman. *The Austin Music Scene Through the Lens of Burton Wilson 1965–1994*. Austin: Eakin Press, 2001.

Wood, Roger, and James Fraher. *Down in Houston: Bayou City Blues*. Austin: University of Texas Press, 2003.

———. *Texas Zydeco*. Austin: University of Texas Press, 2006.

Wyman, Bill, and Richard Havers. *Blues Odyssey: A Journey to Music's Heart & Soul*. New York: DK Publishing, 2001.

Dissertations, Theses, and Related Scholarly Writings

Hillis, Craig D. "The Austin Music Scene in the 1970s: Songs and Songwriters." PhD diss., University of Texas at Austin, 2011.

Krantzman, Phyllis. "Impact of the Music Entertainment Industry on Austin, Texas." MA thesis, University of Texas at Austin, 1983.

Mellard, Jason. "Cosmic Cowboys, Armadillos, and Outlaws: The Cultural Politics of Texas Identity in the 1970s." PhD diss., University of Texas at Austin, 2009.

Menconi, David Lawrence. "Music, Media and the Metropolis: The Case of Austin's Armadillo World Headquarters." MA thesis, University of Texas at Austin, 1985.

Sparks, Hugh Cullen. "Stylistic Development and Compositional Processes of Selected Solo Singer/Songwriters in Austin, Texas." MA thesis, University of Texas at Austin, 1984.

Archival Materials

Gary Cartwright Papers, 1963–1984. Austin History Center, Austin.

Edwin Allen Jr. "Bud" Shrake, Biography File. Austin History Center, Austin.

Armadillo World Headquarters Records, 1971–1980. Center for American History, University of Texas, Austin.

A "Best" Source for Texas Music

The bibliographical information above is the product of research conducted by certain contributors to this volume of essays. Consequently, it reflects specific lines of academic inquiry relevant to specific subjects. It is neither a comprehensive collection of sources, nor is it intended to be. Indeed, the editors feel that the broad sweep of Texas music suggests a massive reservoir of primary and secondary sources. Although a "comprehensive" collection is well beyond the scope of this study, there are exhaustive resources available to Texas music scholars and enthusiasts. Two unique organizations—the Center for Texas Music History at Texas State University and the Texas Music Office (an office of the Governor of Texas)—have worked together over the years to create an outstanding pool of historical sources and contemporary resources. We suggest beginning your search on the Center for Texas Music History website. Check out the Texas Music Bibliography section, which was created in collaboration with the Texas Music Office and includes published and unpublished works relating to Southwestern musical history. Then check out the Texas Music Office, where you will find not only historical sources, but extensive listings on musicians, music business entities, and all items relevant to making and studying music in Texas yesterday and today.

CONTRIBUTORS

COEDITORS

CRAIG CLIFFORD is professor of philosophy and executive director of the Honors College at Tarleton State University in Stephenville, Texas. He is the author of *In the Deep Heart's Core: Reflections on Life, Letters, and Texas* (Texas A&M University Press, 1985), *The Tenure of Phil Wisdom: Dialogues* (University Press of America, 1995), and *Learned Ignorance in the Medicine Bow Mountains: A Reflection on Intellectual Prejudice* (Rodopi, 2009); coeditor with William T. Pilkington of *Range Wars: Heated Debates, Sober Reflections, and Other Assessments of Texas Writing* (Southern Methodist University Press, 1989); and coauthor with Randolph M. Feezell of *Sport and Character: Reclaiming the Principles of Sportsmanship* (Human Kinetics, 2010). His essays, guest columns, and reviews have appeared in numerous newspapers and magazines. Born in Louisiana and raised outside of Houston, Clifford did his undergraduate work in Plan II (the liberal arts honors program) at the University of Texas at Austin. He completed his PhD in philosophy at the State University of New York at Buffalo in 1981, writing a dissertation on Plato and Heidegger. After nine years as expatriates in Buffalo, New York, and Annapolis, Maryland, Clifford and his wife returned to Texas in 1983. Clifford is a prolific songwriter who performs regularly with the Accidental Band and occasionally as a solo singer-songwriter.

CRAIG D. HILLIS is a veteran guitar player who has recorded and toured with Michael Martin Murphey, Steven Fromholz, Jerry Jeff Walker, B. W. Stevenson, Rusty Wier, and an extended list of notable singer-songwriters. As an original member of the Lost Gonzo Band, Hillis played lead guitar on Jerry Jeff Walker's seminal 1973 album *¡Viva Terlingua!* and has an admirable forty-year history of record production and studio engineering with special expertise in artist management and intellectual property issues. Hillis has owned and operated successful nightclubs in Austin, Texas: he bought Steamboat on 6th Street in the early 1980s and developed the venue into a national showcase featuring acts like Christopher Cross and Stevie Ray Vaughan. In 1990, he built the Saxon Pub, another showcase venue designed to feature the talents of exceptional singer-songwriters. With both clubs up and running strong, he enrolled in graduate school at UT in 1994, then sold both businesses in 1996 to devote his attention to his studies. He is a published nonfiction author (*Texas Trilogy: Life in a Small Texas Town*, University of Texas Press, 2002) and has written for academic journals, popular magazines, and regional newspapers. Hillis completed his PhD in American Studies at the University of Texas at Austin in 2011. His dissertation, *The Austin Music Scene in the 1970s: Songs and Songwriters*, focuses on Texas music history and its significance in American cultural history.

WRITERS

BRIAN T. ATKINSON

Brian T. Atkinson is the author of *I'll Be Here in the Morning: The Songwriting Legacy of Townes Van Zandt* (Texas A&M University Press, 2012) and coauthor of *Kent Finlay, Dreamer: The Musical Legacy Behind Cheatham Street Warehouse* (Texas A&M University Press, 2016). He and Jenni Finlay own Eight 30 Records and have co-produced *Cold and Bitter Tears: The Songs of Ted Hawkins, Kent Finlay, Dreamer*, and Danny Barnes's *Got Myself Together (Ten Years Later)*. The Austin-based writer and photographer's work regularly appears in the *Austin American-Statesman* and on CMT.com.

Atkinson's *For the Sake of the Song: The Outlaws of Americana*, an exhibit of live concert photography, has shown in Austin, Denver, and Seattle. He has written liner notes for *Cold and Bitter Tears* (Eight 30 Records), Danny Barnes's *Got Myself Together* (Eight 30 Records), *This One's for Him: A Tribute to Guy Clark* (Music Road Records, 2011), and others. Additionally, he and Finlay own Burgundy Red Films and host the bimonthly house concert series Catfish Concerts in Austin, Texas. For more information about the author, whose writing and photography are archived in the Wittliff Collections at Texas State University, visit squeakystring.com and briantatkinson.com.

PETER COOPER

Peter Cooper is a museum editor at the Country Music Hall of Fame in Nashville. He's also a senior lecturer in country music history at Vanderbilt University's Blair School of Music. He's also a Grammy-nominated producer and a touring singer-songwriter with dozens of fans all over some of the world. He is a winner of The Charlie Lamb Award For Excellence In Country Music Journalism. He is physically dominant, with a good low-post game and a devastating jump shot. He has worked in the recording studio with luminaries including Country Music Hall of Famers Emmylou Harris,

Bobby Bare, Tom T. Hall, and Mac Wiseman. He has profiled music legends including Johnny Cash, Ray Charles, George Jones, John Prine, and, in these pages, Kris Kristofferson.

John T. Davis

John T. Davis has lived in Austin for more than three decades, writing about the music, personalities, and culture of Texas and the Southwest for a variety of regional, state, and national publications. His byline has appeared in the *Austin American-Statesman*, the *Austin Chronicle*, *Texas Monthly*, *Texas Highways*, *San Antonio Magazine*, *Billboard*, *Newsday*, and the website Culturemap.com. He is also a frequent contributor to *Austin Monthly*. He has been interviewed by VH-1, CMT, and NPR and has appeared in the documentary film *Lubbock Lights*.

He is the author of the book *Austin City Limits: 25 Years of American Music* and has assisted in the preparation and editing of several other volumes, including biographies of musicians Jerry Jeff Walker and Johnny Bush, and a travel guide to Texas.

In 2008, he conducted a class of one-on-one interviews with musicians for the Austin Live Music Academy at the University of Texas. That same year, he was a featured panelist at the Association of American Editorial Cartoonists. In 2009, he was awarded a Lone Star Award (Third Place) in the "Magazine/Features" category in a statewide contest sponsored by the Houston Press Club. In 2010 he cowrote a documentary film on Jerry Jeff Walker and contributed a memorial essay on musician Stephen Bruton for the Austin City Limits Music Festival program, among other projects.

As of 2010, his work (including notes, drafts, manuscripts, and more) is featured in the permanent archives of the Southwestern Writers Collection at Texas State University. In 2011, he coauthored *Thin Slice of Life*, a mystery novel published in 2012 by Stephen F. Austin University Press. He and the coauthors are currently at work on a sequel.

Diana Finlay Hendricks

An accomplished editor, writer, reporter, and photographer for more than twenty years—in magazine, newspaper and public relations—Diana has earned statewide and national awards for reporting and photography. She is a frequent contributor to *Lone Star Music* magazine and the *Journal of Texas Music History*. In addition to regular contributions to state and regional magazines, she is currently writing a Delbert McClinton biography and collaborating on two book projects in the fields of Texas music and culture.

For twenty-three years, she was the co-owner of Cheatham Street Warehouse, a historic music venue in San Marcos. Nationally known artists have spent countless nights on that rustic stage, including George Strait, Charlie and Will Sexton, Randy Rogers, Stevie Ray Vaughan, Marcia Ball, Delbert McClinton, Townes Van Zandt, Jerry Jeff Walker, and Willie Nelson. Diana holds a Master of Arts degree with an emphasis in Texas music and culture, and a Bachelor of Arts with an emphasis in Texas music history and creative writing, both from Texas State University.

Jenni Finlay

Jenni Finlay is coauthor of *Kent Finlay, Dreamer: The Musical Legacy behind Cheatham Street Warehouse* (Texas A&M University Press, 2016) and the poetry collection *Table for One* (Mezcalita Press, 2015). Finlay and Brian T. Atkinson own Eight 30 Records and have coproduced *Cold and Bitter Tears: The Songs of Ted Hawkins* (2015), Danny Barnes's *Got Myself Together (Ten Years Later)* (2015), and *Kent Finlay, Dreamer* (2016). Finlay manages acclaimed songwriter James McMurtry and has owned and operated Jenni Finlay Promotions for more than a decade. Her monthly newsletter reaches nearly thirty thousand readers. Additionally, Finlay and Atkinson own Burgundy Red Films and host the bimonthly house concert series Catfish Concerts in Austin, Texas. For more information about the author, visit squeakystring.com and jennifinlaypromotions.com.

Robert Earl Hardy

Robert Earl Hardy has published articles on American music and the arts in various defunct newspapers, obscure journals, and unknown magazines—including in the acclaimed Southern Music Issue of *The Oxford American*. His book, *A Deeper Blue: The Life and Music of Townes Van Zandt*, was published by the University of North Texas Press in 2008 and is now in its seventh printing. He is currently researching a book on American garage bands of the 1960s and 1970s. He is also the proprietor of American Primitive Letterpress in Annapolis, Maryland, where he teaches letterpress printing.

Joe Holley

Joe Holley is a staff writer for the *Houston Chronicle*. Previously, he has been the editor of "Insight," the Sunday opinion section of the *San Antonio Express-News*, editorial page editor of the *San Antonio Light* and *San Diego Tribune*, and editor of the *Texas Observer*. He has also worked as speechwriter for Texas Governor Ann Richards and Texas Land Commissioner Gary Mauro. Holley is coauthor with Tara Holley of *My Mother's Keeper* (William Morrow and Avon Books, 1997), and he is the recipient of the "The Pulliam," a prestigious national award for editorial writing. Holley holds a master's in English from the University of Texas in Austin and a master's in journalism from Columbia.

KATHRYN JONES

Kathryn Jones was born in Hollywood, California, and grew up in South Texas. She is the author of *Ben Johnson: Hollywood's Real Cowboy,* scheduled for publication by University Press of Mississippi. She has been a staff writer at *The Dallas Morning News* and the *Dallas Times Herald.* Currently, she is an instructor in the Department of Communications Studies at Tarleton State University, a contributing editor at *Texas Monthly,* and a regular contributor to *The New York Times.* She lives on a ranch near Glen Rose, Texas.

BOB LIVINGSTON

Bob Livingston is a singer-songwriter, musician, and seasoned road warrior who is also a freelance writer working on his first book, a memoir for Texas Tech University Press.

As a charter member of The Lost Gonzo Band and as an independent studio musician, Livingston has played and recorded with some of Texas' must colorful musicians, including Jerry Jeff Walker, Michael Martin Murphey, Ray Wylie Hubbard, Steven Fromholz, and an array of top Texas songwriters.

Beyond his musical adventures, he as delved into the music and mysteries of many international cultures, taking Texas music as far afield as India, Africa, Southeast Asia, and the Middle East as a Music Ambassador for the US Department of State.

Livingston's latest CD, *Gypsy Alibi,* won "Album of the Year" at the Texas Music Awards in 2011, and he has recently been inducted into the Texas Music Legends Hall of Fame by the Austin Songwriters Association.

JASON MELLARD

Jason Mellard is a lecturer and associate with the Center for Texas Music History at Texas State University, where he coedits *The Journal of Texas Music History* and coauthors the radio program *This Week in Texas Music History.* He is the author of *Progressive Country: How the 1970s Transformed the Texan,* published by the University of Texas Press in 2013. This work builds on a doctoral dissertation in American Studies completed at the University of Texas at Austin in 2009, *Cosmic Cowboys, Armadillos, and Outlaws: The Cultural Politics of Texas Identity in the 1970s.* Delving into the scene surrounding the Armadillo World Headquarters, Mellard has collaborated on a number of memoir, radio, and museum projects in conjunction with the South Austin Museum of Popular Culture, the artist Bob "Daddy-O" Wade, local NPR stations, and others. His work has appeared in a number of academic journals as well as the Italian rodeo press.

JOE NICK PATOSKI

Joe Nick Patoski has been writing about Texas and Texans for four decades. A former cab driver and staff writer for *Texas Monthly* and one-time reporter at the *Austin American-Statesman*, he has authored and coauthored biographies of Selena and Stevie Ray Vaughan, and collaborated with photographer Laurence Parent on *Texas Mountains*, *Texas Coast*, and *Big Bend National Park*, all published by University of Texas Press.

His 2008 book *Willie Nelson: An Epic Life*, published by Little, Brown, was recognized by The Friends of the TCU Library in 2009 with the Texas Book Award for the best book about Texas written in 2007–08. His most recent book for Little, Brown is *The Dallas Cowboys: The Outrageous History of the Biggest, Loudest, Most Hated, Best Loved Football Team in America*. Kirkus Review cited the Cowboys book as one of the ten best football books of the millennium.

Other recent titles include *Generations on the Land*, published by Texas A&M Press in January 2011, and *Texas High School Football: More Than The Game*, published by the Texas Historical Commission.

Patoski's byline has appeared in the *Los Angeles Times*, *The New York Times*, *TimeOut New York*, *Garden and Gun*, and *No Depression* magazine, for which he was a contributing editor. He also recorded the oral histories of B. B. King, Clarence Fountain of the Blind Boys of Alabama, Memphis musician and producer Jim Dickinson, Tejano superstar Little Joe Hernandez, and fifteen other subjects for the Voice of Civil Rights oral history project sponsored by AARP and the Library of Congress, some of which appeared in the book *My Soul Looks Back in Wonder* by Juan Williams, published by Sterling in 2004.

Patoski writes about water, land, nature, and parks for a number of publications including *Texas Parks & Wildlife*, the *Texas Observer*, *National Geographic*, and the *San Antonio Current*.

He is the host of *The Texas Music Hour of Power*, which airs Saturday nights from 6:00 to 8:00 p.m. on KRTS 93.5 in Marfa, and three other frequencies in Far West Texas, and around the world on MarfaPublicRadio .org.

He lives near the village of Wimberley in the Texas Hill Country where he swims and paddles in the Blanco River.

JEFF PRINCE

Jeff Prince is a journalist and musician with deep Texas roots and an affinity for the original outlaws of Texas music. The Fort Worth native has penned more than one hundred investigative cover stories as a staff writer for *Fort Worth Weekly* since 2001, winning more than two dozen awards from the Association of Alternative Weeklies, Society of Professional Journalists, Association of Women Journalists, Dallas Press Club, Houston Press Club, the Associated Press, and the State Bar of Texas. He is a two-time winner of the Houston Press Club's Print Journalist of the Year.

Entertainers profiled by Prince for the *Weekly* and *Texas Music Magazine* include Willie Nelson, Jerry Jeff Walker, Waylon Payne, Steven Fromholz, Jay Milner, Rusty Wier, Tommy Lee Alverson, Larry Joe Taylor, Bugs Henderson, and many others.

As a professional musician and songwriter, Prince has played countless stages in North Texas during the past few decades. He has self-produced four albums of original music for Reload Records in Fort Worth. His song "Hooked on the Bottle," recorded by Blue Boot recording artist Brad Hines, reached the Top 20 on the Texas Music Chart in 2009.

JAN REID

Jan Reid is a writer-at-large for *Texas Monthly* and has contributed to *Esquire*, *GQ*, *Slate*, *Men's Journal*, *The New York Times*, and many other publications. He is the author of 12 books, including *Close Calls: Jan Reid's Texas*, *"Layla" and Other Assorted Love Songs*, *The Bullet Meant for Me*, *Deerinwater*, *Rio Grande*, *Let the People In: The Life and Times of Ann Richards*, and *Comanche Sundown*, an award-winning novel. Jan Reid's first book, *The Improbable Rise of Redneck Rock*, was published in 1974 and in an updated edition in 2004. Reid is working on his thirteenth book and third novel. He makes his home in Austin.

TAMARA SAVIANO

Tamara Saviano is a Grammy- and Americana-award winning producer and music business consultant. Saviano owns and operates a consulting, artist management, and public relations company serving the Americana and folk communities.

She manages the day-to-day operations for Kris Kristofferson's record label, KK Records, and Radney Foster's label, Devil's River Records. Saviano has managed projects and record releases for many acclaimed artists, including Foster and Kristofferson, Guy Clark, Gene Watson, Ashley Monroe,

The World Famous Headliners, Shawn Camp, John Corbett, Dirty Dozen Brass Band, Janis Ian, Beth Nielsen Chapman, and Gretchen Peters.

As a producer, Saviano's contributions include *Beautiful Dreamer: The Songs of Stephen Foster*, honored with a 2004 Grammy for Best Traditional Folk Album; *The Pilgrim: A Celebration of Kris Kristofferson*; the Grammy-nominated *This One's For Him: A Tribute to Guy Clark*, which won Album of the Year at the Americana Honors & Awards in 2012; and 2014's *Looking Into You: A Tribute to Jackson Browne*.

Saviano is the coauthor of *From Art to Commerce: A Workbook for Independent Musicians* and teaches a workshop of the same name with her partner Rod Picott. Her biography of Guy Clark will be published in 2016 by Texas A&M University Press.

Saviano is a former president and six-year board member of the Americana Music Association; and former board member of Folk Alliance, the Recording Academy, and the Future of Music Coalition. She is a member of Leadership Music, class of 2007.

GRADY SMITH

Grady Smith is an entertainment writer and culture critic who currently resides in Charlottesville, Virginia. He worked for *Entertainment Weekly* for three years, writing about the film industry and country music and hosting a program on Sirius XM. His self-made YouTube video, "Why Country Music Was Awful in 2013" received over 3.5 million views in its first six months and became a key point in the ongoing discussion about country music's identity crisis. Grady Smith now writes a weekly column on country music for *The Guardian,* and he is also a contributor to *Rolling Stone.*

ANDY WILKINSON

A poet, songwriter, singer, and playwright whose particular interest is the history and peoples of the Great Plains, Andy Wilkinson has recorded twelve albums of original music and has written eight plays: among them *Charlie Goodnight's Last Night*, a one-man show performed by Barry Corbin; the musical drama *My Cowboy's Gift*; and *The Soul of the West* (written with Red Steagall). His work has received several awards, including the Texas Historical Foundation's John Ben Shepperd Jr. Craftsmanship Award, six National Western Heritage "Wrangler" Awards in four different categories, and the Will Rogers Medallion Award. He is Artist in Residence at the Southwest Collection at Texas Tech University, where he is also visiting assistant professor in the School of Music. In addition to his writing and teaching, he continues to perform.

INDEX

NOTE: The abbreviation (perf.) refers to performers: persons, groups, musicians, etc.

Abbott, Josh, 154
ABC Records, 61
Academy Awards, 213
Academy of Country Music, 48, 54
activism, environmental, 59–60
activism, political. *See* political/social activism
"Adam's Song" (Crowell), 189
African influences, 17
After the Curtain (Elders), 127
After the Fair (Hinojosa), 122
"A Guest in Your Heart" (Fromholz), 128
Ahern, Brian, 46
"Ain't No God in Mexico" (Shaver), 88
"Alabama Pines" (Isbell), 226
alcohol/drug issues: Carll, 206; at festivals, 142–45; Foley, 181; Hubbard, 137; Isbell, 227; Kristofferson, 51–52, 52–53; Shaver, 90, 92; Van Zandt, 20, 124; Walker, 76; women songwriters, 123–24
Alcohol & Salvation (Wonderland), 130
Alexander, Stan, 67
Alice Doesn't Live Here Anymore (film), 55–56
"All-American Boy" (Bare), 164
Allen, Bob, 48
Allen, Terry, 1, 2, 20–22, 26, 110, 146
Allison, J. I., 110
Allman, Greg, 37
Allman Brothers, 85–86
Allmusic.com, 186
Altman, Robert, 173
Alverson, Tommy, 144
"Always" (Berlin), 122

"Amarillo Highway" (Allen), 20
"Americana" classification, 28, 162, 186, 194
Americana Music Awards, 194
American Kid (Griffin), 116
The Americans (television show), 84
American Songwriter, 205
Amram, David, 147
A&M Records, 106, 149
"An American Boy" (Gilkyson), 129
Anderson Fair, Houston (venue), 1, 94, 95
"Angel Eyes" (W. A. Ramsey), 38
"Angel from Montgomery" (Prine), 166, 197
"Another Like You" (Carll), 205
Antler Dave, 146, 147
Antone's, Austin (venue), 181
Appalachia traditions, 17, 86
Archer, Billy, 65
Arger, Fred, 37
Arhos, Bill, 155
"Armadillo Country" (tour), 106–7
Armadillo World Headquarters, Austin (venue), 67, 95, 106, 154, 155, 166, 168
Arnold, Eddie, 124
art and human creativity, 111–13
artistic freedom *vs.* commerciality, 3–4, 118, 153, 187, 219
The Art of Removing Wallpaper (Hendrix), 209–10, 211
Ashby, Dale, 78
"Ashes By Now" (Crowell), 45
Ashley, Roy "The Commander," 140
Asian markets/audience, 122
A Star Is Born (film), 56
Atkins, Chet, 81, 89
Atkinson, Brian T., 181, 207, 209, 244
The Atlantic, 218

Atlantic Monthly, 50

Austin American-Statesman, 125

Austin Chronicle, 89, 130, 179

Austin City Limits, 3, 103, 155

Austin music culture, evolution of, 95, 153, 154–55, 168. *See also* Austin venues

Austin Outhouse (venue), 127

Austin Sun, 146

Austin venues: Antone's, 181; Armadillo World Headquarters, 67, 95, 106, 154, 155, 166, 168; Austin Outhouse, 127; Castle Creek, 166; Chequered Flag, 1, 37, 61–62, 103; Continental Club, 115; Saxon Pub, 1, 104, 166; Soap Creek Saloon, 95; Taco Flats, 17; Texas Opry House, 166

"Baby Took a Limo To Memphis" (Clark), 42

"Backslider's Wine" (Murphey), 80, 81

"Bad Liver and a Broken Heart" (Nolan), 203, 207

"Bad Seed" (Griffith, Kennedy), 121

Baez, Joan, 128

Baker, Sam, 175, 192

Ball, Marcia, 123, 124, 130–31, 135, 168

The Ballad of Calico (Kenny Rogers and The First Edition), 69–73

"Ballad of Penny Evans" (Goodman), 197

"Ballad of Spider John" (Ramsey), 38

"Ballad of the Snow Leopard and the Tanqueray Cowboy" (D. Rodriguez), 22, 24, 172

Ballad of the West (Bridger), 145

"Ballad of the Western Colonies" (D. Rodriguez), 24

Ballad Tree at Kerrville Folk Festival, 139

Balsam Range (perf.), 176

Band of Joy (perf.), 116

Barbra, Jeff, 211

Bare, Bobby, 42

Basement Committee, 167

"Baton Rouge" (Clark, Crowley), 42, 47

The Battalion (Aggie paper), 167

BBC, 179, 183

Beatles, influence of, 162, 198

"Beaumont" (Carll), 207

"Beautiful Despair" (Crowell), 190

Beautiful World (Gilkyson), 129

Be Here to Love Me: A Film About Townes Van Zandt, 19, 155

Belafonte, Harry, 81

Bell, Rex, 207

Bell, Vince, 1, 92–100

Benet, Stephen Vincent, influence of, 42–43

Benson, Ray, 130

Berlin, Irving, 122, 173

"Bermuda Triangle" (V. Bell), 95

Berry, Chuck, 198

The Best of Times (var.), 123

"Bethlehem Steel" (Griffith, Kennedy), 121

Better Days (Clark), 46

"Better Days" (Clark), 44–45

Betts, Dicky, 37

"Big Ball's in Cowtown" (Nix), 110

A Bigger Piece of Sky (Keen), 170

The Big Texan (restaurant), 111

bilingual songs, 121–22

Billboard charts, 54, 73, 152, 221, 222

Billboard magazine, 69, 184

Billy Bob's Texas, Fort Worth (venue), 170

Billy Joe Shaver: Honky Tonk Hero (Shaver and Reagan), 86

Billy Joe Shaver's Greatest Hits (Shaver), 91

Bingham, Ryan, 155, 212–17

Black, Clint, 172

Black Coffee Publishing, 95

"Black Rose" (Shaver), 86

Blake, William, influence of, 49, 51, 52, 102

Blazing Saddles (film), 83

Blessed (L. Williams), 132–33, 184

Bloodless Revolution (Wonderland), 130

Bloodlines (T. Allen), 21

"Blowing Smoke" (Musgraves, Laird, McAnally), 223

"Blue Asian Reds (for Roadrunner)" (Allen), 20–21

"Blue Eyes Crying in the Rain" (Rose), 153

bluegrass, 174, 176, 216

Blue Note label, 133

blues, influence of, 7, 31–32, 34–35, 101, 130, 168, 216

"Blue Skies" (Berlin), 173

BMI (Broadcast Music Incorporated) awards, 126, 152

Boats to Build (Clark), 47

"Boats to Build" (Clark, V. Thompson), 47

Boland, Jason, 142

Bolton, Michael, 124

"Boots of Spanish Leather" (Dylan), 120, 126

"Bosque County Romance" (Fromholz), 63, 64–65, 155

"Bottle in My Hand" (Carll), 205

Box, David, 110

"The Boys of Summer" (Henley, Campbell), 59

Brave Combo, 123

Brazos River, 59–60

"Breakdown" (Hendrix), 209, 210

Brickell, Edie, 123

Bridger, Bobby, 145–48

Bring Me The Head of Alfredo Garcia (film), 55–56

British GQ, 223

British Isles influences, 17, 18, 22–23

"bro country" style, 9–10, 18, 218–19, 221–23, 225

"Broken Fingers" (Baker), 192

"Broken Freedom Song" (Kristofferson), 56

Bromberg, David, 76, 172

Brooks, Mel, 83, 84

Bryan, Luke, 221

Bryant, Boudleaux, 54

Buffalo Springfield (perf.), 103

Buffett, Jimmy, 172, 185

Burnett, T Bone, 213

Burnin' Daylight (Clark, unused title), 45–46

Burns, George, 81

Burton, Brian, 134

Bush, Johnny, 151

"Bus to Baton Rouge" (L. Williams), 182

But What Will The Neighbors Think? (Crowell), 45

"Bye Bye Baby" (Carll), 205

Byrds, 124

Caddo Lake Institute, 59

Cadillac Ranch, 111

Cafe York, Denver (venue), 67

Cajun influences, 7, 17, 130, 177

Cale, John, 97

Calico, California, 69–73

"Calico Silver" (Murphey, Cansler), 70, 71

Camp, Shawn, 48

campfire jams, festival, 137, 138, 139–40

Camus, Albert, 75

Cansler, Larry, 69–70

"The Cape" (G. Clark, S. Clark, J. Janousky), 47

Capote, Truman, 120

Carling, Vachel, 71

Carll, Hayes, 102, 155, 203–8

Carpenter, Mary Chapin, 128, 131

Carrick, "Ma," 93, 94

Car Wheels on a Gravel Road (L. Williams), 131–32, 180–82

"Car Wheels on a Gravel Road" (L. Williams), 132

Cash, Johnny: and Cowboy Jack, 51; and Crowell, 185, 186; and Kristofferson, 51, 53, 55, 56; McMurtry, influence on, 196; Shaver cover, 85

Cash, Rosanne, 45, 128, 169, 186

Cass County (Henley), 60

Castle Creek, Austin (venue), 166

categorization issues: Clark, 42, 45; Earle, 161–63; Griffith, 120; Murphey, 73; Nelson, 156; "ruthlessly poetic" songwriters, 1–2; Williams, L., 179; women songwriters, 118. *See also* "Americana" classification; "Texas Music" classification

Cedar Creek studio, 211

"A Certain Softness" (McCartney), 122

"C'est la Vie" (Berry), 198

"Chances Are" (Carll), 205

"Changed the Locks" (L. Williams), 179

Charles, Ray, 124, 173

Cheatham Street Warehouse, San Marcos, 101, 211

"Cheney's Toy" (J. McMurtry), 195–96

Chequered Flag, Austin (venue), 1, 37, 61–62, 103

Cher, 124

Chestnutt, Mark, 42

Chicago Sun-Times, 189

"Chickens" (Hubbard, Carll), 102, 208
Childish Things (J. McMurtry), 194
children and career, 123
"Children of Children" (Isbell), 230
Chinaberry Sidewalks (Crowell), 186, 187–88
"Choctaw Bingo" (J. McMurtry), 195
"Christmas in Washington" (Earle), 165
Chronicles Volume One (Dylan), 125–26
Circus Maximus (Circus Maximus), 76
Clark, Brandy, 220, 222
Clark, Guy: on *Austin City Limits*, 155; awards/recognition, 47–48; Bingham covering, 215; Carll covering, 204; and Crowell, 185; and Houston music culture, 95; influence of, 102, 162, 169, 192, 211–12; influences, 42–43, 45; poetry and songwriting, 4–5, 39–41, 44–46; recording strategies/techniques, 45–47; "ruthlessly poetic" quality, 1; and Texas folk culture, 2, 152; themes and sources, 41–42; Van Zandt's influence on, 27–28, 35
Clark, Susanna, 48, 95
Clarke, Thurston, 199
classification issues. *See* categorization issues
Clement, Cowboy Jack, 51
"Cleveland County Blues" (Moreland), 226
Clifford, Craig: chapters, 1, 17, 83, 151, 174, 203, 212, 218, 224; profile, 243
Cline, Patsy, 152
Closer to the Bone (Kristofferson), 58
CMT (Country Music Television, Inc.), 191
Coe, David Allen, 42
coffeehouse movement/circuit, 1, 2–3, 37, 93–94, 149, 152, 167
Cohen, Leonard, 32
Cold Dog Soup (Clark), 48
Cole, Katherine, 193
Cole, Nat King, 173
"Coley" (V. Bell), 94
college circuit, 37, 149, 167. *See also* coffeehouse movement/circuit
Columbia Recording Studios, Nashville, 53
Columbia Records, 126, 194
Colvin, Shawn, 122, 172

Come Away With Me (N. Jones), 133–34
commerciality *vs.* artistic freedom, 3–4, 118, 153–54, 187, 219
commercialization of country/folk, 153, 162–63. *See also* "Americana" classification; "bro country" style
Compadre Records, 194
Continental Club, Austin (venue), 115
"Conversation with the Devil" (Hubbard), 102
Cook, Elizabeth, 186
Coolidge, Rita, 55, 56
Cooper, Peter, 49, 244–45
Copeland, Aaron, 5
"Copper Canteen" (J. McMurtry), 199
Copperhead Road (Earle), 164–65
"Copperhead Road" (Earle), 164–65
Cordell, Denny, 38
"Cornmeal Waltz" (Clark, Camp), 48
"Corona Con Lima" (Nunn), 141
"Cosmic Cowboy" persona, 101, 154, 168
Cosmic Cowboy Souvenirs (Murphey), 74
Costello, Elvis, 132–33
Cotton (Baker), 192
counterculture movement, 43, 153, 154, 157
"Count My Blessings" (Hubbard), 101
Country Music, 48
Country Music, U.S.A., 2
Country Music Association, 54
Country Music Hall of Fame, 57, 125
"Cover Me Up" (Isbell), 227
"Cowboy" (B. Elders), 128
Cowgirl's Prayer (E. Harris), 177
"Crack in the Mirror" (B. Elders), 127
Craftsman (Clark), 40
craftsmanship *vs.* songwriting, 40
Crayons (Elders), 127
"Crazy" (Nelson), 152
Crazy Heart (film), 212
Creole influences, 216. *See also* Cajun influences
"Crescent City" (L. Williams), 177
Crosby, Bing, 124
Crosby, David, 95
Crosby, Fanny J., 173
Crosby, Ronald Clyde. *See* Walker, Jerry Jeff
Crosby, Stills & Nash, 103

Cross Canadian Ragweed (perf.), 216
Crow, Mike, 141
Crow, Sheryl, 134
Crowell, Rodney, 42, 44, 45–46, 156, 185–91
Cry Till You Laugh (Hendrix), 210
Curtis, Sonny, 110

Daddy's Coal (Elders), 127
"Daddy's Hands" (Dunn), 126
"Daisy Mae" (Isbell), 226
Dallas venues: House of Blues, 215; Poor David's Pub, 1, 37; Rubaiyat, 1, 36, 73
Damron, Allen Wayne, 137
dance halls, 3, 78, 85
"Dancin' Circles 'Round the Sun (Epictetus Speaks)" (Crowell), 190
Danger Mouse (perf.), 134
"The Dark" (Clark, Mondlock), 211–12
The Dark (Clark), 48
Davis, Frank, 95
Davis, John T., 185, 245
Davis, Mac, 110
Davis, Sammy Jr., 81
"Daybreak" (Fromholz), 63–64
"Day by Day" (Shaver), 92
Dean, Richard, 103
"The Death of Sis Draper" (Clark, Camp), 48
A Deeper Blue: The Life and Music of Townes Van Zandt (Handy), 27
Delirium Tremolos (Hubbard), 101
Denver, John (Deutschendorf), 110, 113
"Desperados Waiting for a Train" (Clark), 5, 41–42, 80, 81
Deunser, Stephen M., 183
Diamond, Neil, 81
Diamonds & Dirt (Crowell), 186
Dickey, James, 177
Diddley, Bo, 198
Dill, Danny, 174
"Dirty Laundry" (Henley, Kortchmar), 59
Dixie Chicks, 118, 168, 171, 210
Doane, W. H., 173
"Don't Get Me Started" (Crowell), 190
"Don't Know Why" (J. Harris), 134
"Don't Let The Bastards (Get You Down)" (Kristofferson), 57

"Don't Let Your Babies Grow Up to Be Cowboys" (E. Bruce, P. Bruce), 18
"Don't Miss You at All" (N. Jones, Ellington), 134
"Don't You Take It Too Bad" (Van Zandt), 34
Dooley, Michael, 212
"Dorsey, the Mail-Carrying Dog" (Murphey, Cansler), 71
Dougherty Theater, Austin, 96
Douglas, Tom, 220
"Down Home Country Blues" (Hubbard), 102
"Dreadful Selfish Crime" (Keen), 171
Drinking Gourd, San Francisco (venue), 66
drugs. *See* alcohol/drug issues
"Drunken Angel" (L. Williams), 8, 132, 181
"Drunken Poet's Dream" (Hubbard, Carll), 101, 102, 204, 208
Dualtone Music, 48
Dublin Blues (Clark), 47
"Dublin Blues" (Clark), 42, 47, 215
Dudley, Dave, 53
Dunn, Holly, 126
Dylan, Bob: Baker, influence on, 192; Bingham, influence on, 214–15; Carll, influence on, 204–5; Elders, influence on, 127; and folk culture, 1–2, 3, 7, 152; Griffith album harmonica, 120; on Hester, 125–26; influence of on Van Zandt, 31, 35; and poetic songwriting concept, 28–29; Shaver cover, 85; Van Zandt cover, 19; Walker cover, 81; and Williams, L., 132, 178, 182
"Dylan's Hard Rain" (Bingham), 214

Eagles, 59
Eakin, Michael, 146, 147
Earle, Steve: and Clark's song editing, 43; and evolution of Austin music, 168; as Kerrville New Folk winner, 138; and Lambert, 219; McMurtry on, 194; profile, 161–66; Van Zandt's influence on, 2, 9, 28; on Van Zandt's songwriting, 19, 32, 34; on Williams, L., 131
"Earthbound" (Crowell), 186, 189

Eaton, Robin, 98
Edie Brickell & New Bohemians, 123
El Corazón (Earle), 165
Elders, Betty, 127–28
Elders, Gene, 127
Elektra/Asylum Records, 47, 123
Eliot, T. S., 30
Ellington, Duke, 134
"Ellis Unit One" (Earle), 165
Ely, Joe, 28, 110, 126, 136, 137, 171
Emerson, Ralph Waldo, 59, 75
Emma Joe's, Austin (venue), 17
"Empty-Handed Compadres" (Murphey,
    Cansler), 70–71
English, Paul, 107, 150, 151
"Enjoy the Ride" (Hendrix), 210
Entertainment Weekly, 10, 218
environmental activism, 59–60
Equal Scary People (Hickman), 123
Essence (L. Williams), 182
European markets/audience, 9; Crowell,
    190; Griffith, 120; Hinojosa, 122;
    Lovett, 168–69; Rhodes, 126–27
Evans, Mike, 197
"Ever Wonder Why" (Bingham), 214
Everybody's Brother (Shaver), 90

Fabulous Thunderbirds (perf.), 168
The Fall (N. Jones), 134
family and career, 123
Family Gathering, Hog Mountain Retreat,
    Mineral Wells, 144
Farar, Donna, 156
Farr, Tyler, 222
"Farther Along" (W. B. Stevens), 146
"Farther Down the Line" (Lovett), 169
Fass, Bob, 76
"Fastest Girl in Town" (Lambert, A. Pres-
    ley), 219
Fate's Right Hand (Crowell), 186, 187,
    188–89
Faulkner, William, 3–4, 20, 24, 177, 192,
    224, 227, 228–29, 230
"Faulkner Street" (Carll), 207
"Feed Me to the Lions" (Wonderland),
    130
Feeling Mortal (Kristofferson), 58
Feels Like Home (N. Jones), 134

Felker, Evan, 216, 224–25
feminism, 218–21. *See also* gender bias
"Fence Post" (T. Hinojosa), 121–22
Ferris, Jerry. *See* Walker, Jerry Jeff
festivals. *See* music festival scene
film careers, 55–56, 173
"The Final Attraction" (Kristofferson), 58
Finlay, Jenni, 101, 246
Finlay, Kent, 52, 211
"The Flag." *See* Chequered Flag, Austin
    (venue)
"Flagship" (Isbell), 229
Flatt, Lester, 174
Flippo, Chet, 107
Florida Georgia Line (perf.), 221
Flowers and Liquor (Carll), 207, 208
"Flowers on the Wall" (DeWitt), 196
"Flyin' Shoes" (Van Zandt), 172
Foley, Blaze, 17, 180, 181
folk music/culture: British Isles, 17, 22–23;
    counterculture movement, 43, 153, 154,
    157; evolution of and "Texas" music,
    1–8, 161–66; Greenwich Village music
    culture, 1–2, 3, 7, 76, 125, 163; histori-
    cal profile, 28; original/traditional, 2,
    17–18; politics and cultural evolution,
    163–64
Folkways Records, 178
"Follow Your Arrow" (Musgraves, McA-
    nally, Clark), 134–35, 219, 223
"For the Good Times" (Kristofferson), 54
"Fort Worth Blues" (Earle), 2, 9, 19
Foster, Fred, 53–54, 125
Foster, Ruthie, 123
Fowler, Rick, 106
Fox, Aaron A., 88
Freedom Folk Singers, 126
Freedom's Child (Shaver), 92
free verse style, 167, 171
The Freewheelin' Bob Dylan (Dylan), 43,
    205
Friedman, Kinky, 83–85, 86, 89
Frisell, Bill, 183
"From Here to Forever" (Bruton, Swan,
    Glen Clark, Kristofferson), 58
Fromholz, Steven: on *Austin City Limits*,
    155; in Frummox, 36, 61–62, 103; "The
    Great Progressive Country Scare of the

1970s," 103, 168; at LJT festival, 142; Lovett covering, 172; on memorable songs, 72; and Murphey, 67; Nelson covering, 156; and poetic songwriting concept, 5; "ruthlessly poetic," 1; songwriting profile, 66; and Texas folk music culture, 2, 95, 152; *Texas Trilogy*, 62–66, 73

"From The Bottle To The Bottom" (Kristofferson), 53

frontier culture, 113–14

"Front Porch Song" (Keen, Lovett), 139, 167–68

Frost, Robert, influence of, 29, 31, 32–33, 42, 127

Frum, David, 164

Frummox (perf.), 36, 61–62, 103

Fry, Segle, 37, 62

Fullbright, John, 217, 225

"Funny How Time Slips Away" (Nelson), 152, 173

Gantry, Chris, 52, 111

Gatlin, Larry, 55

Geldof, Bob, 128

gender bias: sexism in music, 9–10, 18, 218–19, 218–23, 221–23; in Texas music culture, 7–8, 117–19, 124

Genesee (perf.), 103

Gentilly (W. A. Ramsey, unpub.), 39

"Georgia on a Fast Trail" (Shaver), 86, 87–88

Geronimo's Cadillac (Murphey), 73–74, 106, 149

"Get It Out" (J. Walker), 79

"Gettin' By" (J. Walker), 78–79

"Ghost of Travelin' Jones" (Bingham), 214

Gibson, Susan, 111, 118

Gilbert and Sullivan, 198

Gilkyson, Eliza, 119, 128–29

Gilkyson, Terry and Jane, 128

Gill, Vince, 169, 170

Gilley, Mickey, 124

Gilmer, Jimmy, 111

Gilmore, Jimmie Dale, 110

Give Me All You Got (C. Rodriguez), 133

"Glasgow Girl" (Crowell), 190

"God Will" (Lovett), 171

"The Golden Idol" (Kristofferson), 53

Gold Hill, Colorado, 62

"Good Bye Old Missoula" (W. A. Ramsey), 38

Goodbye to a River (Graves), 59–60

"Goodbye to a River" (Henley, Simes, Winding, Lynch), 59–60

"Good-Hearted Woman" (Nelson, Jennings), 154

Goodman, Steve, 197

Goodnight, Charlie, 112

"Good Ol' Boy (Gettin' Tough)" (Earle, Bennett), 161, 164

Gorka, John, 129

gospel music, 90, 205

Gourds (perf.), 168

"Go Wherever You Wanna Go" (Griffin), 116

Grammy Awards and nominations: Clark, 48; Crowell, 186, 191; Dunn, 126; Gilkyson, 128; Griffith, 120; Jones, N., 133, 134; Kristofferson, 57; Lovett, 173; McMurtry, 193; Musgraves, 223; Shaver, 90; Williams, L., 132, 177, 180

Grand Ole Opry, 126, 152

"Grateful for Christmas" (Carll), 205

Graves, John, 2

"Gravities" (Heaney), 25

"The Great Joe Bob (A Regional Tragedy)" (Allen), 22, 153

"The Great Progressive Country Scare of the 1970s," 103–8, 168

Green, Al, 173

Green, Pat, 18, 137, 141–42, 175, 216

"Greensboro Woman" (Van Zandt), 204, 207

"Greenville" (L. Williams), 180

Greenwich Village music culture, 1–2, 3, 7, 76, 125, 163

Griffin, Patty, 115–17

Griffith, Nancy: on *Austin City Limits*, 155; Bell cover, 96; and evolution of Austin music, 168; and Houston music culture, 95; Keen cover, 171; at Kerrville Folk Festival, 126, 139; as Kerrville New Folk winner, 138; profile, 120–21; Van Zandt's influence on, 28

The Grifter's Hymnal (Hubbard), 101

Gringo Honeymoon (Keen), 170–71
"The Gringo's Tale" (Earle), 166
"grrl power," 219
Gruene Hall, Gruene (venue), 170
Guitar Town (Earle), 161, 162, 164
"Guitar Town" (Earle), 164
"Gulf Coast Plain" (D. Rodriguez), 26
"Gunpowder and Lead" (Lambert, Little), 219
Guthrie, Woody: Bridger, influence on, 146; Earle, influence on, 161, 166; and Gilkyson, 128; legacy of, 7, 28, 216, 225; Murphey, influence on, 68; and political activism, 163, 165; Williams, L., influence on, 178
Guy Clark (Clark), 45
Gypsy Songman (J. Walker), 6, 75

Haggard, Merle, 60, 134, 156
Hall, Tom T., 50, 53, 55
Halley, David, 110
Hancock, Butch, 110
"Hang Me in the Tulsa County Stars" (Moreland), 225–26
Happy Prisoner: The Bluegrass Sessions (Keen), 174
Happy Woman Blues (L. Williams), 178
"Harbor for My Soul" (Murphey, Cansler), 71
Hardcore Troubadour: The Life & Near Death of Steve Earle (St. John), 162
"Hard Out Here" (Carll), 205
"Hard Times" (Bingham), 214
The Hard Way (Earle), 162
Hardy, Robert Earl, 27, 192, 246
Harp magazine, 187
Harris, Emmylou, 124, 126, 177, 179, 180, 185, 191
Harris, Jesse, 133, 134
Hartford, John, 55
"The Hawk" (Bridger), 146
"Heal in the Wisdom" (Bridger), 146–48
Heaney, Seamus, 25
Hearne, Bill and Bonnie, 126, 137
"The Heart" (Kristofferson), 50, 56–57
"Heart Like Mine" (Lambert, Monroe, T. Howard), 219
"Hell No (I'm Not Alright)" (Griffith), 121

"Hell on Wheels" (Lambert, Monroe, A. Presley), 219
"Hello Walls" (Nelson), 152
"Help Me Make It Through The Night" (Kristofferson), 54
Hemingway, Ernest, 192
Hendricks, Diana Finlay, 193, 245–46
Hendrix, Terri, 118, 124, 128, 209–12
"He Never Got Enough Love" (B. Elders, L. Williams), 128
Henley, Don, 59–60
"Here Comes the Sun" (Harrison), 198
Here to There (Frummox), 61–62
Here We Rest (Isbell), 226
Hester, Carolyn, 125–256
"Hey Now" (Hendrix, Maines), 209
Hickey, Dave, 89
Hickman, Sara, 122–23
"Hide Me" (Carll), 205
High on Tulsa Heat (Moreland), 225–26
The Highwaymen (perf.), 42, 56
Hillis, Craig D.: book concept, 203; chapters, 1, 61, 103, 145, 148, 151; Moon Hill Management, 95; musician, 8–9, 77, 106; profile, 243–44
Hinojosa, Rolando, 24
Hinojosa, Tish, 121–22, 123
Hispanic music influences, 216. *See also* Mexican music influences
history, American West, 68–69
history, philosophy of, 203
Hollander, John, 29
Holley, Joe, 85, 246–47
Hollinger, John, 175
Holly, Buddy, 109–10, 125
Holzhaus, Chris, 96
Homeland (T. Hinojosa), 121
Homer, 28
"Home to Houston" (Earle), 166
"Honey Bee" (L. Williams), 184
Honky Tonk Heroes (Jennings), 86, 88–89, 198
"Honky Tonk Heroes" (Shaver), 88
Hopkins, Sam "Lightnin,'" 29, 31, 34–35, 45, 95, 102
Horseman, Pass By (L. McMurtry), 25, 194
Hot Band (perf.), 185
"Hot Corn, Cold Corn" (Flatt, Scruggs), 174

House of Blues, Dallas (venue), 215
"The House That Built Me" (Douglas, Shamblin), 220
Houston Folklore Society, 45
The Houston Kid (Crowell), 186, 187, 191
Houston music culture, 43, 93–95, 162. *See also* Houston venues
Houston Press, 90
Houston venues: Anderson Fair, 1, 94, 95; Jester Lounge, 1, 45, 152; Liberty Hall, 94; Old Quarter, 19, 45, 94, 207; Sand Mountain Coffeehouse, 45, 93, 94
Howard, Harlan, 68, 125
Howling Wolf (perf.), 181
Hubbard, Ray Wylie: and Carll, 204, 208; at LJT festival, 137, 142; and Murphey, 67; profile, 101–2; with Three Faces West, 106; and "Up Against the Wall Redneck Mother," 80–81
Hud (film), 194
Hudson, Kathleen, 117, 125
humility and culture of skill, 114–15
"Hurricane" (D. Rodriguez), 24–25

"I Ain't Living Long Like This" (Crowell), 187
"I Can Help" (Swan), 55
Icehouse Music, 128
"I Cry for Love" (C. Rodriguez), 133
"idea morgue," 99
"I'd Have to be Crazy" (Fromholz), 156
"If I Had a Boat" (Lovett), 171
"If I Needed You" (Van Zandt), 20
illness/injuries: Baker, bomb blast, 192; Bell, auto accident, 96; Hendrix, epilepsy, 209–10; Shaver, lumber mill, 88
"I Loved a Lass (She's Gone to Be Wed to Another)," 23
"I'm Just an Old Chunk of Coal" (Shaver), 86, 90
Impossible Dream (Griffin), 117
In A Narrow Grave (L. McMurtry), 194
"I Never Cared for You" (Nelson, Buskirk, Breeland), 152
injuries. *See* illness/injuries
Inmon, John, 147
Inside Job (Henley), 59–60
"Inside Job" (Henley, Campbell), 59

intellectual approach, 84, 86
internal rhyme, 33
Intersection (Griffith), 120–21
"Invisible Girl" (Hendrix), 118
Irish influences, 18, 25, 216. *See also* British Isles influences
"Iron" (Baker), 192
Isbell, Jason, 216, 226–30
Isle of Wight, 55
"It Is What It Is" (Musgraves, Laird, B. Clark), 223
"It's About Time" (Hendrix, Maines), 210–11
"It's a Hard Life Wherever You Go" (Griffith), 120
"It's a Shame" (Carll), 204, 207

Jackson, Alan, 134
"Jackson" (L. Williams), 180, 181
Jagger, Mick, 60
James, Etta, 185
Jansch, Bert, 23
Jason Isbell and the 400 Unit (Isbell), 226
Javors, Marty, 67
jazz, 133
Jennings, Waylon: artistic freedom endeavors, 153; Clark cover, 42; Crowell cover, 185; in The Highwaymen, 42, 56; and Kristofferson, 56; and Lubbock music culture, 110; McMurtry, influence on, 198; and Nelson, 153, 154; Ramsey cover, 172; Rhodes covers/duets, 126–27; Shaver covers, 86, 88–89
Jerry Jeff Walker (Walker), 77–78
Jerusalem (Earle), 165–66
Jester Lounge, Houston (venue), 1, 45, 152
Jesus Was a Capricorn (Kristofferson), 55
Jewel of the South (Crowell), 189
John, Elton, 81
"John Brown's Body" (Benet), 42–43
John Graves Scenic Riverway, 60
"Johnny B. Goode" (Berry), 164
"Johnny Come Lately" (Earle), 164
Johnson, Eric, 96
Johnson, Robert, 178
Johnston, Bob, 36, 73, 106
Jones, Buck, 174–75
Jones, Chris, 183

Jones, Kathryn, 59, 115, 176, 247
Jones, Norah, 125, 133–34
Jones, Tim, 174–76
"Jon Walker's Blues" (Earle), 165
Joplin, Janis, 54, 123–24, 129
Journal of Country Music, 131
"Joy" (L. Williams), 181
Joyce, James, 25
Juarez (T. Allen), 21
"Judgment Day" (Hendrix, Maines), 210
Julian, Richard, 133
Jurek, Thom, 186
"Just Dropped In (To See What Condition My Condition Was In)" (Newbury), 69
"Just The Other Side of Nowhere" (Kristofferson), 54
Just Us Kids (J. McMurtry), 195–96

Kaplansky, Lucy, 129
Karr, Mary, 191
Keats, John, 208
Keen, Robert Earl Jr.: Allen cover, 20; appeal of to small town/rowdy audience, 139, 143, 216; on *Austin City Limits*, 155; Carll, influence on, 205, 208; Hickman cover, 123; Hubbard, influence on, 102; as Kerrville New Folk winner, 138; Lovett covering, 172; profile, 166–74
Keltner, Jim, 183
Kennedy, Rod, 17, 126, 139, 147–48
Kenny Rogers and The First Edition, 69
"Kerosene" (Lambert, Earle), 219
Kerrville Folk Festival: Ballad Tree, 139; history and profile, 137–40, 145; New Folk Songwriter Competition, 127, 138, 170; performers banned from, 17; theme song, 147–48; women performers, 126
Kidd, Wayne, 106
Kierkegaard, Søren, 229
Kin (Crowell and Karr), 191
King, Carole, 125
King, Stephen, 193, 195
Kingston Trio, 23
KLRN (PBS station), 3, 155
KMAG YOYO (Carll), 204–6
"KMAG YOYO" (Carll), 204–5

"Knockin' Over Whiskeys" (Carll), 207
"KNON Super Roper Redneck Review," 140
Knott, Walter, 69
Knox, Buddy, 110
Kopperl, Texas, 2, 62, 63, 64
Krauss, Alison, 60, 134
Kristofferson (Kristofferson), 54–55
Kristofferson, Fran, 50
Kristofferson, Kris: awards and recognition, 54, 57; background and early profile, 49–52; Clark cover, 42; film career, 55–56; "ruthlessly poetic," 1; Shaver cover, 86; songwriting years, 53–55; success and influence of, 4, 54–55, 56–58, 196; on Van Zandt, 26
Kristofferson, Lisa, 57

"Ladies Love Outlaws" (Clayton), 154
LaFarge, Peter, 68
LaFave, Jimmy, 123, 168
"Lafayette" (L. Williams), 178
"LA Freeway" (Clark), 41, 42
Laird, Luke, 222
Lake, Janey, 62
"Lake Charles" (L. Williams), 180–81, 185
Lake Whitney, 63, 64
Lambert, Miranda, 60, 155, 218–21, 222, 223
The Land of Milk and Honey (Gilkyson), 128
language skills and techniques: Van Zandt, 33
La Pista de Vida Agua, 114
Larry Joe Taylor Texas Music Festival (& Chili Cookoff) (LJT), 118, 136–37, 140–45
Last of the True Believers (Griffith), 120
"Last Think I Needed First Thing This Morning" (Nunn, Farar), 156
"Last Train to Amsterdam" (Hubbard), 102
Late Night Grande Hotel (Griffith), 96
Latino influences, 17
Lauderdale, Jim, 186
Lavender Hill Express (perf.), 103
Lead Belly, 163
"Leaving Louisiana In the Broad Daylight" (Crowell, Cowart), 187

LeDuff, Charlie, 84

Legg, Mabel, 87, 92

Lehning, Kyle, 47

Lennon, John, 34, 92

Leon, Craig, 45–46

Leslie's Chicken Shack, Corsicana, 86

"Levelland" (J. McMurtry), 195

Liberty Hall, Houston (venue), 94

Lightning Rod Records, 194

"Lights of Cheyenne" (J. McMurtry), 197

"Lil' Jack Slade" (Hendrix, M. Maguire, N. Maines, E. Robison), 210

Lindh, John Walker, 165

Lindsay, Vachel, 43, 68

Lipscomb, Mance, 45, 95, 102

literary influences: and brotherhood of "ruthless poetry," 18; Henley, 59; Murphey, 6, 67; overview, 4–6; Walker, 6, 75; Williams, L., 131, 177. *See also* poets (classic), influence of; *individual poets/writers*

Little, Heather, 219

"Little Bird" (J. Walker), 79

Little Broken Hearts (N. Jones), 134

Little Honey (L. Williams), 184

"Little Joe, the Wrangler" (Thorp, Ritter), 110

Little Love Affairs (Griffith), 120

Little Willies (perf.), 125, 134

Live at the Old Quarter, Houston, Texas (Van Zandt), 19

Live In Aught-Three (J. McMurtry), 195

live-music venues (small), 1

"Live Oak" (Isbell), 227

Live @ the Fillmore (L. Williams), 183

Living Room, NYC (venue), 133

Livingston, Bob: and Lubbock music scene, 110; and Murphey, 67, 73, 74, 104, 106; profile, 247; Ramsey, article on, 36; with Three Faces West, 106; and Walker, 77, 80–81

Llano Estacado music culture, 2, 109–15

Lomax, John (also Alan and John III), 163

"London Homesick Blues" (Nunn), 78, 81, 103

Lonesome, On'ry and Mean (Jennings), 153

"Lonesome, On'ry and Mean" (Clayton), 154

Lone Star Beer, 106

Lone Star Music, 210

Lone Star State of Mind (Griffith), 120

"Long Bed from Kenya" (B. Elders), 127

"Long Black Veil" (Dill, Wilkin), 174

"Long Island Sound" (J. McMurtry), 198–99

"The Long Ride Home" (K. S. Taylor), 211

The Lonliest Man I Ever Met (Friedman), 85

"Loretta" (Van Zandt), 204, 207

Los Angeles folk culture, 67–68

The Lost Notebooks of Hank Williams (Dylan), 134

Love and Circumstance (C. Rodriguez), 133

"Love at the Five and Dime" (Griffith), 120

Loveless, Patty, 179

Lovett, Lyle: on *Austin City Limits*, 155; and Bell, V., 96, 97; on Clark's songwriting, 4; film career, 173; Friedman cover, 84; Fromholz cover, 172; Keen cover, 172; at Kerrville Folk Festival, 139; as Kerrville New Folk winner, 138; Murphey cover, 172; profile, 166–74; Ramsey, W. A. cover, 172; Rodriguez, D. cover, 22, 172; Van Zandt's influence on, 28

Lubbock (on everything) (T. Allen), 2, 20

Lubbock, Texas, 20

Lubbock East (Nashville), 110

Lubbock Lake Landmark, 114

Lubbock music culture, 2, 109–15

Lubbock North, 110–11

Lubbock South (Austin), 110

Lubbock West (Los Angeles), 110

"Lubbock Woman" (Allen), 22

Lucinda Williams (L. Williams), 176–77

Luckenbach, Texas, 78

"Luckenbach, Texas" (Moman, Emmons), 18

Luckenbach Dance Hall, 78, 85

Lucky Star (B. Jones), 174

Lyle Lovett and His Large Band (Lovett), 171

Lynch, Stan, 59, 60

"Madame De Lil and Diabolical Bill" (Murphey, Cansler), 70–71
"Magnolia Wind" (Clark, Camp), 48
Maines, Lloyd, 118, 210
Maines, Natalie, 110
Malone, Bill C., 2
"Mama's Broken Heart" (Musgraves, B. Clark, McAnally), 220, 222–23
"Mamas Don't Let Your Babies Grow Up to Be Cowboys" (E. Bruce, P. Bruce), 154
"Mama You Sweet" (L. Williams), 183–84
Manassas (perf.), 66–67
"Man Came Up From Town" (Murphey, Cansler), 71
Mandela, Nelson, 84
Mandrell, Louise, 126
"The Man in Me" (Crowell), 188
"Man of God" (Gilkyson), 128–29
Mansfield, David, 97, 99
"Many a Fine Lady" (Van Zandt), 19
Manzarek, Ray, 68
Marley, Bob, 57
Marsh 3, Stanley, 111
Martin, Mary, 65
Masters, Edgar Lee, 68
Mattea, Kathy, 120
"Maybe You Heard" (Kristofferson), 56
McAnally, Shane, 220, 222
MCA Records, 77, 79, 139, 169
McCarthy, Cormac, 21, 192
McCartney, Paul, 122
McClinton, Delbert, 168
McConnell, Sean, 215
McCormick, Robert "Mack," 45
McCrimmon, Dan, 36, 61–62, 103
McGeary, Michael, 74, 77, 80, 106
McGee, David, 162, 163
McGraw, Tim, 185
McGuire, Martie, 210
McMurtry, Curtis, 197–98
McMurtry, James, 138, 155, 193–99
McMurtry, Larry, 24, 25, 26, 196–97
McTell, Blind Willie, 35
"Me and Billy the Kid" (Ely), 136
Me and Bobby McGee (Kristofferson), 55
"Me and Bobby McGee" (Kristofferson), 5, 54
"Meet Me in the Morning" (Dylan), 129

Meier, Heinz, 173
Mellard, Jason, 161, 247–48
Mellencamp, John Cougar, 194
Melody Mountain Ranch, 137, 143
"Memphis" (Berry), 198
Memphis Minnie, 178
"Memphis Pearl" (L. Williams, L. Rall), 179–80
"Mercedes Benz" (Joplin, Neuwirth, McClure), 124
Mercy (Baker), 192
Meridian, Texas, 143
"Merry Christmas from the Family" (Keen), 171, 205
"Merry Go 'Round" (Musgraves, McAnally, Osborne), 135, 219, 222, 223
"Metal Firecracker" (L. Williams), 181
Mexican music influences, 7, 121, 122, 216
Midler, Bette, 124
military careers: Fromholz, 66; Kristofferson, 50–51; Shaver, 88
Millay, Edna St. Vincent, 130
Miller, Roger, 54
Miller Outdoor Theater, Houston, 95
"Million-Air" recordings, 152
Mills, Irving, 173
Mingus, Texas, 136, 141
"Minneapolis" (L. Williams), 183
Miss Understood (Wonderland), 130
Mitchell, Joni, 125
Moffatt, Katy, 125
"Monopoly" (Hendrix, Maines), 210
Monroe, Ashley, 60, 219, 222
Montrose area culture, Houston, 43, 93
Monument Records, 53–54
Moon Hill Management, 95
Moore, Marianne, 68
Moreland, John, 225–26
More of Roy Orbison's Greatest Hits (Orbison), 152
"Moritat (Mack the Knife)" (Brecht, Weill), 173
Morrison, Jim, 68
Morrison, Van, 124
Morrow, Cory, 142
Morton, Jelly Roll, 163
Moser, Margaret, 130, 179, 180–81, 184–85

"Mother Blues" (Hubbard), 102

"Move Over" (Joplin), 124

movie/film careers: Kristofferson, 55–56; Lovett, 173

Mr. Bojangles (J. Walker), 79

"Mr. Bojangles" (J. Walker), 76–77, 81

Muldaur, Geoff, 97

Muncey, Jennifer, 213

Murphey, Michael Martin: on *Austin City Limits*, 155; background and influences, 67–68, 152; *The Ballad of Calico*, 68–73; Bell opening for, 95; and Hinojosa, 121; at Kerrville Folk Festival, 137; Lovett covering, 172; and Nunn, 105; "ruthlessly poetic," 1; Texas, return to, 73–74

Musgraves, Kacey, 10, 134–35, 155, 218–20, 221–23

music festival scene: and evolution of Texas music culture, 3; Family Gathering, Hog Mountain Retreat, Mineral Wells, 144; Larry Joe Taylor Texas Music Festival (& Chili Cookoff) (LJT), 118, 136–37, 140–45; Raz On The Braz (festival), 144. *See also* Kerrville Folk Festival

"Music School" concept of Vince Bell, 98

"Muskrat Love/Candlelight" (W. A. Ramsey), 38

My Baby Don't Tolerate (Lovett), 173

My Favorite Picture of You (Clark), 48

"My Favorite Picture of You" (Clark, Sampson), 42, 48

"My Old Friend the Blues" (Earle), 163

Nall, Kathy and Frances, 133

Nash, Alanna, 177, 178

Nashville (TV drama), 223

Nashville music culture, 9–11, 18, 49–51, 52–53, 153, 162

Nashville Songwriter's Hall of Fame, 186

Natural Forces (V. Bell), 96

Necessary Angels (Hickman), 123

neighboring, 114

Nelson, Willie: Clark cover, 42; Crowell cover, 156, 185; early career, 152; Friedman cover, 84; Fromholz cover, 156; Hickman cover, 123; Keen, influence on, 167; at Kerrville Folk Festival, 138; and Kristofferson, 56; legal troubles, 91; music culture, influence on, 4, 151–57, 168; and Nunn, 107–8; Nunn cover, 156; and outlaw movement, 18, 153–55; Rhodes, duets with, 127, 156; Shaver, inspiration to, 87; Shaver cover, 86; on Shaver's songwriting, 85; songwriting strategies, 108; style, consistency of, 149–51; Van Zandt cover, 156; Walker, C. covers, 124, 125

neo-traditional country, 162

Neuwirth, Bob, 54, 97–98, 99

Neverland Revisited (Circus Maximus), 76

Newbury, Mickey, 27–28, 33, 34, 55, 102, 185

New Folk Songwriter Competition (Kerrville Festival), 127, 138, 170

"newgrass" music, 120

New Orleans, 75

Newport Folk Festival, 127, 138

"New South Wales" (Isbell), 228

New York Magazine, 221

New York Times, 117, 171, 196

Niehardt, John G., 68

Nietzsche, Friedrich, 203, 204

"Night Life" (Nelson, Breeland, Buskirk), 107, 108, 152

"The Night's Too Long" (L. Williams), 179

Nitty Gritty Dirt Band, 81

Nix, Hoyle, 110

No. 2 Live Dinner (Keen), 170

Nocturne Diaries (Gilkyson), 129

No Depression (journal), 198

No Kinda Dancer (Keen), 139

North Texas State University, 59, 67, 69

"Not a Bad Man" (Griffin), 116–17

Not Too Late (N. Jones), 134

Nunn, Gary P., 74, 77, 103–5, 140, 156

"The Obscenity Prayer" (Crowell), 189–90

O'Connor, Flannery, 131, 177–78, 230

O'Connor, Sinead, 57

Oklahoma music, 101, 214–17, 224–26

Old Five and Divers Like Me (Shaver), 90

"Old Five and Divers Like Me" (Shaver), 86

Old Friends (Clark), 46–47

"Old Mojave Highway" (Murphey, Cansler), 71

Old No. 1 (Clark), 39–40, 41–42

Old Quarter, Houston/Galveston (venue), 19, 45, 94, 207

Old Yellow Moon (Crowell and E. Harris), 191

Once in a Very Blue Moon (Griffith), 120

"One Lonely Room" (Murphey, Cansler), 71

One Man's Music (V. Bell), 98

One Man's Music: A Monologue with Song (V. Bell), 98

"One Night Stand" (Hendrix, Fukunaga), 210

Oneonta, New York, 74–75

"One Way" (Hendrix, Maines), 210

"On the Advantage and Disadvantage of History for Life" (Nietzsche), 203

"On the Road Again" (Nelson), 154

Orbison, Roy, 110, 124, 152

Osmond, Marie, 126

"The Other Texas" (D. Rodriguez), 23

Other Voices, Other Rooms (Griffith), 120

"Ourland" (Allen), 21, 22

"Our Mother the Mountain" (Van Zandt), 19

outlaw movement (country), 9–11, 18, 88–89, 142, 153–56. *See also* progressive country

The Outsider (Crowell), 186, 187, 189–90

Overby, Tom, 184

"Over Yonder" (Earle), 165

Page, Patti, 124

"Painted Ladies" (W. A. Ramsey), 172

"Painting By Numbers" (J. McMurtry), 194

Palo Duro Canyon, 111

"Pancho and Lefty" (Van Zandt), 5, 19, 30, 156

Pancho & Lefty (Nelson, Haggard), 156

Panhandle music culture, 2, 109–15

Pantex nuclear weapons factory, 111

Papa Joe's Texas Saloon, 90–91

Paradise Hotel (Gilkyson), 128

Pareles, Jon, 117

Parton, Dolly, 60

The Party Never Ends (Keen), 170

Passenger (perf.), 95

"Passionate Kisses" (L. Williams), 131, 177

"Pass Me Not" (F. Crosby, Doane), 173

"Pastures of Plenty" (W. Guthrie), 161

Patoski, Joe Nick, 8, 92, 248

Patsy Cline Showcase, 152

Patterson, Dow, 110

Peaceful Existence (Elders), 127

Peace Meal (Wonderland), 129

Pearl (Joplin), 54, 124

Pearls in the Snow (Friedman), 84

Perskin, Spencer, 67

Peter, Paul and Mary, 138

Pettibone, Doug, 183, 185

Petty, Tom, 179

Phoenix (V. Bell), 97, 98

physical environment and art, 112–15

Pickens, Slim, 42

Pickin' in the Pines festival, 137

Picture in a Frame (Rhodes), 156

Pierce, Jo Carol, 110

"The Pilgrim, Chapter 33 (Kristofferson), 52

Pilkington, Tom, 20

"Pineola" (L. Williams), 179

Pirkle, Sarah, 211

Pistol Annies (perf.), 219

Pitchfork.com, 183

Plant, Robert, 116, 117

Poet: A Tribute to Townes Van Zandt (var.), 4

poetic songwriting concept, 4–8, 28–29

Poet in My Window (Griffith), 120

Poetry, Texas (V. Bell), 100

"Poetry" (Wilkins, Raines), 175

poets (classic), influence of, 4–8, 28–29, 32, 43, 68. *See also* literary influences; *individual poets/writers*

Poet's Award (Academy of Country Music), 48

Pogues (perf.), 164

political/social activism: Crowell, 189–90; Earle, 161–62, 163–66; Gilkyson, 128–29; Griffith, 120–21; Guthrie, W., 163, 165; Hinojosa, 121; Kristofferson, 50, 56–57; McMurtry, 193, 194–96; Musgraves, 222–23; and outlaw movement, 18; Rodriguez, D., 23–25

politics and folk culture evolution, 163–64
Poor David's Pub, Dallas (venue), 1, 37
populism, 165
"Positively" (W. A. Ramsey), 39
Possum Kingdom Lake, 141
Post, Shania, 213–17
"Preachin' To the Choir" (Crowell), 188
Presley, Angaleena, 219
Presley, Elvis, 85, 124
Presumed Innocent (Ball), 130
"Pretty Boy Floyd" (W. Guthrie), 216
"Pretty Paper" (Nelson), 152
Pretty World (Baker), 192
Price, Ray, 54, 152
Pride, Charley, 51
Prigg, Jack (character), 41–42
Prince, Jeff, 136, 249
Prine, John, 166, 197
progressive country, 103–8, 142, 162, 168.
    See also outlaw movement (country)
punk era in Austin, 168
Purcell, Henry, 6
Pure Prairie League, 169

"Quiet Me" (Barbra, Pirkle), 211
Quiet Valley Ranch, 138. *See also* Kerrville
    Folk Festival

"Rabbit" (Hubbard), 101
"Rachel's Song" (J. McMurtry), 197
Racing Aimless (D. Rodriguez), 26
racism: against Mexicans, 21, 50; in music
    business, 51; and redneck culture, 88;
    and satire, 83–84
radio, influence of, 31, 32, 87, 93
"ragged but right" concept, 77–78, 83
Ramblin' (L. Williams), 178
"Ramblin' Jack and Mahan" (Clark, Leigh),
    42
"Ramblin' Man" (Williams, Hank), 154
Ramsey, Buck, 111, 113–14
Ramsey, Willis Alan, 36–39, 171–72
"The Randall Knife" (Clark), 42, 47
Raphael, Mickey, 97, 99
Raye, Collin, 10–11, 218
Raz On The Braz (festival), 144
Razor, Terry, 144
RCA Records, 45

Reagan, Brad, 86, 90
"Real Live Bleeding Fingers and Broken
    Guitar Strings" (L. Williams), 132
"red dirt" music, 101, 214–17, 224–26
Redemption Road (Gilkyson), 128
Red Headed Stranger (W. Nelson), 18, 153
Red Horse (Gilkyson, Gorka, Kaplansky),
    129
redneck cultural identity, 88. *See also* "bro
    country" style
"redneck rock," 154–55
Reeves, Eddie, 111
Reid, Jan, 8, 154, 166, 249
religion and spirituality, 175–76, 219–20
"Rendezvous USA" (Allen), 21
Repossessed (Kristofferson), 56
Reprise Records, 73
"Requiem" (Gilkyson), 128
research and songwriting, 72–73
Reshen, Neil, 153
"Rex's Blues" (Van Zandt), 5, 20, 27, 230
Rhett, Thomas, 222
Rhodes, Kimmie, 126–27, 156
Rhodes Scholarship, 49, 50
Rhyder, Brandon, 175
Rhythmaires (perf.), 188
"Ride 'Em, Jewboy" (Friedman), 84–85
"Ride Me Down Easy" (Shaver), 87
"Ridin' Out the Storm" (Crowell), 189
"Righteously" (L. Williams), 182
Rilke, Rainer Maria, 102
"Rita Ballou" (Clark), 40, 41
"Rivertown" (Clark, Carll), 204
"Road Agent" (Murphey, Cansler), 71
"The Road Goes On Forever" (Keen), 173
Roadside Attractions (Ball), 130–31
The Road to Ensenada (Lovett), 173
"Road Trippin'" (Abbott), 154
Robison, Charlie/Bruce, 141–42, 168, 208
rock 'n' roll, influence of, 31, 154–55, 215,
    216
"The Rock of My Soul" (Crowell), 188
Rodgers, Jimmie, 174
Rodriguez, Carrie, 133
Rodriguez, David, 1–2, 17, 22–26, 95, 172
Rogers, Kenny, 69, 124
Rogers and Hammerstein, 198
"Rollin' By" (Keen), 172

Rolling Stone, 60, 88–89, 107, 116, 196

Rolling Stones, influence of, 198

"Rolling Wheels." *See* "Wheel"

roots music: "Americana" classification, 28, 162, 186, 194; contemporary highlights, 224–30; country and western, 35, 86; and folk genre evolution, 161–66; and the outlaw movement, 89, 153; by Texans for Texans, 1–2, 19, 119–20, 176; "Texas Music" classification, 1, 162, 215–16, 224–30. *See also* folk music/culture

Rose, Fred, 153

"Rosemary Lane" (D. Rodriguez), 23

Rosen, Jody, 221

Roses at the End of Time (Gilkyson), 129

Rosin, Hanna, 218

Rossetti, Christina, 112

Rough Trade Records, 177

"Rowing Song" (Griffin), 117

Rubaiyat, Dallas (venue), 1, 36, 73

"Ruby, Don't Take Your Love To Town" (Tillis), 69

Rush, Tom, 128

Russell, Kevin, 168

Russell, Leon, 36, 37, 172

Russell, Shake, 95

"ruthlessly poetic" concept, 1–2, 17–27, 61, 224

Sahm, Doug, 168

"Sally Grey's Epitaph" (Murphey, Cansler), 71

Same Trailer Different Park (Musgraves), 10, 134–35, 222–23

"Sam Stone" (Prine), 166

Sandburg, Carl, 68

Sanders, Don, 95

Sand Mountain Coffeehouse, Houston (venue), 45, 93, 94

San Francisco folk culture, 66

"Sangria Wine" (J. Walker), 79–80

"Satan and St. Paul" (Fullbright), 217

satire, 83–84

Saturday Night Live, 57

Saviano, Tamara, 39, 249–50

Saving Country Music, 206

Saxon Pub, Austin (venue), 1, 104, 166

Say Grace (Baker), 192

"Say You Love Me" (Crowell), 186, 189

Schmitt, Al, 38

"School Teacher" (Murphey, Cansler), 71

Screen Gems, 67–68

"Screw You, We're From Texas" (Hubbard), 102

Scruggs, Earl, 174

Seeger, Pete, 2, 23

"Seeing Black" (L. Williams), 132–33

Seely, Mike, 198

Seger, Bob, 185

self destructive behaviors, 181. *See also* alcohol/drug issues

Servant of Love (Griffin), 117

Service, Robert, 43

Seven Angels on a Bicycle (C. Rodriguez), 133

Sex and Gasoline (Crowell), 191

sexual themes, 55, 179, 223

"Shadowboxing" (Hickman), 123

Shakespeare, influence of, 29, 30, 51

Shamblin, Allen, 220

"Shandy (The Perfect Disguise)" (Kristofferson), 56

Shankar, Ravi, 133

Shaver, Billy Joe, 85–92, 102

Shaver, Brenda, 91–92

Shaver, Eddy, 90, 92

Shaver, Victoria "Tincie," 86–87

Shaver, Virgil "Buddy," 86–87

"She Ain't Goin' Nowhere" (Clark), 74

"She Left Me for Jesus" (Carll), 204, 205, 219

"Shelter from the Storm" (Dylan), 190

Shelter Records, 36, 38, 172

Shelton, Blake, 221

Sherrill, Billy, 53

"She's So Innocent" (Ball), 130

She's the One (Tom Petty and the Heartbreakers), 179

Shinyribs (perf.), 168

Shires, Amanda, 110, 227

Shiva's Headband (perf.), 67

Shortstop (Hickman), 123

Sign of Truth (T. Hinojosa), 121–22

Silverman, Sarah, 84

Simes, Frank, 59

Simone, Nina, 81

Sinatra, Frank, 81

"singer-songwriter" label, 1–2, 7, 28, 163

Sirens of the Ditch (Isbell), 226

"Sis Draper" (Clark, Camp), 48

"Sister Sinead" (Kristofferson), 57

Skanse, Richard, 210

Skelton, John, 40

Skunks (perf.), 168

"Sleepwalking" (W. A. Ramsey), 172

"Slippin' Around" (Tillman), 110

small town America in music, 2, 62–66, 69–73, 155, 222, 229. *See also* working-class themes

Smile: Songs from the Movies (Lovett), 173

Smith, Grady, 10, 218, 221, 250

Snake Farm (Hubbard), 101

"Snake Farm" (Hubbard), 101, 102

Snider, Todd, 52, 208

Soap Creek Saloon, Austin (venue), 95

social activism. *See* political/social activism

"Sold American" (Friedman), 84

Soldier, Dave, 99

"Soldier's Joy, 1864 (Clark, Camp), 48

Somedays The Song Writes You (Clark), 48

Something More Than Free (Isbell), 226, 227

"Something More Than Free" (Isbell), 228

"Song of the South Canadian" (Murphey, Nunn), 5

"songwriter's songwriter," 26–27

The Sound in Your Mind (Nelson), 156

"South Canadian River Song" (Murphey, Nunn), 105–6

"The South Coast of Texas" (Clark), 42

The South Coast of Texas (Clark), 45–46

Southeastern (Isbell), 226, 227

Souther, J. D., 111

"Southside of Heaven" (Bingham), 214

Space Dance Theater, 95

Spacek, Sissy, 186

Spanish language music, 121–22

Sparkles (perf.), 104

"Speed Trap Town" (Isbell), 229–30

"Spider John, Ballad of" (W. A. Ramsey), 38, 172

spirituality, 175–76

Spooky Lady's Sideshow (Kristofferson), 56

Spoon River Anthology (Masters), 68

Stanley, Carter, 174

Stardust (W. Nelson), 153–54, 168

"Star-Spangled Bummer (Whores Die Hard)" (Kristofferson), 56

State Musician of Texas, 122

Statler Brothers, 196

Steagall, Red, 5

"Steel" (Baker), 192

Steiner, Herb, 74, 80, 82, 106

Stephenville, Texas, 140, 212–13, 215

Step Inside This House (Lovett), 22, 44, 172

"Step Inside This House" (Clark), 28, 43–44, 172

Steve Earle: Fearless Heart, Outlaw Poet (McGee), 162

Stevens, Wallace, 68

Stevenson, B. W., 138, 155

Stevenson, Robert Louis, 127

"Still Learning How to Fly" (Crowell), 188–89

Stills, Stephen, 66–67

St. John, Lauren, 162

Stovall, Babe, 75

"Straighten Up and Fly Right" (N. Cole, Mills), 173

Strait, George, 171

"Stuff That Works" (Clark, Crowell), 42, 47

"Subterranean Homesick Blues" (Dylan), 204–5

Sugar Hill Records, 46, 48, 170, 194

"Suite: Judy Blue Eyes" (Stills), 36

"Summer Wind" (Bradtke, Meir, Mercer), 173

"Sunday Morning Coming Down" (Kristofferson), 54

Sun & Moon & Stars (musical), 96–97

"Sun & Moon & Stars" (V. Bell), 96–97, 99

Sun Records, 51

Swan, Billy, 55

"Sweet Love" (L. Williams), 184

Sweet Old World (L. Williams), 131, 179–80

"Sweet Old World" (L. Williams), 179

"Swervin' In My Lane" (Keen), 139

Swift, Taylor, 222

Swindell, Cole, 222
Swinney, Cary, 110
Sykes, Keith, 37

Taco Flats, Austin (venue), 17
talking blues style, 167–68, 171
"Talkin' World War III Blues" (Dylan), 205
Tally Ho Tavern, Nashville, 52
Tarleton State University, 140, 141,
    212–13, 215
Tarpaper Sky (Crowell), 191
Taylor, Chip, 133
Taylor, Eric, 95
Taylor, K. S., 211
Taylor, Sherry, 141
"Tears of Joy" (L. Williams), 184
"Tecumseh Valley" (Van Zandt), 120
Telling Stories, Writing Songs (Hudson),
    125, 126
Ten in Texas (var.), 128
Terlingua International Chili Cookoff, 136
Terri Hendrix: Live in San Marcos
    (Hendrix), 211
"Texas 1947 (Clark), 41, 42
Texas A&M University, 166–67
The Texas Campfire Tapes, 138
Texas Cookin' (Clark), 45
Texas Folk Music Foundation, 140
Texas Heritage Music Foundation, 117
Texas Heritage Songwriters' Hall of Fame,
    117, 173
Texas Monthly, 116
"Texas Music" classification, 1, 162,
    215–16, 224–30
Texas Opry House, Austin (venue), 166
Texas Plates (V. Bell), 98
Texas Tech University, 104, 110
Texas Trilogy (Fromholz, 3-song suite), 2,
    62–66, 73, 155, 172
"Tex-Deutsch folk pop," 122
"T for Texas" (J. Rodgers), 174
"Thank You for a Life" (Kristofferson), 58
The Improbable Rise of Redneck Rock (Reid),
    8
There's a Light Beyond These Woods
    (Griffith), 120
"They Ain't Making Jews Like Jesus Any-
    more" (Friedman), 83, 84

"They Killed Him" (Kristofferson), 56
"Things I've Come to Know" (J. McMurtry),
    199
Third Coast Music, 22
"The Third World" (D. Rodriguez), 24
Third World Warrior (Kristofferson), 57
Thirty Tigers, 117
"This Old Porch" (Keen, Lovett), 139,
    167–68
This Old Road (Kristofferson), 58
This One's For Him: A Tribute to Guy Clark
    (var.), 45, 204, 211
"This Too Will Pass" (Crowell), 189
"This Used To Be Paradise" (Ball), 131
Thomas, Dylan, influence of, 5, 18, 31, 43,
    206
Thoreau, Henry David, 59, 75
Thorp, N. Howard "Jack," 110
"Those Three Days" (L. Williams), 182
Threadgill, Kenneth, 137–38
Three Faces West (perf.), 106
"Til I Gain Control Again" (Crowell), 156,
    187
Tillman, Floyd, 110
TIME magazine, 132, 182
"Time To Go Inward" (Crowell), 187
"To Beat The Devil" (Kristofferson), 52,
    54–55
"To Live Is To Fly" (Van Zandt), 43, 215
Too Long in the Wasteland (J. McMurtry),
    194
Tootsie's Orchid Lounge, 53
"Too Weird for Kerrville" gathering, 17
"Topsy Turvy" (Crowell), 188
"Tour of Duty" (Isbell), 226–27
"Tower of Song" (Cohen), 32
tragedy, appeal of, 20
Train a Comin' (Earle), 162
"Train in the Distance" (Henley, Lynch), 60
"Trainride" (Fromholz), 63, 64
"Trains I've Missed" (Wilkins, Godard,
    Witt), 176
Tramp On Your Street (Shaver), 90
The Traveling Kind (Crowell and E.
    Harris), 191
Tres Rios campground, 143
"Trigger Happy Kid" (Murphey, Cansler),
    71

The Troubadour, Los Angeles (venue), 55
Trouble in Mind (Carll), 205, 207–8
"The True Cross" (D. Rodriguez), 24
"Try and Try Again" (Shaver), 90
Turner, Joe "Mad Dog," 91
Turnpike Troubadours (perf.), 215, 216, 217, 224–25
Two Dollar Shoes (Hendrix), 210

UCLA (University of California, Los Angeles), 67
"Undermine" (Musgraves, Dabbs), 223
Underwood, Carrie, 222
University of North Texas, 59, 67, 69, 133
University of Oxford, 49
"Unsuffer Me" (L. Williams), 184
Untimely Meditations (Nietzsche), 203
"Up Against the Wall Redneck Mother" (Hubbard), 78, 80–81, 101, 102
Urban, Keith, 185
urban folksingers, 1–2
USA Today, 126

"Vachel Carling's Rubilator" (Murphey, Cansler), 71
Vandiver, John, 67
Vanguard Records, 76
Vanity Fair, 183
Van Zandt, Townes: on *Austin City Limits*, 155; Baker, influence on, 192; Bell, influence on, 94; Bingham covering, 215; Carll, influence on, 204, 208; Clark, influence on, 27–28, 35, 43; Crowell, influence on, 185; Earle, influence on, 2, 162; and folk culture, 95, 152; Houston music culture, influence on, 95; Hubbard, influence on, 102; influences and direction, 29–35; Kerrville Folk Festival, banned from, 17; at Kerrville Folk Festival, 138; Kristofferson on, 26; Lovett covering, 172; Nelson covering, 156; Old Quarter annual wake, 207; and the outlaw movement, 155; on perfect songs, 18, 28, 32; and poetic songwriter concept, 4–5, 27–29; Ramsey, influence on, 39; Rhodes duet, 127; "ruthlessly poetic" quality, 1, 19–20; Texas Heritage Songwriters'

Hall of Fame, 173; Williams, L., influence on, 180, 181
Vaughan, Stevie Ray, 96, 168
"Ventura" (L. Williams), 182–83
venues, evolution of, 2–3
"Viet Nam Blues" (Kristofferson), 53
Vietnam War, 164–65
Village Voice, 193
violence: at festivals, 142–45; music themes, 21–22
¡Viva Terlingua!, 78–83
Voice of America, 193
Vollenweider, Andreas, 128

Waco area, 86–87
Walden Pond, 59
Walden Woods Project, 59
Walker, Billy, 53, 152
Walker, Cindy, 117, 124–25
Walker, Jerry Jeff: Clark cover, 42; Crowell cover, 185; early years and background, 74–76; and Houston music culture, 95; Hubbard, influence on, 102; at Kerrville Folk Festival, 138; literary influences, 6, 75; "Mr. Bojangles," 76–77, 81; !Viva Terlingua!, 78–83, 101
Wall Street Journal, 135
"Wanna Rock and Roll" (Hubbard), 101, 102
"War" (Marley), 57
Warner Bros. Records, 45
Washington Post, 199
Waters, Muddy, 102
Watson, Birdie Lee, 87
Wayfarers (perf.), 23
"The Way It Used to Be" (Murphey, Cansler), 70
WBAI Pacifica Radio, 76
"The Weary Kind" (Bingham, T. Burnett), 212, 213, 214
Weavers (perf.), 23
"We Can't Make It Here" (J. McMurtry), 194, 195
Welk Music Group, 48
Welty, Eudora, 2, 224
West (L. Williams), 183–84
West Point (USMA), 50–51
"West Side of Town" (T. Hinojosa), 121

West Texas Heaven (Rhodes), 127, 156
"West Texas Highway" (Murphey, Castleman), 172
West Textures (Keen), 170, 172
"What'd I Say" (Charles), 173
"What Good Can Drinkin' Do" (Joplin), 129
"Wheel" (J. Walker), 81–82
"When the Fallen Angels Fly" (Shaver), 86
"Whiskey River" (Bush), 151
Whisky a Go-Go, Los Angeles (venue), 106
White, Lari, 186
"White Dove" (C. Stanley), 174
Whitman, Walt, influence of, 32, 68
"Who Showed You the Way to Your Heart" (T. Hinojosa), 122
"Who's To Bless and Who's To Blame" (Kristofferson), 56
Why Country Music Was Awful in 2013 (Smith, video), 10
"Why Don't We Talk About It" (Crowell), 186
"Why Me?" (Kristofferson), 55
"Why You Been Gone So Long" (Newbury), 54
"Wide Open Spaces" (Gibson), 118
Wier, Rusty, 142
"Wild as a Turkey" (Carll,), 208
"Wild Cowboy Gravy" (Shaver), 86
"Wildfire" (Murphey, Cansler), 68, 73
Wild Seeds (perf.), 168
Wilkin, Marijohn, 51, 174
Wilkins, Walt, 174–76
Wilkinson, Andy, 109, 250
Wilkinson, Miles, 46, 47
Williams, Andy, 185
Williams, Billy, 169
Williams, Hank Sr.: Dylan, influence on, 28; Kristofferson, influence on, 49; *The Lost Notebooks of Hank Williams* (var.), 134; McMurtry, influence on, 197; Murphey, influence on, 68; Nelson covering, 154; Poet's Award, 48; and rhythm of language, 33; Van Zandt, influence on, 31, 32, 33, 35; Williams, L., influence on, 177–78
Williams, Holly, 222

Williams, Lucinda, 60; on *Austin City Limits*, 155; and categorization dilemmas, 118; Elders collaboration, 128; on happiness and creativity, 123; and Houston music culture, 95; *The Lost Notebooks of Hank Williams* (var.), 134; profiles, 8, 131–33, 176–85; on Rodriguez, D., 22
Williams, Miller and Lucy, 177–78, 181–82
Williams, Victoria, 97
Williams, William Carlos, 68
Willie and Waylon: outlaw movement, 18. *See also* Jennings, Waylon; Nelson, Willie
Willie Nelson: An Epic Life (Patoski), 8
"Willing to Love Again" (Carll, D. Scott), 208
Willis, Kelly, 168
Willis Alan Ramsey (Ramsey), 36–39, 172
Willner, Hal, 183
Wills, Bob, 113, 124
Wilson, Eddie, 67, 106
Winding, Jai, 59
A Winter Moon (D. Rodriguez), 24–25
WKIT radio, 195
Womack, Lee Ann, 134
Women in Texas Music: Stories and Songs (Hudson), 117, 124, 125, 130
women songwriters (Texas): addiction and depression issues, 123–24; Ball, Marcia, 123, 124, 130–31, 135, 168; contemporary paradigms, 11, 209–12, 218–23; Dunn, Holly, 126; Elders, Betty, 127–28; Gilkyson, Eliza, 119, 128–29; Griffin, Patty, 115–17; Hester, Carolyn, 125–256; Hickman, Sara, 122–23; Hinojosa, Tish, 121–22, 123; Jones, Norah, 125, 133–34; Joplin, Janis, 54, 123–24, 129; Lambert, Miranda, 60, 155, 218–21, 222, 223; Musgraves, Kacey, 10, 134–35, 155, 218–20, 221–23; Rhodes, Kimmie, 126–27, 156; Rodriguez, Carrie, 133; Walker, Cindy, 117, 124–25; Wonderland, Carolyn, 129–30. *See also* gender bias; Griffith, Nancy; Williams, Lucinda
Wonderland, Carolyn, 129–30

Woodward, Clyde J., 180–81
Workbend Songs (Clark), 48
working-class themes, 34, 87–88, 164, 165.
 See also small town America in music
World Without Tears (L. Williams), 132,
 182–83
"Worry Be Gone" (Clark, Nicholson,
 Parnell), 204
Wrecking Ball (E. Harris), 179
"Write Me Down (Don't Forget My
 Name" (Murphey, Cansler), 70
"Writers Talk" program, 122

Yarrow, Peter, 138
Yearwood, Trisha, 60, 126

Yeats, W. B., 2, 26
Yellowhouse Canyon, 114
"Yellow Rose of Texas" (trad.), 26
"Yoknapatawpha of the Texas panhandle,"
 2, 20
"You Asked Me To" (Shaver), 88
"You Don't Know Me" (C. Walker,
 Arnold), 124–25
*You Don't Know Me: The Songs of Cindy
 Walker* (Nelson), 125
Young, Faron, 152
Young, Neil, 103

Zimmerman, David, 126